PLAY BRIDGE

WITH

REESE

PLAY BRIDGE
WITH
REESE

by

Terence Reese

DOVER PUBLICATIONS, INC.

NEW YORK

Published in Canada by General Publishing Company, Ltd., 30 Lesmill Road, Don Mills, Toronto, Ontario.

This Dover edition, first published in 1969, is an unabridged and unaltered republication of the second (1961) printing of the work originally published in 1960. It is reprinted by special arrangement with Sterling Publishing Company, publisher of the original edition.

Standard Book Number: 486-22313-2
Library of Congress Catalog Card Number: 70-84636

Manufactured in the United States of America
Dover Publications, Inc.
180 Varick Street
New York, N.Y. 10014

Contents

Introduction

"Mr. Reese, how did you know that West had no more hearts?"

"Why did you take that deep finesse in clubs?"

"What made you play for the drop of the King of spades?"

This is the kind of question that the kibitzers fire at the experts after watching a session of play.

As a rule, there is no short answer. From the beginning of a hand a good player tries to play all fifty-two cards—not just the twenty-six he can see. As he goes along he builds up a picture of the opposing hands. That is how he performs the apparent miracles.

In the present book I have tried to show how it is done. The reader sits at my elbow from the moment I pick up my cards and considers how to bid them. (The bids printed in bold face are those which are not only contemplated but actually made.) He follows my thoughts— briefly in the bidding, more fully in the play after the dummy has gone down. In a post-mortem we review the main inferences that have been drawn and extract some general principles.

The setting of the hand is given sometimes as rubber bridge, sometimes as duplicate bridge of one kind or another. The lesson of the hand is usually the same, but the non-tournament player may appreciate a few explanations:

In a team-of-four event there is a comparison of the play between two tables. Scoring and tactics are, in effect, much the same as in rubber bridge. When there is a big difference between the scores at two tables one side is said to have gained, the other to have lost, a "swing."

In a pairs event the score on each hand obtained by each pair is compared with that of several others who have played the same cards, the principle being that a pair scores one "match point" in respect of every pair whom it outstrips. The pair that does best on a particular hand is said to score a "top," the pair that does worst a "bottom." When a player wants to be safe and get a not-worse-than-average score, he may decide to make the same bid or play that he expects to be made at other tables; he is said to "go with the room."

Apart from these duplicate terms, there will be a few words or phrases that are more common in Britain than America. Thus I may have written "third in hand" for "in third position," "game all" instead of "both sides vulnerable." So long as the meaning is clear these "Briticisms" have been allowed to stand, for essentially the book is a record of my thoughts as I tackle a tricky problem and to have made too many changes would have destroyed its flavor (*sic*)!

Terence Reese

PLAY BRIDGE

WITH

REESE

1. Disclosing a Doubleton

"Medium no-trump, Stayman responses, and Blackwood?" asked my partner at the beginning of a rubber. Not my favorite methods by any means, but I agree. On the first hand I deal myself the following in the South position:

♠ 10 8 2 ♡ K 10 7 5 2 ◇ K 6 ♣ A K 9

An awkward type of hand because I don't like opening one heart and perhaps, over two diamonds, having to rebid two hearts. Medium no-trump, he said; having a couple of tens and a five-card suit I think I'll "borrow" a point or two and open **1NT**.

West passes and partner, looking learned, responds **two clubs**, a conventional request for my four-card major. After a pass by East I bid a dutiful **two hearts**. Partner now alarms me with a raise to **six hearts** and all pass. The bidding has been:

South	West	North	East
1NT	pass	2♣	pass
2♡	pass	6♡	pass
pass	pass		

West leads the 9 of spades and partner puts down with pride:

♠ A Q
♡ A J 9 8 4
◇ A 8 3
♣ J 7 3

♠ 9 led

♠ 10 8 2
♡ K 10 7 5 2
◇ K 6
♣ A K 9

Partner has his bid, I suppose, but if he had responded three hearts instead of that idiotic two clubs he would have been playing the hand and we would have avoided this awkward spade lead through the A Q.

(Against any other lead declarer can draw trumps, eliminate diamonds, and play off Ace, King and another club, with various chances.)

I suppose the spade finesse is wrong but it is not unknown for players to underlead a King against a small slam, so I will put in the Queen. East wins with the King and returns the 3, on which West plays the 7. Now, how shall I play the trumps? The only indication I have is that West appears to be short in spades. He led the 9 and I held the 8; with a long suit headed by the 9 7 he would presumably have led low. If anyone is void in hearts, therefore, it is more likely to be East. So I play the 4 of hearts from table; East plays the 6 and I win with the King, West playing the 3. I draw a second trump, West playing the Queen and East discarding a spade.

Somehow I have got to avoid losing a club and superficially the best chance is to find East with Q 10. Before committing myself I must try to find out more about the distribution. I play a diamond to the King and lead the 10 of spades. West discards a club and dummy ruffs.

So East has six spades! I continue with the Ace and another diamond; on the third diamond East plays the 9 and West the 10. The following cards are left:

♠ —
♡ J 9
♢ —
♣ J 7 3

♠ —
♡ 10 7
♢ —
♣ A K 9

I can still enter dummy twice and play East for Q 10 x in clubs, but is that likely? East has six spades, one heart and at least three diamonds. I wonder whether it is four diamonds and two clubs or three diamonds and three clubs. I haven't seen the Jack or Queen of diamonds yet. West played the 10 on the third round, didn't he? Of course! He can't have the Queen and Jack as well, or he would have led a diamond from five to the Q J 10.

Then East must have a doubleton club and my only chance is to drop the Queen. This I am lucky enough to do, for the full hand turns out to be:

                        ♠ A Q
                        ♡ A J 9 8 4
                        ◇ A 8 3
                        ♣ J 7 3
    ♠ 9 7   ♠ K J 6 5 4 3
    ♡ Q 3   ♡ 6
    ◇ Q 10 5 2   ◇ J 9 7 4
    ♣ 10 8 5 4 2   ♣ Q 6
                        ♠ 10 8 2
                        ♡ K 10 7 5 2
                        ◇ K 6
                        ♣ A K 9

Partner is sufficiently pleased with the result not to notice that I was under-weight for my medium no-trump.

Post-mortem

This was not a difficult hand to play once certain inferences were drawn.

First, West's lead of the 9 of spades from a holding that did not include the 8 suggested that he might be short in spades. That was an indication as to how to play the trump suit, though in practice it would not have mattered had the Ace been led first.

The play of the diamonds, in conjunction with the fact that West had not led a diamond, established that East had at least four cards of the suit.

Then the count became exact. South could tell that he had to play East for Q x in clubs (or Q single) and not for Q 10 x.

2. A Slip in Defense

Playing in a pairs event against average opposition, I hold the following hand:

♠ K 6   ♡ A J 8 5 2   ◇ 9 7 5 2   ♣ 10 2

No one is vulnerable and East, on my right, deals and passes. I pass and West opens **one spade** third in hand. My partner **doubles** and East bids **two spades**. If my King were not in spades I might bid four hearts now, but as it is I think that **three hearts** is enough. West passes and partner raises to **four hearts**.

The bidding has gone:

South	West	North	East
—	—	—	pass
pass	1♠	double	2♠
3♡	pass	4♡	pass
pass	pass		

West opens the Queen of diamonds and partner puts down:

```
              ♠ 9 7
              ♡ K Q 10 6
              ◇ A 10 8
              ♣ A K 7 4

◇ Q led

              ♠ K 6
              ♡ A J 8 5 2
              ◇ 9 7 5 2
              ♣ 10 2
```

Somehow I have to avoid losing two diamonds and two spades. I'm not sure what this Queen of diamonds signifies. It could be from Q J and it could be a false card from K Q. At any rate, I don't want to make it easy for East to come in to lead a spade through my King, so for the moment I shall play low from dummy. East plays the 6. As the 4 and 3 are missing, that looks like the beginning of a signal. West continues with the 3 of diamonds. Now I go up with the Ace and East plays the 4, completing an echo.

I am still unsure about the diamonds. West could have Q 3 or Q J 3 or even K Q J 3. K Q 3 is not likely, for then he would have played the King so as not to be thrown in later on. My best hope is that he has led from a doubleton Q 3.

In fact, assuming that West has the Ace of spades I don't see that I stand a chance unless I find him with a doubleton diamond. In that case I may manage some sort of ruff-and-discard elimination if I can eliminate clubs and pass the lead to West with a spade. After making two spade tricks he may have to give me a ruff and discard.

To negotiate that I shall want entries to table, and I don't think I should play a round of trumps just yet. I will start with Ace, King and another club. On the third round of clubs East plays the Queen and I ruff with the 8. Now I lead a heart to dummy's Queen, West playing the 4 and East the 3. The position is now:

♠ 9 7
♡ K 10 6
♢ 10
♣ 7

♠ K 6
♡ A J 5
♢ 9 7
♣ —

The Jack of clubs is still out and the elimination I am planning will not succeed unless the trumps are 2 — 2. So I may as well ruff the fourth club and see if both opponents follow to a second heart. West plays the Jack on the fourth club, which is good news for it suggests that he is short in diamonds. Then both opponents follow to the second round of hearts.

Now I think I'm going to make it if I can duck a spade into West's hand. Is the 7 or the 9 the better card to lead? I think the 7 because if East has something like J 8 x he may be asleep and not put in the 8. So I lead the 7 and East, I am glad to see, plays low. Naturally I do not put in the King, for I don't want West to be able to give his partner the lead on the next trick. West wins with the 8 and heaves a deep sigh.

Evidently he is wondering whether to underlead the Ace now. Well, it makes no difference, for if he cashes the Ace of spades he will have to give me a ruff and discard on the next lead, the full hand being as follows:

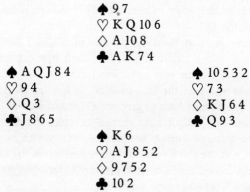

♠ 9 7
♥ K Q 10 6
♦ A 10 8
♣ A K 7 4

♠ A Q J 8 4
♥ 9 4
♦ Q 3
♣ J 8 6 5

♠ 10 5 3 2
♥ 7 3
♦ K J 6 4
♣ Q 9 3

♠ K 6
♥ A J 8 5 2
♦ 9 7 5 2
♣ 10 2

West eventually plays the Ace of spades and surrenders when I show him my remaining cards.

Post-mortem

This contract could have been defeated had East overtaken the Queen of diamonds at trick 1 and returned a spade. The defenders then cash two spade tricks and later make another diamond.

As to declarer's play, it may be noted that an early round of trumps would have been fatal. Suppose that the King of hearts is played from dummy at trick 3. Declarer follows with three rounds of clubs, enters dummy with a second trump and ruffs a fourth club. Now he has only one trump left and if he uses this to enter dummy there will be no trumps for a ruff-and-discard elimination. If South does find himself in this position the best he can do is lead the King of spades from hand. When West wins with the Ace he will have to underlead the Q J to put his partner in with the 10.

3. Short Circuit

In a rubber bridge game of average standard I deal myself the following at game all:

♠ A K 2   ♡ Q 6 4 2   ◇ K J   ♣ A K Q 3

This adds up to 22 points, enough on our system for an opening 2NT, but that does not strike me as at all a good bid with so much strength in the black suits and no tenace combinations. I open **one club.** Partner responds **one diamond** and now I cannot bid less than **3NT.** So it has been a simple auction:

South	West	North	East
1♣	pass	1◇	pass
3NT	pass	pass	pass

West leads the 3 of hearts and partner puts down:

> ♠ 9 5 3
> ♡ A 8
> ◇ Q 10 7 6 4
> ♣ 8 7 4

♡ 3 led

> ♠ A K 2
> ♡ Q 6 4 2
> ◇ K J
> ♣ A K Q 3

For all our 28 points, this isn't going to be easy if they knock the heart entry out at once. At any rate, I must play low from dummy; East wins with the King and returns the 5 to dummy's Ace.

I can see eight tricks: two spades, two hearts, one diamond and three clubs. No problem if I can induce them to take the Ace of diamonds on the first round. The best chance is to lead the King of diamonds from my hand; if West has A x or A x x he may perhaps put it on.

To enter hand, I play a club to the King. East drops the 2 and West the 6. I lead the King of diamonds now but the result is negative: West plays the 2 and East the 3.

Now it looks as though I haven't got much chance except the club break. I should imagine that West has led from four hearts and the diamonds may well be 3 — 3 since no one began an echo. If the diamonds are 3 — 3 I wonder whether I can force them to give dummy a diamond trick at the finish. To do that, I have got to eliminate their cards of exit.

I think it might be a good move now to lead and pass a low spade. They will knock out my Queen of hearts and then I can test the clubs. If the clubs don't break I may find one opponent with four clubs and three diamonds, to his disadvantage.

In any event it cannot cost to play a spade. I lead the 2; East wins with the 10 and exits with the 10 of hearts, which I take with the Queen. The situation is now:

♠ 9 5
♡ —
◇ Q 10 7
♣ 8 4

♠ A K
♡ 6
◇ J
♣ A Q 3

I cash Ace and King of spades, followed by Ace and Queen of clubs. Now I exit with a diamond and after making his Jack of clubs East has to give the last trick to the table.

This was the full deal:

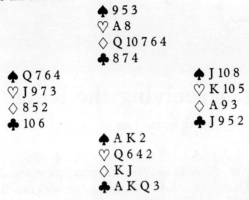

```
                    ♠ 9 5 3
                    ♡ A 8
                    ◇ Q 10 7 6 4
                    ♣ 8 7 4
♠ Q 7 6 4                           ♠ J 10 8
♡ J 9 7 3                           ♡ K 10 5
◇ 8 5 2                             ◇ A 9 3
♣ 10 6                              ♣ J 9 5 2
                    ♠ A K 2
                    ♡ Q 6 4 2
                    ◇ K J
                    ♣ A K Q 3
```

Post-mortem

West started to blame his partner for not cashing the Ace of diamonds when he was in. That would have made no difference, for I could have exited with a club at the finish just as well. East would still have had a diamond left and would have had to play to dummy.

While there is nothing complicated in the play, the ending has to be foreseen in good time. Suppose that after the King of diamonds has held declarer plays a second diamond. East wins this and exits with his 10 of hearts. Now it is too late for South to duck a spade: West can go in with the Queen, cash his good heart and exit in either black suit.

4. Deceiving the King

In a team-of-four match against keen opposition I hold the following hand as South:

♠ A J 8 5 3   ♡ K 9 7 2   ◇ J 4   ♣ 10 5

Neither side is vulnerable and West deals and opens **one diamond**. Partner overcalls with **two clubs** and East contests with **two diamonds**. I can join in this: **two spades**. West bids **three diamonds** and North supports me to **three spades**. No one has anything more to say, so the bidding has gone:

South	West	North	East
—	1◇	2♣	2◇
2♠	3◇	3♠	pass
pass	pass		

West leads the King of diamonds and partner puts down:

```
            ♠ K Q 9
            ♡ J 3
            ◇ 9 7 5
            ♣ A Q J 8 7

◇ K led


            ♠ A J 8 5 3
            ♡ K 9 7 2
            ◇ J 4
            ♣ 10 5
```

It is going to be a close struggle, I can see that. East plays the 8 of diamonds on the King and the 2 when West continues with the Ace. A third diamond is led to East's Queen and I ruff.

This appears to be one of those hands on which, if the important finesse is right, one does not need to take it! That is to say, if West has the King of clubs then I can lead a club to the Ace and let him win the next trick with the King. Nothing that he can play will embarrass me. The clubs will be established and if the spades are 3 – 2 I shall lose at most two diamonds, a heart and a club. Meanwhile, there is always the chance that if I lead a small club to the Ace and a small one back East, if he has the King, will not put it on. There's nothing to lose: I'll try that.

On the 5 of clubs West plays the 2 and North the Ace. The 7 of clubs is led back from dummy, East plays the 6 and my 10 holds, West playing the 4. That's one small success achieved. These cards are left:

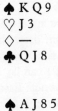

♠ K Q 9
♡ J 3
◇ —
♣ Q J 8

♠ A J 8 5
♡ K 9 7 2
◇ —
♣ —

If West had had a doubleton club he would probably have begun an echo, so I am inclined to think that the clubs are 3 – 3. If the spades are breaking as well, I can play Ace and another spade, ruff out the King of clubs and enter dummy to make two long clubs. But I am not so sure that the spades are going to break. They did bid up to three diamonds and West hasn't shown much yet. He should have some shape. In any case I am reckoning to lose two heart tricks, so it cannot lose to play a heart now and see what that produces. Should the spades be 4 – 1 that will leave me more room for maneuvering.

So I lead the 2 of hearts and put on the Jack from dummy. East wins with the Queen and returns the 5. West must have the Ace, so I put in the 9; West wins with the 10 and after some thought plays the Ace, which I ruff with dummy's 9 of spades. Now I have lost four tricks and the hand is still not over. We are down to five cards:

♠ K Q
♡ —
◇ —
♣ Q J 8

♠ A J 8 5
♡ K
◇ —
♣ —

Still no problem if the trumps are 3 – 2: I can simply play King of spades, then overtake the Queen, draw the last trump and make my King of hearts. But that will be the wrong play if East has four spades to the 10. Before thinking it out I can lay down the King of spades in case the singleton 10 falls. It does not: East plays the 2 and West the 7.

Now what about these spades? I have seen all the outstanding honors. West started with five diamonds to the A K 10 and either three or four hearts to the A 10. With that meager holding in high cards he made a free bid of three diamonds over my two spades. As I thought before, he must have distribution. 2 – 3 – 5 – 3 is impossible. I have got to play him for one of two hands:

    (a)   ♠ 10 x   ♡ A 10 x x   ◇ A K 10 x x   ♣ x x
    (b)   ♠ x   ♡ A 10 x x   ◇ A K 10 x x   ♣ x x x

Both the bidding and the play in clubs make (b) more likely. More-over, if he is 2 – 4 – 5 – 2 the cross-ruff will still be all right unless his second spade is the 10. There doesn't seem much doubt that the cross-ruff is the right play.

So I play a club from dummy. East plays the King and I ruff with the Jack. West follows suit with the 9. Now the hand is a certainty, for if West is going to follow to the King of hearts he can have only one trump and the cross-ruff will succeed. If by any chance West has only three hearts and has a doubleton trump then he will have to ruff the King of hearts and again I shall have a trump position at the twelfth trick. As expected, West follows suit on the King of hearts; I ruff in dummy and win the last two tricks with the A 8 of spades. My picture of the hand was about right:

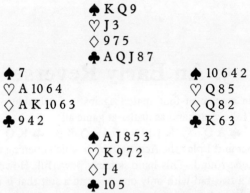

♠ K Q 9
♡ J 3
◇ 9 7 5
♣ A Q J 8 7

♠ 7   ♠ 10 6 4 2
♡ A 10 6 4   ♡ Q 8 5
◇ A K 10 6 3   ◇ Q 8 2
♣ 9 4 2   ♣ K 6 3

♠ A J 8 5 3
♡ K 9 7 2
◇ J 4
♣ 10 5

The East hand does not meet the requirements for a free raise as laid down by most American authorities. In other countries a different view is taken of this matter, the general theory being that in competitive situations it is essential to show a modicum of strength while one safely can.

Post-mortem

If East-West had been the sort of players who always signal their length—and I am far from saying that is the best way to play the defense —they would not have let me slip through the second trick in clubs. West's 2 of clubs on the first round would have told his partner that he had three, for with an even number he would have begun an echo. If East takes the King of clubs and exits with either a spade or a club declarer can make only eight tricks.

After the 10 of clubs had held, the rest of the play depended on not making the too ready assumption that the trumps would divide according to the customary 3 – 2. In general, when opponents have bid to the level of three or more on a scanty holding of high cards one must expect the suits to break badly.

5. An Early Reverse

Playing in a team-of-four match against redoubtable opposition, I pick up the following hand as dealer at game all:

♠ A Q   ♡ K J 10 9 7 5 4   ◇ K 3   ♣ K Q

My partner and I play the Acol system in which opening two-bids are forcing for one round. This hand is fairly powerful. However, I don't like to open a two-bid with only one Ace and a suit that is not solid, so I call simply **one heart**.

After a pass by West partner responds **1NT**. East passes and now, clearly, I can go to **four hearts**.

The bidding has been:

South	West	North	East
1♡	pass	1NT	pass
4♡	pass	pass	pass

West leads the Jack of diamonds and dummy goes down as follows:

♠ 10 7 6 4
♡ 6 3
◇ A Q
♣ 10 9 5 4 2

◇ J led

♠ A Q
♡ K J 10 9 7 5 4
◇ K 3
♣ K Q

Two Aces to lose, two finesses to take, and I can only be in dummy twice. The question is, which finesse should I take first? That requires a little thought.

Suppose I take the spade finesse first and it loses. I shall get back to dummy with the second diamond and finesse in hearts. But one heart finesse may not see me home even if East has the Queen. For example,

West might have the singleton Ace and in that case I should need to finesse twice. Alternatively, East might have A Q x; then again I should need to lead through him twice.

It is beginning to look as though the heart finesse should come first. Supposing I finesse the Jack and it fetches the Ace. Then unless West is playing a deep game from A Q or A Q x the Queen will be marked, and when I am next in dummy I can take another finesse in hearts. So long as I lose only one heart it will not matter about the spades, so I'll take the heart finesse first.

I win the first trick with the Queen of diamonds and lead the 3 of hearts from the table. East plays the 8 and I put in the Jack, which holds, West playing the 2. It looks as though East has A Q 8. I think I have played it the right way, giving myself the chance of two heart leads. I play the King of diamonds to dummy's Ace and lead another heart from the table.

Disaster! East discards a diamond on the second heart and West wins with the Queen. West cashes the ace of hearts and exits with a diamond, which I ruff. I am now in this unenviable position:

♠ 10 7 6
♡ —
♢ —
♣ 10 9 5 4

♠ A Q
♡ K 10 9
♢ —
♣ K Q

This is most humiliating because I am sure the spade finesse is right all the time. The only remaining hope is that they let me slip through a club and bring off some sort of three-card end-play. I try the Queen of clubs. As expected, East takes it with the Ace and returns a small club. Now I must go through the motions of leading out my hearts. But the story has no happy ending—at least not for me. I have to surrender the last trick to the King of spades and my worst fears are confirmed when the hand turns out to be:

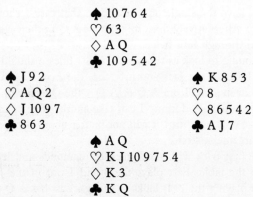

♠ 10 7 6 4
♡ 6 3
◇ A Q
♣ 10 9 5 4 2

♠ J 9 2
♡ A Q 2
◇ J 10 9 7
♣ 8 6 3

♠ K 8 5 3
♡ 8
◇ 8 6 5 4 2
♣ A J 7

♠ A Q
♡ K J 10 9 7 5 4
◇ K 3
♣ K Q

With murder in my heart I congratulate West on his good defense.

Post-mortem

I trust that the reader has not missed the point of this deal: if West had taken the Jack of hearts with the Queen, then when next in dummy I would have taken the spade finesse and made the contract.

West might also have tried to deceive me by winning the first heart with the Ace. (If he had had A Q alone that would have been a brilliant play). You may remember that I did envisage the possibility of West winning with the Ace when he had the A Q. Somehow he caught me napping by ducking on that first trick.

The defense followed a sound general principle, that when declarer takes an early finesse in a critical suit it is generally good play to hold up. This applies both to a side suit and to the trump suit. The value of such defense is two-fold for it causes declarer to misplace the cards and may induce him, as on the present hand, to expend an entry from dummy on a useless cause.

6. Friendly Return

This is a hand from a pairs contest against opponents of, so far as I know, not more than average skill. We are vulnerable and I hold:

♠ A J 5 2   ♡ Q 8 2   ◇ J 5   ♣ A 8 5 4

My partner, North, deals and opens **one diamond**. East comes in with **one heart**.

My own preference on this sort of hand is for 2NT, which most players would consider uncouth. My experience is that partners seldom have four spades and the usual effect of mentioning the suit is that the defense to 3NT is made easier. However, in a pairs contest it is wiser to play with the room and not to risk a bad result should this be one of the rare occasions when partner can support the spades. So I bid **one spade**.

West passes and North raises to **two spades**. Now I introduce **2NT** and he raises me to **3NT**. The bidding has been:

South	West	North	East
—	—	1◇	1♡
1♠	pass	2♠	pass
2NT	pass	3NT	pass
pass	pass		

West leads the Queen of clubs and partner goes down with this moderate collection:

> ♠ Q 7 4
> ♡ A 7 5
> ◇ A K 9 6 2
> ♣ 6 3

♣ Q led

> ♠ A J 5 2
> ♡ Q 8 2
> ◇ J 5
> ♣ A 8 5 4

I don't like the look of this; I wish he'd left me in 2NT. East overtakes the Queen of clubs with the King and I duck. East returns the 9 and I play low again. Now East switches to the 10 of spades.

Obviously the clubs are 5 – 2. This spade return seems friendly. I play low from hand, West puts on the King and returns the Jack of clubs. North and East throw a heart and I win with the Ace.

I have got to make some tricks from diamonds and since I cannot afford to let West in I lead the Jack and run it. East wins with the Queen and returns the 9 of spades. This is won by dummy's Queen, leaving the position as follows:

♠ 7
♡ A 7
♢ A K 9 6
♣ —

♠ A J
♡ Q 8 2
♢ 5
♣ 8

The lead is in dummy and I want the rest of the tricks. I wonder if I can get a count on the diamonds. The clubs were 5 – 2 and the hearts most probably 6 – 1. (If West had had a doubleton he would probably have led his partner's suit.) I shall find out about the spades on the next round but for the moment I am inclined to place West with either two or three of them. If he had had K 8 x x he would not have played the King when his partner led the 10 at trick 3. It looks as though West has at least four diamonds and possibly five. If he has five then I can squeeze him in diamonds and clubs. I must play off the Ace of hearts before coming to hand, so that the timing will be right.

On the Ace of hearts West plays the Jack. Now I play a spade to the Ace and West throws a club. That is good news because it means, almost certainly, that he is 2 – 1 – 5 – 5, so I need not worry about losing to a doubleton Q 10 of diamonds in East's hand. On the Jack of spades West throws a diamond. Then I finesse dummy's 9 and make the last four tricks in diamonds. As can be seen from the diagram of the full hand, West was squeezed on the last spade:

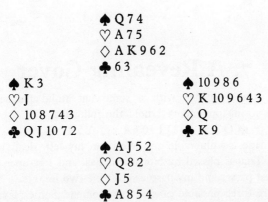

♠ Q 7 4
♡ A 7 5
◇ A K 9 6 2
♣ 6 3

♠ K 3
♡ J
◇ 10 8 7 4 3
♣ Q J 10 7 2

♠ 10 9 8 6
♡ K 10 9 6 4 3
◇ Q
♣ K 9

♠ A J 5 2
♡ Q 8 2
◇ J 5
♣ A 8 5 4

East's return of the 10 of spades at trick 3 made the hand easier to play, but one can see that he had no good alternative.

Post-mortem

Like most hands, this one was not difficult to play so long as declarer kept track of what was going on. Where some players would have gone wrong is that they would not have cashed the Ace of hearts when in dummy. To do that, declarer does not have to foresee the squeeze. He is going to make the contract only if he takes the right view of the diamonds. Playing off the Ace of hearts may help him to assess the distribution and if it results in his going more than one down that will make little difference to the match-point score.

7. A Revealing Cover

Playing rubber bridge with a somewhat stolid partner against reasonably strong opponents I hold the following:

♠ Q 7 3   ♡ Q J 10 6 4   ◇ A 5 2   ♣ A J

Neither side is vulnerable and West, on my left, deals and opens **one club.** That is passed by North and East and I re-open with **one heart.** West passes and my partner gives me **two hearts.**

There are three possible calls at this moment. Some players would say that I had a maximum for a bid of one (as opposed to a double) in the protective position and that I should go straight to four hearts. There are too many losers for that and anyway I am not sure it will be the best contract. As I see it, the choice is between 2NT and three hearts. With my present partner I shall make the most straightforward bid: **three hearts.** Partner raises this to **four hearts** after some thought. The bidding has been:

South	West	North	East
—	1♣	pass	pass
1♡	pass	2♡	pass
3♡	pass	4♡	pass
pass	pass		

West leads the Queen of diamonds and partner, remarking that he was thinking of 3NT, puts down:

♠ K 8 4
♡ A 8 2
◇ K 7 3
♣ 9 8 4 3

◇ Q led

♠ Q 7 3
♡ Q J 10 6 4
◇ A 5 2
♣ A J

Yes, 3NT would have been better, especially played from my hand.

Prospects are not too good in four hearts. Even if the heart finesse is right I have four apparent losers.

Dummy plays low on the first trick, East plays the 6 and I win. Now can it make any difference which heart I lead? If I lead the 10 and West puts in the King it will be fair to assume that it's a singleton, whereas if I lead the Queen and West puts on the King that won't tell me anything. So I lead the 10 and West does play the King. I put on the Ace from dummy and return the 2. If I am going to play East for the 9 7 5 3 I've got to finesse at once. Surely West couldn't have put in the King from a doubleton? No, I'm going to finesse the 6.

The 6 holds and East looks aggrieved. I follow with the Queen of hearts and then the Jack to draw East's last trump. West, meanwhile, has had to make three discards. The first is the 6 of clubs, the second the 5 of spades and the third, after much thought, the 9 of diamonds. I have to discard from dummy on the fourth trump. I don't want to let a spade or a club go, for they exercise some sort of threat against West, so I discard dummy's 7 of diamonds. The following cards are left:

♠ K 8 4
♡ —
♢ K
♣ 9 8 4 3

♠ Q 7 3
♡ 4
♢ 5 2
♣ A J

I have a fairly good picture of West's hand. He has let one club go, so I place him with five clubs. He let one spade go quite gaily but would not release a second; that looks like A J x x or A 10 x x. One heart I know of and his diamonds were presumably Q J 9, for he led the Queen and has played the 9.

I think the game now must be to extract his diamond and duck a club into his hand. East may well have a club honor (since the King of clubs was not led) and in that case dummy's 9 8 of clubs may assume some significance. So in the diagram position I lead a diamond to the King, on which West plays the Jack, and return a club, finessing the Jack and losing to West's King.

West returns a club on which East's Queen falls. Now dummy's 9 8 of clubs are equals against the 10 and I can make the contract in several ways. I lead a spade to the King and return the 9 of clubs, discarding my losing diamond. Now West must either lead into my Queen of spades or concede a trick to dummy's 8 of clubs. There was no defense, the full hand being as follows:

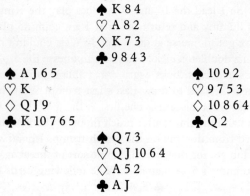

♠ K 8 4
♡ A 8 2
◇ K 7 3
♣ 9 8 4 3

♠ A J 6 5
♡ K
◇ Q J 9
♣ K 10 7 6 5

♠ 10 9 2
♡ 9 7 5 3
◇ 10 8 6 4
♣ Q 2

♠ Q 7 3
♡ Q J 10 6 4
◇ A 5 2
♣ A J

Post-mortem

That lead of the 10 of trumps is worth noting. In such situations it is generally possible to gauge whether the defender has the King alone or K x.

Note, also, how from West's three discards on the trumps it was possible to assess his exact distribution. That made it safe to release the King of diamonds. West could not discard in any other way. If he had let go a second club, for example, South would have led out Ace and Jack and would have established the fourth club in dummy.

8. They Talk Too Much

This is a hand from rubber bridge of not particularly high standard. As dealer at game all I pick up a hand more in keeping with my average holding than the majority in this book:

♠ J 9 7 3   ♡ Q 8 2   ◇ 9 7 2   ♣ 9 6 3

I pass and West on my left opens **one heart**. Partner **doubles** and East passes. No choice—I have to bid **one spade**. West now bids **two diamonds** and partner, very intense, **three diamonds**. What does he expect me to do? I can only say **three spades**. Now West passes and partner raises to **four spades,** which nobody doubles. The bidding has been:

South	West	North	East
pass	1♡	double	pass
1♠	2◇	3◇	pass
3♣	pass	4♠	pass
pass	pass		

West leads the Queen of diamonds and I see that partner's excitement was justified, for he puts down:

♠ K 8 6 5 4 2
♡ A 5
◇ A K
♣ A Q 8

◇ Q led

♠ J 9 7 3
♡ Q 8 2
◇ 9 7 2
♣ 9 6 3

I win the diamond on table. Now the trouble is that I cannot come to hand to lead a spade. Since I have to play from table, which is better —King of spades or a small one? As West has bid two suits it is quite likely that he has a singleton spade, and that card may be the Ace. So I play the 4 of spades from dummy, East plays the 10 and my Jack is headed by the Queen. That's one chance that has gone amiss! West cashes the Ace of spades on which his partner discards the 3 of hearts. Now West puts dummy back with a diamond. I have lost two tricks and the position does not seem very hopeful:

♠ K 8 6 2
♡ A 5
♢ —
♣ A Q 8

♠ 9 7
♡ Q 8 2
♢ 9
♣ 9 6 3

I can come to hand with a spade and finesse the Queen of clubs, but that won't save me from losing a heart and a club. Can I do anything with my 9 of diamonds in some sort of loser-on-loser elimination? Let me think about the club position. West has bid hearts and diamonds and has turned up with the A Q of spades. He is vulnerable, too, so his suits should be five-carders. If that's right he must have a singleton club. In that case I can save a trick by cashing the Ace of clubs, coming to hand with a spade and giving West the lead with a diamond, throwing a club loser from table.

On the Ace of clubs—a happy sight—West drops the King. I am going to make the contract now unless East has a diamond higher than the 9. I play the Queen of Clubs from dummy, West discarding a heart, come to hand with a spade and play the 9 of diamonds. West plays the 10 and I discard the losing club from dummy. Showing signs of strain,

West leads the Jack of hearts. This runs up to the Queen and the rest is straightforward. The full hand:

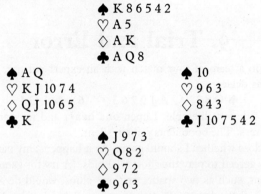

♠ K 8 6 5 4 2
♡ A 5
◇ A K
♣ A Q 8

♠ A Q
♡ K J 10 7 4
◇ Q J 10 6 5
♣ K

♠ 10
♡ 9 6 3
◇ 8 4 3
♣ J 10 7 5 4 2

♠ J 9 7 3
♡ Q 8 2
◇ 9 7 2
♣ 9 6 3

"I thought you'd make *six* with my hand," said my partner.

Post-mortem

One lesson from this hand is that it is silly to talk just for the pleasure of hearing one's own voice. Had West not bid two suits, South would not have thought of playing off the Ace of clubs. After the double by North and the pass by his partner, West was not going anywhere. His bid of two diamonds could only help the opposition.

9. Trial and Error

Playing in a team-of-four match with an expert partner, I hold the following as dealer:

♠ Q 8 3   ♡ A J 9 7 6 3   ◇ 6   ♣ A Q 4

Neither side is vulnerable. I open **one heart** and my partner raises to **two hearts.** The opponents remain silent.

Rather close whether I should go on. As it happens, my partner and I have lately agreed to play the short trial bids. (A try for game by South at this point, such as two spades or three clubs, would be a trial bid.) The idea is that when a player makes a trial bid he should choose a short suit—as a rule, a singleton. That will help partner to judge whether or not the hands fit well.

As this is a borderline hand I think I might give this convention a try-out. I bid **three diamonds.** Partner jumps to **four hearts** and all pass.

So the bidding has been:

South	West	North	East
1♡	pass	2♡	pass
3◇	pass	4♡	pass
pass	pass		

West leads the King of diamonds and, proudly remarking that he has remembered the convention, partner puts down:

♠ J 7 2
♡ K 10 5 2
◇ 9 5 4
♣ K 10 6

◇ K led

♠ Q 8 3
♡ A J 9 7 6 3
◇ 6
♣ A Q 4

I see that I am in some danger of losing a diamond and three spades, not to mention a possible heart, but I don't blame the convention: we both forced the pace a little and there is some duplication in clubs.

East plays the 8 of diamonds on the first trick. West continues with the 7 of diamonds, East plays the Ace and I ruff. The first point to consider is which opponent, if either, is likely to have three hearts to the Queen.

So far as one can judge from the play of the diamonds, West is slightly more likely to have length. His play of the King followed by the 7 could well be from a five- or six-card suit. I should imagine that the spade honors are divided, for West appears to have K Q of diamonds and East the A J. If either had A K of spades as well, he might have entered the bidding. Now, if West had a void heart together with a diamond suit and a high honor in spades, he would perhaps have come in over one heart.

I don't think actually that either opponent is void of hearts. I am not going to spend more time on this. I lay down the Ace and all is well. Both follow.

When I lead a second heart, West plays the Queen and North the King, East discarding the 3 of diamonds.

So much for that, but the main battle is still ahead: avoiding the loss of three spade tricks. If either opponent held A K I could lead through him, but I am still disposed to think the honors are divided. Then could either player have a doubleton honor? For example, if West had K x or A x I could lead from hand towards the Jack and duck on the way back. Again I don't think it's likely since they might well have maneuvered to take a spade ruff if the distribution were 5 – 2; also, on the second heart East discarded a diamond, and if he had had five spades he would probably have thrown a spade.

I am coming more and more to the conclusion that it cannot be done by brute force. If the spades are 4 – 3 and the honors are divided my only chance is to induce a misplay. I'll lead the Jack of spades from dummy and hope that East does not play the Ace or King. The sooner I do it the better.

On the Jack of spades East plays low. Better! West wins with the King and plays a third diamond. I can shorten it now: I cross to dummy in clubs and lead another spade from table. East plays the Ace and the rest are mine.

While West is having his say about his partner's failure to play the Ace of spades on the Jack, let us look at the full deal:

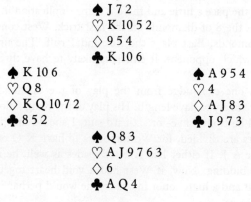

```
                 ♠ J 7 2
                 ♡ K 10 5 2
                 ◇ 9 5 4
                 ♣ K 10 6
    ♠ K 10 6                    ♠ A 9 5 4
    ♡ Q 8                       ♡ 4
    ◇ K Q 10 7 2                ◇ A J 8 3
    ♣ 8 5 2                     ♣ J 9 7 3
                 ♠ Q 8 3
                 ♡ A J 9 7 6 3
                 ◇ 6
                 ♣ A Q 4
```

Post-mortem

There were a number of small indications on this hand of a sort that are liable to be overlooked. The fact that the high diamonds were divided between the two hands, taken in conjunction with the fact that neither opponent entered the bidding, suggested that the spade honors would also be divided. Also, the fact that the opponents had not taken a ruff in spades suggested that they were not 5 – 2.

It should be mentioned that the lengthy reflection about the spades took place after the second trick and not when declarer was in dummy with the King of hearts. The narrative of the play was differently arranged for convenience.

As to the defense, presumably East placed South with some such holding as K 10 x x in spades. His failure to play the Ace on the Jack was a mistake but not such an unlikely one. Note that the defense would have been easier had South played off three rounds of clubs before leading the spade Jack. Then East would have known that the defense had to take three spade tricks and would surely have covered the Jack.

10. A Profitable Exchange

Playing in a team-of-four match against strong opponents, I pick up this swing hand:

♠ A Q 7 6 3   ♡ 7   ◇ A Q 10 6 5 4 2   ♣ —

We are vulnerable, our opponents not. Though promising, my hand is not solid enough for a two-bid, so I open **one diamond**. West, on my left, passes and partner responds **two clubs**. East comes in with **two hearts** and I show my second suit, **two spades**. Partner raises to **three spades**, which is unexpected but gratifying. I bid **four spades** and when this goes round to East, he **doubles**. It is tempting in a way to redouble, but this sort of hand can go sadly astray if the breaks are bad, so I shall pass.

The bidding has been:

South	West	North	East
1◇	pass	2♣	2♡
2♠	pass	3♠	pass
4♠	pass	pass	double
pass	pass	pass	

West leads the Jack of hearts and I await partner's hand with interest. He puts down:

♠ K J 4
♡ Q 8 4
◇ K
♣ K 10 8 6 4 3

♡ J led

♠ A Q 7 6 3
♡ 7
◇ A Q 10 6 5 4 2
♣ —

I play low from table and ruff the second heart. I am glad to see that King of diamonds in dummy but no doubt both suits are going to break badly. Let me see what I can work out about the distribution at this stage.

The hearts, I should imagine, are 6 – 3. If West had had four hearts he would probably have taken some part in the bidding. No doubt East has the Ace of clubs, quite possibly the A Q. Whether he has doubled on length or shortage in spades I cannot be sure. No doubt he has a singleton or void in either spades or diamonds.

At any rate, it is certain that I must play a diamond first and see what happens. On the King of diamonds East plays the 7 and West the 8. The 3 is missing but one of those cards could easily be a false card from J x x x. If the diamonds are 3 – 2 and the spades not worse than 4 – 1 I can make two overtricks. Could East have six hearts, four clubs, a singleton spade and two diamonds ? It's not impossible.

However, I must think about making the contract, not about overtricks. If I lead out four rounds of spades and then find that the diamonds are 4 – 1 I shall be in bad trouble. I may need dummy's spades to ruff a diamond, so I think that the first move should be a low trump to the Queen. If the trumps turn out to be 5 – 0 I shall have to scramble as many tricks as I can. If they are 4 – 1 I don't think I can be defeated.

So I lead the 4 of spades from dummy. East plays the 2, I win with the Ace and West plays the 8. That's a relief. It cannot cost to play the Ace of diamonds now; it will probably be ruffed but I shall still have the situation in hand. On the Ace of diamonds West plays the 3, dummy discards a club and East ruffs. That was not unexpected. East plays a high heart, which I ruff, and the position is now:

♠ K J
♡ —
◇ —
♣ K 10 8 6 4

♠ Q 7
♡ —
◇ Q 10 6 5 4
♣ —

There are two diamonds still out and two spades. I ruff a diamond with the King of spades and return the Jack of spades. Naturally I overtake, though this establishes a trump trick for East. Apart from that the rest of my hand is high, the full deal being:

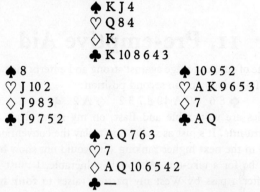

♠ K J 4
♡ Q 8 4
◇ K
♣ K 10 8 6 4 3

♠ 8   ♠ 10 9 5 2
♡ J 10 2   ♡ A K 9 6 5 3
◇ J 9 8 3   ◇ 7
♣ J 9 7 5 2   ♣ A Q

♠ A Q 7 6 3
♡ 7
◇ A Q 10 6 5 4 2
♣ —

The defense has made one heart and two trump tricks.

Post-mortem

This hand is an instructive example of how to manage a two-suiter when bad breaks are to be expected. Once the South hand has been shortened at trick 2, declarer's policy must be to establish his side suit even if the opponents ruff meanwhile. East was allowed to make two trump tricks but obviously it was in a good cause, for if the declarer takes the King of diamonds and then draws four rounds of trumps he ends up with only eight tricks. East's double was a warning of bad breaks but even without the double the play should follow the same general lines.

11. Pre-emptive Aid

In a game of rubber bridge against strong and enterprising opposition I hold the following hand in second position:

♠ 8 6   ♥ A 10 8 7 3 2   ♦ A 2   ♣ A J 4

Both sides are vulnerable and East, on my right, deals and opens **three diamonds.** It's just as well I don't play the convention in which an overcall in the next higher ranking suit would not show hearts at all but would be for a take-out. Although vulnerable, I must risk **three hearts.** After a pass by West my partner raises to **four hearts** and all pass.

So the bidding has gone:

South	West	North	East
—	—	—	3◇
3♡	pass	4♡	pass
pass	pass		

West leads the 4 of diamonds. Remarking, "I haven't much for you," partner puts down:

♠ A Q 7 4
♥ Q 9 4
♦ 9 7 6
♣ 8 5 2

◇ 4 led

♠ 8 6
♥ A 10 8 7 3 2
♦ A 2
♣ A J 4

The lead looks like a singleton, though it could possibly be from a doubleton, East having opened on a six-card suit with 100 honors. At any rate, I cannot risk having my Ace ruffed, so I play the 6 from dummy and win the 10 with the Ace.

Prospects are not too good. It looks like a diamond and two clubs to lose, apart from the spades and hearts. There are two slender chances of not losing a heart: I can play West for the singleton Jack, leading the Queen from dummy, or East for the singleton King. In view of East's pre-emptive bid, the better chance must be to play him for the singleton, so I lay down the Ace of hearts, on which West plays the Jack and East the 5. Have I done the wrong thing? No, West's Jack was not single. On the next round he plays the King and East the 6.

West now switches to the Jack of spades through dummy's A Q. I finesse and the Queen holds. West's 4 of diamonds was obviously a singleton. I don't know yet whether I can do anything about the clubs, but I'm going to play off Ace and another spade to build up a picture of the hand. All follow to the Ace of spades and on the next round East plays the 10. I ruff and West drops the King. There are now seven cards left and I have lost only one trick:

♠ 7
♡ 9
◇ 9 7
♣ 8 5 2

♠ —
♡ 10 8 7
◇ 2
♣ A J 4

The 9 of spades is still out and no doubt West has it. What was his hand exactly? Two hearts and one diamond I know; four spades and six clubs, that must be it. Some light is beginning to appear. I can cross to dummy's 9 of hearts and throw West in with a spade, forcing him to lead clubs for what that is worth. If West's clubs are headed by the K Q I can play an old-fashioned Bath Coup and make him lead into my A J.

But can his clubs be as good as six to the K Q? True, he wouldn't have bid four clubs over three hearts but he might well have doubled four hearts. Also, he would probably have led the King of clubs at some point.

It is beginning to look as though East has the singleton King or Queen. In that event it is no use crossing to dummy and playing a spade, for West will exit perforce with a low club. If I have the picture right the Ace of clubs will drop the singleton King or Queen and then I can go for the end-play.

So in the diagram position I play off the Ace of clubs. East, I am glad to see, plays the Queen. Then I cross to dummy and lead the 7 of spades, discarding my 2 of diamonds. West wins with the 9, cashes the King of clubs and concedes the last trick to my Jack. I just make the contract, losing a spade (when I threw the diamond), a heart and a club.

This was the full hand:

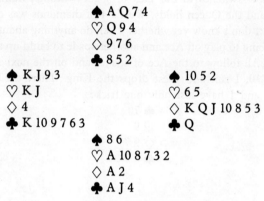

♠ A Q 7 4
♡ Q 9 4
◇ 9 7 6
♣ 8 5 2

♠ K J 9 3   ♠ 10 5 2
♡ K J   ♡ 6 5
◇ 4   ◇ K Q J 10 8 5 3
♣ K 10 9 7 6 3   ♣ Q

♠ 8 6
♡ A 10 8 7 3 2
◇ A 2
♣ A J 4

Post-mortem

As often happens, East's weak pre-emptive bid pushed us into a game that we might not otherwise have reached and might not have made. A perceptive reader may have noted that there was another quite elegant way to make the contract. After ruffing the third spade and cashing the Ace of clubs South can exit with a diamond. East wins and plays another diamond on which South discards a club. Then East must concede a ruff and discard.

Weak pre-emptive bids undoubtedly make the play easy for the opponents when they gain the declaration. I hold strongly to the view that in rubber bridge especially it pays to vary one's three bids, making them often on two to three quick tricks. A pre-empt that is known to be weak is a blunt sword.

12. High Pressure

In a team of four match, with both sides vulnerable, I hold the following third in hand:

♠ 5 2   ♡ 10 5 4   ◇ A 10 5   ♣ K J 6 3 2

North, my partner, deals and opens **two clubs**. That is the conventional forcing bid in our system, promising a game or near-game hand. With a five-card suit, together with an Ace and a King, I have enough for a positive response, so after a pass by East I bid **three clubs**. With the opponents remaining silent, my partner bids **three spades**. I have nothing more to show for the moment, so I bid **3NT**.

Partner's next call is a little unexpected: he raises to **5NT**. That is a natural call, I presume. We do play some five no-trump conventions but only when a suit has been clearly agreed. He knows I have a club suit and I cannot support his spades, so my natural call is **6NT**.

The full bidding:

South	West	North	East
—	—	2♣	pass
3♣	pass	3♠	pass
3NT	pass	5NT	pass
6NT	pass	pass	pass

West leads the 7 of spades and partner puts down:

♠ A Q J 9 8 3
♡ A K 7
◇ K Q
♣ A 8

♠ 7 led

♠ 5 2
♡ 10 5 4
◇ A 10 5
♣ K J 6 3 2

My partner's 5NT was a good call, in my opinion. Certainly we are in the best contract.

If I can make five tricks in the spade suit that will be enough except that there may be entry trouble. I wonder what that lead of the 7 means, through dummy's suit. Is anything to be gained by putting up the Ace? Only if East has the singleton King, and I don't think it is likely that West would have led from 10 x x x. If the spades are all on the wrong side I shall have to make the tricks from clubs. For the moment, I will put in the Jack and see what happens.

On the Jack of spades East throws a diamond. Pity I didn't finesse the 8 of spades; I might have done, at that. Now I can't make more than three spade tricks. Three spades, two hearts and three diamonds make eight so on the surface four club tricks will see me home, but it's not so simple as that. Entries are a problem. Suppose I play Ace of clubs, finesse the Jack and find East with Q x x x. I can set up a fifth club but I'll have to overtake one of dummy's diamonds in order to enter hand.

The difficult question is whether or not to play off the K Q of diamonds before taking the club finesse. If the clubs are 3 – 3 and West has the Queen it is essential to keep the diamond entry to my hand. On the other hand, since the spades are 5 – 0 it is more likely (a) that East will have the Queen of clubs and (b) that the clubs will break 4 – 2 or worse.

Suppose I play off the diamonds and the Ace of clubs and successfully finesse the Jack of clubs: how do I stand then? Counting three tricks in spades, that will give me eleven tricks on top. And surely West will be in some trouble, for he won't be able to let a spade go.

I find these chances hard to estimate and I haven't considered the extra possibility that the Jack of diamonds might fall in two rounds. I am going to take the simple view that if the club finesse is right I shall surely be able to exert pressure on West. I play off the K Q of diamonds and everyone follows. Since East threw a diamond on the first trick I assume he began with at least five, very likely six. Now I play Ace of clubs and finesse the Jack of clubs. That passes off all right, West playing the 10 on the second round. I play the King of clubs and West throws a heart. The hand is developing much as I expected. The following cards are left:

♠ A Q 9 8
♡ A K 7
♢ —
♣ —

♠ 5
♡ 10 5 4
♢ A
♣ 6 3

West has four spades still left and I am pretty sure I have him now. If he follows to the Ace of diamonds his other two cards will be a couple of hearts. Let's put that to the test. On the Ace of diamonds West throws the 8 of hearts. Now it's a certainty. I throw a heart from table, finesse the Queen of spades and cash the top hearts. Dummy's last three cards are the A 9 8 of spades and West has K 10 6. Like a well brought up chess player, West resigns, not waiting for the inevitable end-play. This was the full hand:

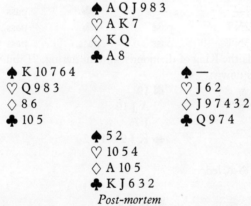

♠ A Q J 9 8 3
♡ A K 7
♢ K Q
♣ A 8

♠ K 10 7 6 4
♡ Q 9 8 3
♢ 8 6
♣ 10 5

♠ —
♡ J 6 2
♢ J 9 7 4 3 2
♣ Q 9 7 4

♠ 5 2
♡ 10 5 4
♢ A 10 5
♣ K J 6 3 2

Post-mortem

The long spades in dummy were like a tin can attached to West's tail. Declarer had to foresee the possibility of exerting pressure on West in spades and hearts. As was remarked in the narrative, playing off the K Q of diamonds at an early stage, giving up the diamond entry to the South hand, would have been a mistake if West had had Q x x of clubs. It became the right play once declarer realized that three tricks in diamonds plus three in clubs would put him in a commanding position.

13. . . . But the Patient Died

In a hotly contested game of rubber bridge I hold the following in third position:

♠ A Q 6   ♡ Q 8 5 2   ◇ 10 8 6 3   ♣ A 10

With both sides vulnerable, my partner deals and opens **one club**. In such positions I hold strongly to the natural and uninformative 2NT rather than the scientific approach of one diamond or one heart. So I respond **2NT** and partner bids **three clubs**. That is a weak bid in our system and strictly I ought to pass. However, he has opened vulnerable and I have the Ace of his suit. I shall have to take the blame if it goes wrong, but I'm going to battle on with **3NT**. All pass, so bidding has been:

South	West	North	East
—	—	1♣	pass
2NT	pass	3♣	pass
3NT	pass	pass	pass

West leads the King of diamonds, and muttering, "I did warn you," partner puts down:

     ♠ 10
     ♡ A J 10
     ◇ J 7
     ♣ K J 9 6 4 3 2

◇ K led

     ♠ A Q 6
     ♡ Q 8 5 2
     ◇ 10 8 6 3
     ♣ A 10

They can't run more than four diamonds against me, so this is going to depend on the Queen of clubs at worst. West's King of diamonds holds the first trick and he follows with the 2 of diamonds to his partner's Ace. East returns a diamond and I try the 8 but West wins with the 9 and cashes the Queen. Meanwhile, I have to discard twice from the table. There are more hazards to this contract than I realized at first. I have got to rely on making seven club tricks, so I throw two hearts from dummy, leaving the Ace bare. On the last diamond East throws the 4 of hearts.

West, inevitably, leads the 7 of hearts, taking dummy's Ace off the table. East plays the 3, completing an echo. I lead a club to the Ace and the 10 back. No Queen appears, so now I have to work out whether or not to finesse, with about 1000 points depending on it.

All I know for certain is that West began with four diamonds. As to the hearts, I can't be altogether sure but the indications are that they are 4 – 2. If East had had only three hearts he would probably have discarded a spade rather than a heart either from three small or from K x x. If West has four diamonds and two hearts, is he likely to have a doubleton club? With five spades he might surely have led a spade. These inferences are not very secure but I can't think of anything better. I'm going to play the Jack.

East produces the Queen and partner fixes me with a steely glare. East now leads the Jack of spades, pinning dummy's 10.

Every trick costs money, so I must get out of this as best I can. I still think that West began with short hearts. If so, the reason why he didn't lead a spade from a five-card suit must be that it was headed by the King and he preferred to lead from K Q 9 x of diamonds. If West has the King of hearts as well—that echo by East doesn't mean anything—I may still emerge with a few tricks. So I'm not going to finesse the spade now. After the Ace has won, the following cards are left:

$$\spadesuit —$$
$$\heartsuit —$$
$$\diamondsuit —$$
$$\clubsuit\ K\ 9\ 6\ 4\ 3$$

$$\spadesuit\ Q\ 6$$
$$\heartsuit\ Q\ 8\ 5$$
$$\diamondsuit —$$
$$\clubsuit —$$

There are three hearts still out—the King, the 9 and the 6. If the King is held by East I probably shan't make another trick anyway. If

West has K 6 and East the 9 I do better to play the Queen, keeping East out of the lead. West will throw me back with a heart and I shall make two more tricks that way. On the other hand, if West has the King of hearts alone I can make three more tricks if I exit with a low heart now. That is just as likely, so I lead the 5. West has to put the King on this: he makes his King of spades and I win the last three tricks. That's 300 away, not so brilliant when one looks at the full hand:

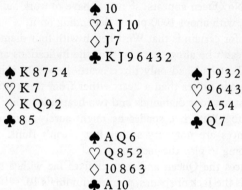

♠ 10
♥ A J 10
♦ J 7
♣ K J 9 6 4 3 2

♠ K 8 7 5 4
♥ K 7
♦ K Q 9 2
♣ 8 5

♠ J 9 3 2
♥ 9 6 4 3
♦ A 5 4
♣ Q 7

♠ A Q 6
♥ Q 8 5 2
♦ 10 8 6 3
♣ A 10

"It might have been worse," I begin to tell my partner. "For example, if I finesse the Queen of spades all I make is my three Aces and . . . " But he isn't listening.

Post-mortem

Declarer could have protected himself from disaster on this hand by discarding a couple of clubs on the long diamonds instead of the J 10 of hearts. That would be somewhat cowardly play, however, for to make the contract he would still have to find the Queen of clubs as well as the heart finesse. Despite the result, the play was well thought out. The operation was successful but the patient died.

14. A Tactical Incident

Vulnerable against non-vulnerable opponents in a team-of-four match, I hold the following two-suiter:

♠ A 3   ♡ Q J 10 8 6 3   ◇ K 8 7 4 2   ♣ —

North, my partner, deals and opens **one club**. East passes and I respond **one heart**. West comes in with **one spade** and this is followed by two passes.

I must show some life now. Neither three hearts nor two diamonds would be forcing according to my methods. I shall jump to **three diamonds**. West passes and partner jumps to **four hearts**. The bidding so far has gone:

South	West	North	East
—	—	1♣	pass
1♡	1♠	pass	pass
3◇	pass	4♡	pass

Am I worth a slam try now? Partner has opened one club, of which I am void, and passed over one spade. His jump to four hearts over my three diamonds suggests that the diamond bid improved his hand in some way. I should imagine he has a balanced hand with a fit in diamonds and probably A x x or K x x in hearts. Suppose I give him K x x of hearts and A x of diamonds; add the Ace of clubs to take care of my losing spade and that still doesn't add up to an opening bid. Or he could have A K of hearts and something like Q J of diamonds. Yes, I can certainly make a slam try and the most helpful bid should be **four spades**.

To four spades partner responds **five diamonds**. That looks like Ace of diamonds and an honor in hearts at the least. I shall bid **six hearts**.

The full bidding:

South	West	North	East
—	—	1♣	pass
1♡	1♠	pass	pass
3◇	pass	4♡	pass
4♠	pass	5◇	pass
6♡	pass	pass	pass

West leads the King of clubs and partner goes down as follows:

♠ 10 9 7 4
♡ K 9 5
◇ A Q 5
♣ A 10 7

 ♣ K led

♠ A 3
♡ Q J 10 8 6 3
◇ K 8 7 4 2
♣ —

The dummy is actually better than I expected. If I had bid only five hearts I imagine he would have given me six.

If the diamonds are 3 – 2 I can hardly fail. If they are 4 – 1, how do I stand? No problem if the trumps are 2 – 2, for in that case I can simply ruff the fourth diamond. Then let's take the more pessimistic view that the diamonds are 4 – 1 and the trumps 3 – 1.

I would still be all right if the hand that held the three trumps also had the four diamonds. After either one or two rounds of trumps I could play three rounds of diamonds and ruff my fourth diamond as before. But I see a slight difficulty in all this. Suppose I take a round of hearts and the Ace is not played. Do I play another round or not? If the trumps are 2 – 2 I don't want to risk having a diamond ruffed; but if I play another round of trumps to find out, an opponent with A x x may win and draw a third round. If I can force out the Ace of hearts on the first round, I can avoid this dilemma. Then I can take a second round and if I find them 3 – 1 I can switch to diamonds. How can I play the hearts in such a way as to make it difficult for them to hold up the Ace? After discarding my spade on the Ace of clubs, I must play the *King* of hearts from dummy. In that way, I should be able to form an impression about the Ace even if they hold it up.

So I take my discard on the Ace of clubs and lay down the King of hearts. This holds the trick, East playing the 2 and West the 7. Now what am I to make of that? Would either player hold up with A x? It would be very far-sighted and I doubt it. I am inclined to think that one opponent, probably East, has A x x. If that's so I mustn't play another trump and give them a chance to draw a third round. Instead I must test the diamonds.

I play off Ace and Queen of diamonds, and on the second round West discards a club. It looks as though West has two red singletons! I play a third round of diamonds to the King, ruff a fourth diamond and then play the third trump from table. All the defense makes is the Ace of hearts, the full deal being as follows:

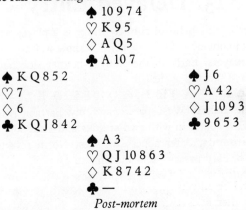

♠ 10 9 7 4
♡ K 9 5
◇ A Q 5
♣ A 10 7

♠ K Q 8 5 2
♡ 7
◇ 6
♣ K Q J 8 4 2

♠ J 6
♡ A 4 2
◇ J 10 9 3
♣ 9 6 5 3

♠ A 3
♡ Q J 10 8 6 3
◇ K 8 7 4 2
♣ —

Post-mortem

The play of the King of hearts from dummy at trick 2 was one of those inconspicuous tactical maneuvers that make the game easier for good players. An onlooker might think that the lead of a small heart could make no difference. That it can is shown by what happened at the other table in this match. There South, also playing in six hearts, won the opening lead with the Ace of clubs and led a low heart to the Queen. Now he was nervous about testing the diamonds lest the diamonds be 4 – 1 while all the time the hearts were 2 – 2. He therefore returned a heart. East won and drew a third round of trumps, after which a diamond had to be lost. The essential difference between the two lines of play is that when the King of hearts is not taken there is a fair inference that the hearts are 3 – 1; but when the low heart slips through there is nothing to show that East has not started with A x.

While on this hand declarer wanted to force out the opponent's trump winner on the first round, there are just as many on which he would prefer that the Ace be held up. With a sequence of this kind it is always wise to consider, with reference to the tactical situation, what is the best way to slip past the Ace and the best way to smoke it out.

15. Delayed Entry

My partner in this hand of rubber bridge is a player with whom I have small acquaintance. The opponents I know well to be strong and enterprising players. Early in the rubber, neither side having scored below the line, I pick up as dealer:

♠ K   ♡ A Q 10 3   ◇ Q 10 8 5   ♣ K 7 6 4

I open **one heart**, West passes and my partner responds **two diamonds**. East comes in with **two spades** and I support my partner to **three diamonds**. After a pass by West North reverts to **three hearts**, which East passes. The bidding so far:

South	West	North	East
1♡	pass	2◇	2♠
3◇	pass	3♡	pass
?			

I don't know if he intends this sequence to be forcing or not. It is not so in my book. The hand could play awkwardly in hearts if he had only three trumps, so I am certainly not going four hearts. The question is whether I should leave it in three hearts or put him back to four diamonds. If his diamonds are not good he may return to four hearts, which will probably be doubled. In fact, I rather distrust the whole affair. I am going to pass although, technically, the right bid is probably four diamonds.

But West is still there and he re-opens with **three spades**. Partner is nodding his head and looking serious. Eventually he bids **four hearts** and to my relief no one doubles. The full bidding has been:

South	West	North	East
1♡	pass	2◇	2♠
3◇	pass	3♡	pass
pass	3♠	4♡	pass
pass	pass		

West leads the Ace of spades and with well-founded apprehension partner puts down:

> ♠ J 7 3
> ♡ K 9 8 4
> ◇ A 7 6 3
> ♣ Q 9

♠ A led

> ♠ K
> ♡ A Q 10 3
> ◇ Q 10 8 5
> ♣ K 7 6 4

I suppose he thought he wasn't good enough to give me three hearts on the first round. When the spades were supported he placed me with a singleton. A scientific sort of player, I can see that.

After the Ace of spades West continues with the 9 and I ruff with the 3 of hearts. Since no one doubled I think I can assume that the hearts are going to break 3 – 2. I shall have to ruff spades twice, so I can't draw trumps yet awhile. I must force out the Ace of clubs first.

On the lead of the 4 of clubs West plays the 3, dummy the Queen and East the Ace. East returns the Queen of spades. As West supported spades I imagine he has three, so I trump with the 10 and West follows suit. Now I draw Ace and Queen of hearts and on the second round East drops the Jack. That leaves the cards as follows:

> ♠ —
> ♡ K 9
> ◇ A 7 6 3
> ♣ 9

> ♠ —
> ♡ —
> ◇ Q 10 8 5
> ♣ K 7 6

Sooner or later I have to develop the diamonds to lose only one trick. The simplest line is to enter dummy with the Ace of diamonds, draw the last trump and lead a low diamond, hoping that East has a doubleton honor. Before I do that, let me see if I can reconstruct the hand.

East surely has six spades and a doubleton heart, unless that Jack of hearts was a peculiar false card. He could have a doubleton diamond and three clubs to the Ace. Alternatively, he could have one diamond and four clubs. I can't see any strong clue from his bidding or play.

What about West? Could he have, for example,

$$\spadesuit A x x \quad \heartsuit x x x \quad \diamondsuit J x x \quad \clubsuit J x x x ?$$

He would pass three diamonds on that but would he re-open with three spades? Unlikely. Similarly, with a diamond more and a club less, he would probably pass three hearts.

He must have thought he had good defense against four hearts—I am sure that that is the explanation! He must have reckoned on tricks in diamonds, probably holding K J x or even K J x x. If that's so I cannot lose by leading the Queen of diamonds from hand. I may as well do that at once while I have the trumps and clubs under some control.

On the Queen of diamonds West plays low and East drops the 9. On that play West could have K x x and East J 9 but I feel it is more probable that West has K J x x and East the singleton 9. Either way, it is safe for me to lead another diamond (unless East has the third trump all the time). I lead the 5 of diamonds, West plays low again and I put in the 6 from table. This holds the trick, East discarding a spade. Now I draw the trump and lose only to the King of diamonds. This was the full hand:

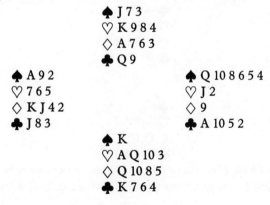

Post-mortem

After the Queen of diamonds held, declarer could also have played King of clubs, ruffed a club and drawn the last trump. Then a small diamond from table would leave West on play. That line of play would fail, however, if West had three diamonds and four clubs.

The main point of the play was the lead of the Queen of diamonds in the diagram position instead of the lazy play of a low diamond to the Ace. West, it will be remembered, passed three diamonds and then came late into the bidding with three spades. When a player follows such a sequence it is usually possible to define his hand within fairly close limits.

16. Something up my Sleeve

Playing in a pairs contest against expert opponents, I hold:

♠ A K J 9 6 5 4   ♡ J 10 3   ◇ 10 4   ♣ 5

With both sides vulnerable, my partner, North, opens **1NT** and East passes. This would be a good hand for Texas. Playing the Texas convention, I would bid four hearts and my partner (always assuming that he remembered the convention) would transfer to four spades. It might well be better that he, the no-trump bidder, should play the hand in spades.

However, we have not agreed to play Texas, so that possibility does not arise. I might bid three spades and pass if partner rebid 3NT. That could produce a good match-point score but it is the sort of bid that I would try only if I were desperate for a "top." As it is, I shall bid a straightforward **four spades.** Everyone passes, so the bidding has been simple:

South	West	North	East
—	—	1NT	pass
4♠	pass	pass	pass

West leads the Jack of clubs and partner puts down:

♠ Q 7 2
♡ A Q 6 4
◇ K 6 5
♣ A K 6

♣ J led

♠ A K J 9 6 5 4
♡ J 10 3
◇ 10 4
♣ 5

That's a friendly lead. I cannot fail to make eleven tricks, for at most I shall lose a heart and a diamond. To make a good score, I may need two overtricks. If the King of hearts is wrong, how can I stop East from playing a diamond?

It would be foolish to play off two top clubs and throw a diamond. If I have to lose a heart I want to do that before the enemy can sum up the situation. To begin with, I win the first club with the Ace and come to hand with a spade, on which East plays the 10 and West the 3.

Now if I lead the 10 or Jack of hearts and East wins with the King he will see that there is not much future for the defense and will play a diamond even if he has the Ace himself, sitting over the King. He is that sort of player.

I think I can make it more difficult for him by leading my 3 of hearts. I won't help him to count the hand by playing off a second round of spades. On the 3 of hearts West plays the 5, dummy the Queen and East the King. This is the critical moment. If East does not have the Ace of diamonds he will certainly play one, but if he has the Ace he may not realize that he must make it now or never.

Better! East returns a club. I ruff, draw the second trump, cash J 10 of hearts and cross to dummy's Queen of spades. Then my two losing diamonds go away on the Ace of hearts and the King of clubs and I end up with twelve tricks for what should be a good score!

This was the full deal:

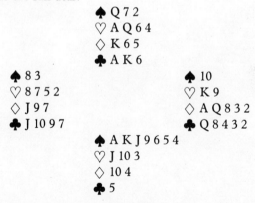

Post-mortem

This hand is instructive in the sense that players of different degree would play it in a number of different ways. A weak player would hastily take the discard on the second club and after that the defenders could not fail to cash their diamond when they won a heart. A better player would avoid that pitfall but would probably draw two trumps and then run the 10 of hearts. An average defender in East's position might still fail to cash the Ace of diamonds, but not a good defender, for he would see that South had seven tricks in spades, two in clubs and at least two in hearts. That being so, he would cash the Ace of diamonds—a play that could lose only if South were void in diamonds.

With regard to the line of play actually followed, a good technician may have noted that leading the 3 of hearts destroys certain squeeze possibilities should West have K 9 x x of hearts and Ace of diamonds. With that holding, West can be squeezed in the red suits so long as South does not block the run of the hearts by leading the 3 originally. Even then, the situation can be restored if South is allowed to slip through the 10 on the next round. Setting one chance against the other, I still think that the deceptive lead of the 3 is more likely to bring in the extra trick.

17. Recovery

Playing in a pairs event where the standard of play is theoretically high all round, I hold the following second in hand:

♠ J 5 2   ♡ J 8 7   ◇ K J 4   ♣ K 10 6 2

Neither side is vulnerable and East, on my right, opens **one club**. This is passed round to my partner, who re-opens with **two clubs**.

I assume this shows a strong hand with short clubs, either singleton or void. The question is whether I am to bid 2NT or 3NT. I think I will give him a picture that I hold fair values by jumping to **3NT**. This is passed all round, so the bidding has been:

South	West	North	East
—	—	—	1♣
pass	pass	2♣	pass
3NT	pass	pass	pass

Now that partner has passed 3NT I wonder if I have made the wrong bid. I am sure of it when West leads the 7 of clubs and dummy goes down:

♠ A 9 7 6 4
♡ A K 10 6 3
◇ A Q 5
♣ —

♣ 7 led

♠ J 5 2
♡ J 8 7
◇ K J 4
♣ K 10 6 2

I ought to have said 2NT and then we would have found a contract of four hearts or four spades. Most pairs will be in four hearts, I should think, and will make four or five according to whether they drop the

Queen of hearts. How I'm going to make as many tricks at no-trump I don't know. This 7 of clubs may be top of nothing or it may be from three or four cards to an honor. For the moment all I can do is throw a spade from dummy and see what develops.

East wins with the Ace of clubs and returns the King of spades. Unexpected, but I can guess what has happened. East's clubs are headed by the A Q and he is placing me with the K J and others. If I take this spade in dummy and return a spade East will realize that there is no future for him in spades. He will take the Queen and play a club. That way, I shall be able to run only nine tricks (having thrown a spade at trick 1) and will have a bad score unless I drop the Queen of hearts.

I think the game must be to conceal my spade holding and encourage East to play a second round. On the King of spades I play the 5, West the 8 and dummy the 6. East continues with the Queen of spades, so my little stratagem has succeeded. West drops the 10, so now I have three spade tricks and can afford to open up the hearts. It remains to decide whether to try to drop the Queen of hearts or finesse.

I play a spade to the Jack, return to dummy with the Ace of diamonds and cash the last spade. East throws a club meanwhile, and West throws two diamonds. The following cards are left:

♠ —
♡ A K 10 6 3
◇ Q 5
♣ —

♠ —
♡ J 8 7
◇ K J
♣ K 10

East has shown up with K Q x of spades and a suit of clubs headed by the A Q. He doesn't have to have the Queen of hearts for his opening bid. As I am going to make as many tricks in no-trump as the others will in a suit I think I will go with the majority and play to drop the Queen of hearts. I may as well do that before I get into any difficulty with entries. The Queen of hearts does not fall under the Ace or King but I am relieved to find that it is East who has the Queen guarded. I make ten tricks for what should be a good score, the full hand being:

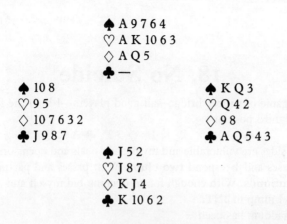

♠ A 9 7 6 4
♡ A K 10 6 3
◇ A Q 5
♣ —

♠ 10 8
♡ 9 5
◇ 10 7 6 3 2
♣ J 9 8 7

♠ K Q 3
♡ Q 4 2
◇ 9 8
♣ A Q 5 4 3

♠ J 5 2
♡ J 8 7
◇ K J 4
♣ K 10 6 2

Post-mortem

East was not so much to blame for misreading the club position. It looked to him as though his partner had led the 7 from something like 10 8 7 and that I had K J 9 6 2.

This hand presented a problem of a sort that occurs only at match-point pairs. Realizing that he was in an inferior contract declarer had to take a considerable risk (when he ducked the spade return at trick 2) to give himself a chance of making sufficient tricks to beat the other pairs. Once he had drawn level, as it were, he had to play with the room and refuse the heart finesse.

18. No Suicide

In a game of rubber bridge—all good players—I hold the following hand in third position:

♠ J 10 6 5   ♡ K 4   ◇ 3 2   ♣ A K Q 7 3

Both sides are vulnerable and my partner deals and opens **one heart**. East passes and I respond **two clubs**. West passes and partner rebids **two diamonds**. With enough for an opening bid myself and a reasonable fit, I jump to **3NT**.

The bidding has been:

South	West	North	East
—	—	1♡	pass
2♣	pass	2◇	pass
3NT	pass	pass	pass

West leads the 3 of spades and this dummy goes down:

                        ♠ K
                        ♡ Q J 9 7 5
                        ◇ A K J 10 8
                        ♣ 5 4

♠ 3 led

                        ♠ J 10 6 5
                        ♡ K 4
                        ◇ 3 2
                        ♣ A K Q 7 3

I can't form much of a plan until I know what is going to happen in spades. East heads the King with the Ace and returns the 2. If that's a true card the spades are 4 – 4. East may have the Queen, so I must go in with the Jack. This is covered by the Queen and I have to consider what to throw from dummy. I think a heart, because one extra heart will be enough for the contract.

West returns the 8 of spades and again I have to discard from table. I have more or less made up my mind that the spades are 4 – 4, so I shall be knocking out the Ace of hearts and can spare a diamond. East plays the 4 of spades. Now, is there any point in holding up? The missing spades are the 9 and 7 and if East had them both he would surely have overtaken the 8. That is further confirmation that the spades are 4 – 4, so I win with the 10 and lead the King of hearts. West plays the Ace and leads a spade in the following position:

♠ —
♡ Q J 9
◇ A K J 10
♣ 5 4

♠ 6
♡ 4
◇ 3 2
♣ A K Q 7 3

I have made one trick and seven more are visible. Meanwhile, I have got to find another discard from dummy At first sight it looks as though I can throw a club, but I am not so sure about that. I want to give myself all the chances and if I throw a club now and East returns a club, as he probably will, I shall have to find discards on the second and third rounds of clubs. From all points of view, it must be better to throw another diamond from table.

East wins the spade trick with the 9 and returns a club. I win with the Ace and cross to dummy to play off the Queen and Jack of hearts. Both follow to the first round but East shows out on the second, discarding a diamond. I play off one top diamond, then return to the King of clubs. Now only three cards are left:

♠ —
♡ 9
◇ K J
♣ —

♠ —
♡ —
◇ 3
♣ Q 7

On the Queen of clubs West throws a diamond. As I know that West has the 10 of hearts, I throw the 9 of hearts from table. Now the two diamonds must be good, for West has a heart and a diamond, and East a diamond and a club.

The diamond finesse, if I had taken it earlier, would have been wrong, for this was the full hand:

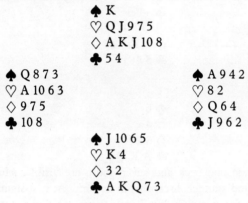

♠ K
♡ Q J 9 7 5
◇ A K J 10 8
♣ 5 4

♠ Q 8 7 3
♡ A 10 6 3
◇ 9 7 5
♣ 10 8

♠ A 9 4 2
♡ 8 2
◇ Q 6 4
♣ J 9 6 2

♠ J 10 6 5
♡ K 4
◇ 3 2
♣ A K Q 7 3

Post-mortem

The main trap in this hand was one that in reading you may have underestimated. Declarer must at no point discard one of the apparently useless clubs on the table. Both are vital as entries to his hand. Having counted up that he needs to develop only one extra trick in either hearts or diamonds or clubs, he must take care not to be put in the position where he has to cash his high clubs before testing the red suits.

Although declarer could not know at the time, the squeeze on East began when the third heart on the table was cashed. As on many such hands, it would have been better play for West to hold up his Ace of hearts. Declarer can still make the contract in more than one way, but he can also go wrong.

19. A Hail of Bullets

Playing rubber bridge with a somewhat excitable partner, I hold the following second in hand:

♠ Q 8 4   ♡ A K J 6 3   ◇ 8 4   ♣ A Q 5

No one is vulnerable and East, on my right, deals and passes. I open **one heart** and West overcalls with **four spades.** Never one to be shut out, my partner bids **five diamonds** and East **doubles.** I pass, so does West, and partner now retreats to **five hearts.** East **doubles** again, surprising no one. All pass. The bidding has gone:

South	West	North	East
—	—	—	pass
1♡	4♠	5◇	double
pass	pass	5♡	double
pass	pass	pass	

West leads the King of spades and partner's hand is not encouraging:

> ♠ 3
> ♡ Q 9 2
> ◇ K Q 10 6 3 2
> ♣ K J 10

♠ K led

> ♠ Q 8 4
> ♡ A K J 6 3
> ◇ 8 4
> ♣ A Q 5

I don't think I'm going to enjoy this. On the first spade East plays the 5. West switches to the 9 of clubs, which I win in dummy with the 10, East playing the 2.

There is a slight reason for leaving the lead in dummy. I am going to play a diamond next, for no doubt East has the Ace, and by leading from dummy I force East to play before his partner. If I lead from my hand and West has a doubleton, he will begin an echo which will give East a count and enable him to hold off.

On the King of diamonds East plays the Ace, I the 4, and West the 9. East now leads the 6 of spades and dummy has to ruff with the 2 of hearts.

Let's see if I can count the hand. I should imagine West has seven spades and East a doubleton. West's 9 of diamonds could be a singleton, or it could be the beginning of an echo from a doubleton. I can't tell about the clubs. As to the hearts, I should imagine that East has all five. If his only values had been a couple of tricks in diamonds he would probably have passed five diamonds. Players who double in such circumstances usually have even better defense against the first suit named. Moreover, this play of a spade to force the dummy is also suggestive of long trumps.

I can't draw his trumps by straight leads but I can exert some pressure by leading the 9 and forcing him to cover. That will leave me with a major tenace of sorts. So I lead the 9 of hearts from table, East plays the 10, I win with the King and West, as expected, shows out.

It looks as though East's distribution is two spades, five hearts, and either three diamonds and three clubs or four diamonds and two clubs. If he has three diamonds I think I can do it. My trumps are K J 6 3 with the Queen in dummy. East has the 8 7 5 4.

I play my second diamond to dummy, West playing the 5. I ruff a third diamond with my 3 of hearts, East playing the Jack, and take two rounds of clubs, finishing in dummy. Now I know the cards exactly, so I can show all four hands:

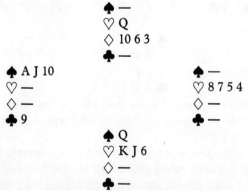

On the lead of a diamond from dummy East is caught in the diagonal crossfire of my trumps. Shaking his head, he plays the 7. I over-ruff,

ruff my spade with the Queen of hearts and win the last two tricks with the Jack and 6 of hearts, just making the contract.

This was the full deal:

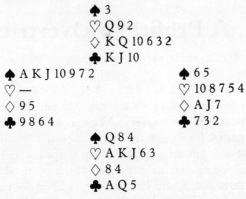

♠ 3
♡ Q 9 2
◇ K Q 10 6 3 2
♣ K J 10

♠ A K J 10 9 7 2   ♠ 6 5
♡ —   ♡ 10 8 7 5 4
◇ 9 5   ◇ A J 7
♣ 9 8 6 4   ♣ 7 3 2

♠ Q 8 4
♡ A K J 6 3
◇ 8 4
♣ A Q 5

Post-mortem

Looking at the full diagram I see that it would not have helped East to hold off the first diamond. In fact, there is no defense. The play shows the enormous power that can be exerted in an end-game when there are high trumps in both hands. That struck me some years ago when I constructed the following deal:

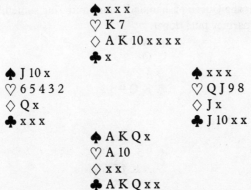

♠ x x x
♡ K 7
◇ A K 10 x x x x
♣ x

♠ J 10 x   ♠ x x x
♡ 6 5 4 3 2   ♡ Q J 9 8
◇ Q x   ◇ J x
♣ x x x   ♣ J 10 x x

♠ A K Q x
♡ A 10
◇ x x
♣ A K Q x x

If you were by some odd chance to land in a contract of six hearts you could make it against any lead but a trump! You cash eight winners in the side suits and then lead a club from hand. Dummy's K 7 of hearts and your own A 10 will suffice to win four of the last five tricks!

20. A Profitless Overtrick

In a multiple team event, present opponents not the strongest in the field, I hold the following:

♠ 9 5   ♡ A K J 8 6 2   ◊ K 7 5 3   ♣ 4

The enemy are vulnerable, we are not. My partner, North, deals and opens **one spade**. East passes and I respond **two hearts**. Partner rebids **two spades**. I have two possible calls now. Three hearts is the more obvious one, but on some hands three spades could turn out better. If the bidding goes the same way at the other table South is likely to bid three hearts, and I think I'll play along with him. Three hearts in this sequence is fairly encouraging, so there is no reason to jump to four. I bid **three hearts,** therefore, and all pass. The bidding has been:

South	West	North	East
—	—	1♠	pass
2♡	pass	2♠	pass
3♡	pass	pass	pass

West leads the Queen of diamonds, and muttering something about a second suit partner puts down:

♠ A Q 10 8 4
♡ Q
◊ 4 2
♣ K Q 9 5 3

◊ Q led

♠ 9 5
♡ A K J 8 6 2
◊ K 7 5 3
♣ 4

With the Ace of diamonds on the right side, it looks as though we have underbid this. I play low from dummy; East puts on the Ace and returns a trump, which I run to dummy's Queen.

I would like to lead up to dummy's clubs but I don't feel disposed to take out my King of diamonds at this stage. If I do that I shall make nine tricks at most, for when they take the Ace of clubs they will cash a couple of diamonds. Though it may cost a trick in the suit I lead the King of clubs from dummy. East plays the 8 and West wins with the Ace. West returns the 6 of clubs; slightly unexpected, but not un-welcome. Trusting that it will not be ruffed, I put up the Queen. East drops the Jack and I discard a diamond. I come to hand by ruffing a club and on this trick East discards the 3 of spades.

It takes four rounds to draw the trumps, for West turns up with 10 9 x x, East with a doubleton. On the third and fourth rounds East discards two more spades. The following cards are left:

♠ A Q 10
♡ —
◇ 4
♣ 9

♠ 9 5
♡ 8
◇ K 7
♣ —

It is time to do some reconstruction. West appears to have had four hearts and five clubs. What has he got in spades and diamonds? He must have at least two diamonds and probably more. Odd that he didn't play a spade when he was in with the Ace of clubs! He may have a singleton King but hardly a low singleton, for that he would surely have led at some point. And East has thrown three spades, which is rather significant. In fact, I am beginning to think that the spades are 6 – 0.

If I lead a spade in the diagram position and West shows out, East will win and return a diamond. Then I shall have to lose another trick. But suppose I play off my last trump now? That may embarrass East and in any case it will be safe to finesse a spade afterwards, for East has no more clubs. On the 8 of hearts West throws a club, North a club, and East, after some reflection, the 6 of diamonds. Now I cash the King of diamonds, on which West plays the 9 and East the 10. At trick 11 a spade is led and West shows void. Dummy plays the 10, East the

Jack and a spade return into the A Q gives me a diamond discard. Thus I end up with ten tricks. This was the full hand:

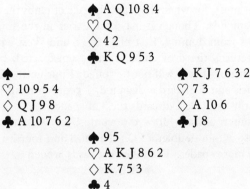

```
                 ♠ A Q 10 8 4
                 ♡ Q
                 ◇ 4 2
                 ♣ K Q 9 5 3
♠ —                              ♠ K J 7 6 3 2
♡ 10 9 5 4                       ♡ 7 3
◇ Q J 9 8                        ◇ A 10 6
♣ A 10 7 6 2                     ♣ J 8
                 ♠ 9 5
                 ♡ A K J 8 6 2
                 ◇ K 7 5 3
                 ♣ 4
```

Making ten tricks at hearts against less than brilliant defense did not suffice to win the board, for at the other table the bidding went differently. North opened one club, East came in with one spade and South bid two hearts. Somewhat awkwardly placed for a rebid, North bid 2NT and South raised to 3NT. When East opened a spade declarer cashed the Queen of hearts and led a diamond, with the prospect of making about five tricks or nine, according to the position of the Ace of diamonds. His luck was in.

Post-mortem

This may seem a straightforward hand on which no one could go wrong, but the fact is that a declarer playing blind, in the sense of not thinking about the enemy hands, would play a spade after drawing trumps. He would not realize the advantage of playing off the last trump.

There was no defense to the end game, but it would have been better play for East, at trick 1, to let the Queen of diamonds run up to the King. That would have left the defense in better control. The contract would also have been held to nine tricks had West exited with a heart or a diamond when he was in with the Ace of clubs. The timing is different since the Queen of clubs has not been cashed.

21. The Diamonds Were Paste

Playing rubber bridge against opponents of average standard, I pick up the following hand as South:

♠ Q 10 7 6 4 2   ♡ Q 10   ◇ J 5   ♣ Q 6 3

With no one vulnerable, West deals and passes. North opens **one club** and East overcalls with **one diamond.**

Some would say my hand wasn't good enough for a free bid but I don't hold with that. By passing you only create future problems. If the opponents jump the bidding, then on the next round you either have to pass again or come in at a high level. Besides, it's a fair hand, with a six-card major and the Queen of partner's suit. So, I call **one spade.**

After a pass by West, North bids **2NT** and East passes.

So far:

South	West	North	East
—	pass	1♣	1◇
1♠	pass	2NT	pass
?			

The choice now, as I see it, is between three spades and 3NT. It would be timid to pass and there is little point in three clubs. As I have doubletons in both the red suits I think I will make one more try to play in a suit and bid **three spades.** My partner may not take that as forcing but I don't care if he passes.

After some thought, however, he gives me **four spades,** so the full bidding has gone:

South	West	North	East
—	pass	1♣	1◇
1♠	pass	2NT	pass
3♠	pass	4♠	pass
pass	pass		

West leads the 8 of diamonds and the dummy goes down:

♠ A K 5
♡ 9 7 4 2
◇ A Q 10
♣ A 10 4

◇ 8 led

♠ Q 10 7 6 4 2
♡ Q 10
◇ J 5
♣ Q 6 3

Wrong contract, I should think. We play a weak no-trump not vulnerable, so North couldn't open 1NT, but with his strong diamonds and good spades he might have preferred 3NT to four spades. Maybe I should have given him 3NT myself—I nearly did.

However, here we are in four spades and in danger of losing a diamond, two hearts and one or two clubs.

If they don't cash their two hearts at once I may get rid of a heart on the third diamond. At any rate, I'll take the slight risk of a ruff in diamonds and put up the Queen. Then if a low heart comes back West may play another diamond, thinking his partner has the K J.

East covers with the diamond King and leads back the 5 of hearts. I was expecting that, of course. I want to give an impression of strength in hearts, so I shall play the Queen. West wins with the King and returns the 3 of diamonds.

Thus far, my little deception has succeeded. After drawing trumps I can discard the 10 of hearts and the contract will depend on losing only one club. Before putting that suit to the test I want to find out as much about the hand as I can. I'd like to ruff a couple of hearts to get a count of that suit. I shall want entries to the table after drawing trumps, so I play the Queen of spades first. (Of course, that is not the normal way to play such a combination, but it is impossible that East should have J 9 x x and West, who passed throughout, a void.)

Everyone follows to two rounds of spades, West showing up with J 9. After taking my discard on the third diamond I ruff a heart, East playing the 8, cross to dummy with the Ace of spades and ruff another heart, bringing down the Ace from East. Only four cards are left:

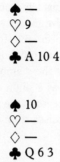

```
      ♠ —
      ♡ 9
      ◇ —
      ♣ A 10 4


      ♠ 10
      ♡ —
      ◇ —
      ♣ Q 6 3
```

Let's see. West threw a club on the third diamond and another club on the third spade. I know that East started with six diamonds and two spades. Were his hearts A 8 5 or A J 8 5? I can't be certain, but in any event he has at most two clubs. Would he have overcalled on

♠ x x   ♡ A x x   ◇ K x x x x x   ♣ x x ?

It looks a bit naked, even not vulnerable. I think I'll assume that he has one of the honors. In that case, the play is Ace of clubs and a small club back, winning against K x or J x and losing only to x x.

Actually, East turns up with J x. The full hand was:

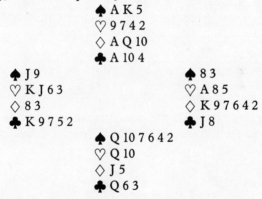

```
              ♠ A K 5
              ♡ 9 7 4 2
              ◇ A Q 10
              ♣ A 10 4
  ♠ J 9                      ♠ 8 3
  ♡ K J 6 3                  ♡ A 8 5
  ◇ 8 3                      ◇ K 9 7 6 4 2
  ♣ K 9 7 5 2                ♣ J 8
              ♠ Q 10 7 6 4 2
              ♡ Q 10
              ◇ J 5
              ♣ Q 6 3
```

Post-mortem

There are quite a few points to note in the play:

The Queen of diamonds at trick 1, the best way to induce West to continue diamonds when next in.

The Queen of hearts at trick 2, to give an impression of strength in hearts, either A Q or K Q.

The use of entries to ruff hearts and obtain a fair count.

The play of the clubs. Observe that it would have been a losing play to finesse the 10. Had South been able to place East with a singleton club he would have played a low club from dummy at trick 10.

As to the defense, East knew the diamond position better than West and his return of a low heart was a slight error. He should have played Ace and another, to make sure that the defense took its heart tricks before declarer could obtain a discard on diamonds.

22. When the Trumps Are Thin

Playing in a pairs contest against competent opposition I hold:

♠ A 8 4 3   ♡ Q 7 6   ◇ J 8 5   ♣ A 9 2

Both sides are vulnerable and East, on my right, deals and passes. I pass and so does West. My partner opens fourth in hand with **one club** and East passes again. This is a situation I always dislike. We play that a response of 1NT to one club shows better than a minimum —say about 7 to 9 or 7 to 10 points. This hand is theoretically a little too good for 1NT, but at the same time I don't fancy one spade on a poor suit with a balanced hand. Nevertheless, I suppose I must go with the room and respond **one spade.** This is passed all round, so the bidding has been uneventful:

South	West	North	East
—	—	—	pass
pass	pass	1♣	pass
1♠	pass	pass	pass

West opens the Jack of hearts and partner displays:

♠ 7 6
♡ A K 2
◇ Q 9 4 3
♣ K J 7 4

♡ J led

♠ A 8 4 3
♡ Q 7 6
◇ J 8 5
♣ A 9 2

I wish I had followed my judgment and responded 1NT. Now, how am I to make one spade? I am bound to lose at least three spades and two diamonds. The opponents will probably establish a long heart and I may have to take finesses in the minor suits. I must play trumps and see what develops.

The first trick is won with the King of hearts, East playing the 5.
I play a trump from dummy and duck it to West's 9. West continues
with the 10 of hearts which I take in hand, East playing the 3. I may
as well knock the trumps together. I lead the Ace, on which West plays
the 2 and East the 10. On a third round of trumps West goes up with
the King, dropping his partner's Queen, as no doubt he intended.
Then West draws my last trump with his Jack. Dummy, meanwhile,
has thrown two diamonds and East has discarded a club. West exits
with a heart to dummy's Ace, East following with the 8. That leaves
the cards as follows:

♠ —
♡ —
◇ Q 9
♣ K J 7 4

♠ —
♡ —
◇ J 8 5
♣ A 9 2

I have got to lose Ace and King of diamonds and someone has the
thirteenth heart. I can afford to lose three more tricks but if I take a
losing finesse in clubs I shall be down for sure. On the other hand, if
I run the 9 of diamonds and that loses to the 10 they still may not be
able to cash three diamonds. A diamond must be the better play, since
even if I guess wrong I may be able to play on clubs later.

When the 9 of diamonds is led from dummy East goes into a trance.
He must have a doubleton honor and be wondering whether to play it.
Eventually he goes up with the King of diamonds and cashes a
thirteenth heart. I discard a club from both hands and concede a trick
to the Ace of diamonds, making my contract of one spade.

If East had played low on the 9 of diamonds I would have run it to
West's 10, but the diamonds would have been blocked, for this was the
full hand:

```
                  ♠ 7 6
                  ♡ A K 2
                  ◇ Q 9 4 3
                  ♣ K J 7 4
  ♠ K J 9 2                      ♠ Q 10 5
  ♡ J 10 4                       ♡ 9 8 5 3
  ◇ A 10 6 2                     ◇ K 7
  ♣ 10 5                         ♣ Q 8 6 3
                  ♠ A 8 4 3
                  ♡ Q 7 6
                  ◇ J 8 5
                  ♣ A 9 2
```

Since the hearts were 4 – 3 I could have made the hand rather more
easily by cashing the third heart before playing Ace and another trump.
The defense would then have had to open up one of the minor suits.

Post-mortem

This may not seem to have been a particularly interesting or significant hand. The reason I include it is that so many players, when faced
with such a threadbare assortment in the trump suit, will not touch
trumps at all. They fiddle away in the side suits until the defenders
set up a cross-ruff position and make their trumps separately. When
opponents have all the master trumps it is still good play to draw two
for one.

23. Avoiding Promotion

Playing in a game of rubber bridge of mixed quality I deal and pick up one of my usual hands:

♠ Q 7 6 3   ♡ 9 7 5   ◇ 7 2   ♣ J 6 5 2

Both sides are vulnerable. I pass, West opens **one heart** and my partner **doubles**. East passes and I respond **one spade**. West bids **two diamonds** and partner jumps to **four spades**. I hope he knows what he's doing. West gives the matter some consideration but finally passes. The bidding has been:

South	West	North	East
pass	1♡	double	pass
1♠	2◇	4♠	pass
pass	pass		

West leads the King of diamonds and North puts down a good hand, though not quite so good as he thinks.

> ♠ K J 9 5
> ♡ A K
> ◇ A 10 4
> ♣ A Q 7 3

◇ K led

> ♠ Q 7 6 3
> ♡ 9 7 3
> ◇ 7 2
> ♣ J 6 5 2

There are only two certain losers but as West has bid two suits I can't rely on good breaks. For one thing, West may well have a singleton Ace of spades. For that reason I would prefer to lead the first round of spades from my own hand. I can come to hand only by ruffing a diamond, so I will hold off the first round.

West continues with the diamond Queen. I take the Ace and ruff the third round, East following suit throughout. I play a low spade, West plays low and the King of spades wins in dummy. Now if I lead a low spade back to the Queen West may play a fourth diamond and that may promote his partner's trump 10. Apart from that, I want an entry to my hand, so I play the Jack of spades from table. West takes this with the Ace and plays a low heart to dummy's King. The position is now:

♠ 9 5
♡ A
♢ —
♣ A Q 7 3

♠ Q
♡ 9 7
♢ —
♣ J 6 5 2

I have only lost two tricks but I am not too happy about the club situation. West bid two suits, has shown up with at least two spades and has not led a club at any point, as he might have done with a singleton. I don't think he has 2 – 5 – 4 – 2 for he obviously thought about bidding over four spades. He could be 2 – 6 – 5 – 0 or possibly 2 – 5 – 5 – 1 and in that case the singleton club could well be the King.

If West is void in clubs I can make the contract all right by end-playing East. At the finish I can play a low club to the Jack and then return a club, ducking the trick. But all that will be a mistake if West has the singleton King. Come to think of it, I can maneuver to play a third round of hearts and discover how that suit is distributed.

In the diagram position I play off the Ace of hearts, then draw the last trump, which is held by East. Now I play a heart and ruff with dummy's last spade. On this trick East discards the 4 of clubs.

Now it does look as though West is 2 – 6 – 5 – 0 and East has all the clubs. I play a low club from table, East puts in the 8 and the Jack holds. Then I duck a club to East's 9 and win the last two tricks with dummy's A Q. This was the full hand:

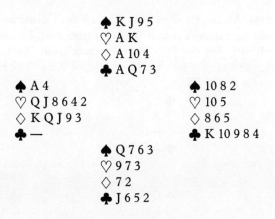

♠ K J 9 5
♥ A K
♦ A 10 4
♣ A Q 7 3

♠ A 4
♥ Q J 8 6 4 2
♦ K Q J 9 3
♣ —

♠ 10 8 2
♥ 10 5
♦ 8 6 5
♣ K 10 9 8 4

♠ Q 7 6 3
♥ 9 7 3
♦ 7 2
♣ J 6 5 2

Post-mortem

Note that it was advisable to play the first trump from hand in case West had a singleton Ace. Also, it would have been a mistake to lead a low trump from dummy on the second round, giving West a chance to promote the 10 in his partner's hand. As the hand developed it became clear that West was short in clubs. If he had held a low singleton he would probably have led it, but he might be void or he might have the singleton King.

Towards the end, declarer wanted to count the clubs. That is why he played off the Ace of hearts when in dummy so that a third heart could be ruffed. Had East followed to that trick declarer would have read him for 3 – 3 – 3 – 4 distribution and would have laid down the Ace of clubs, expecting West's singleton to be the King.

24. Message in Time

Playing in a team-of-four match against expert opposition, I hold:

♠ J 7 6 ♡ A Q J 6 5 ◇ Q 8 2 ♣ Q 7

The opponents are vulnerable, we are not. My partner, North, deals and passes and East passes. At the score I think I can chance a third hand opening of **one heart** which may keep them out of 3NT. West overcalls with **two clubs** and my partner bids **two hearts**. East bids **three clubs** and this is passed to my partner. I hope he has his eye on the score and will allow for my having opened light third in hand. No, he bids **three hearts**. Both opponents give this consideration but neither doubles. So I end up as declarer in three hearts after the following bidding:

South	West	North	East
—	—	pass	pass
1♡	2♣	2♡	3♣
pass	pass	3♡	pass
pass	pass		

West leads the King of clubs and the following dummy goes down:

♠ A Q 10 3
♡ 9 7 4 2
◇ K J 6
♣ 9 5

♣ K led

♠ J 7 6
♡ A Q J 6 5
◇ Q 8 2
♣ Q 7

Yes, I see he had a bit in reserve when he bid only two hearts on the first round. It looks as though I can make it with one out of two finesses.

West begins with King and Ace of Clubs, East playing the 3 and 6. West then switches to the 10 of diamonds. I want to find out where the

Ace is, so I put in the Jack from dummy. East plays the Ace and returns a diamond.

The simple game is to take that in dummy and finesse the Queen of hearts. However, there is no point in doing that if the finesse is bound to be wrong. How can I find out who has the heart King? If East had both missing kings in addition to the Ace of diamonds, he would have bid 2NT on the way around. If I test the spades first and find that East has the King of spades then West must have the King of hearts.

But if I take this diamond in hand and finesse the Queen of spades, is there any danger of my running into a diamond ruff? It is just possible that East has five diamonds. On the other hand, if the spade finesse is wrong then the heart finesse will be wrong and I shall also go down if I take the diamond in dummy and finesse the Queen of hearts. So I really don't have to worry about a possible ruff in diamonds. I decide to win with the Queen of diamonds and finesse the Queen of spades.

When I lead the 6 of spades West plays the 5, dummy the Queen and East the King. East plays a third diamond to dummy's King, everyone following. The position is now:

♠ A 10 3
♡ 9 7 4 2
♢ —
♣ —

♠ J 7
♡ A Q J 6 5
♢ —
♣ —

On the lead of the 2 of hearts from dummy East plays the 8. I am not going to pay any attention to that as it could easily be a false card from 10 8 x. I go up with the Ace of hearts and, happy sight! West drops the King. I had the message about the two Kings just in time.

This was the full hand:

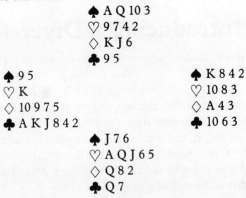

♠ A Q 10 3
♥ 9 7 4 2
♦ K J 6
♣ 9 5

♠ 9 5
♥ K
♦ 10 9 7 5
♣ A K J 8 4 2

♠ K 8 4 2
♥ 10 8 3
♦ A 4 3
♣ 10 6 3

♠ J 7 6
♥ A Q J 6 5
♦ Q 8 2
♣ Q 7

Post-mortem

East made an interesting point at the end of the play.

"If you had played your 9 of spades on the first round," he told his partner, "I would have known you had a doubleton and would have held up my King. Then declarer would have taken the finesse in hearts and you would have made your singleton King."

That is true. Also, if East had led a trump after the Ace of diamonds I would have had to finesse. From East's point of view, however, it was possible that his partner had Q 10 9 or Q 10 8 of diamonds and that the defense could establish a second diamond trick before the King of spades was forced out.

25. Introducing a Diversion

Playing rubber bridge against strong opponents, I hold the following:

♠ K 9 6 ♡ J 8 6 5 ◇ K J 8 2 ♣ A J

Both sides are vulnerable and my partner is the dealer. He opens **one diamond** and the next player passes. I am too strong for three diamonds, as we play it, and I'm certainly not going to make a scientific approach bid of one heart. The hand will probably be played in no-trump and I'm going to bid an old-fashioned **2NT**. Partner raises to **3NT** and that is the end of a simple auction:

North	West	South	East
1◇	pass	2NT	pass
3NT	pass	pass	pass

West leads the 6 of clubs and partner goes down with this disappointing collection:

♠ A 8 4
♡ K 10 7
◇ A Q 9 6 3
♣ 8 3

♣ 6 led

♠ K 9 6
♡ J 8 6 5
◇ K J 8 2
♣ A J

Both short in clubs! That's annoying—not that we'd have much chance of game in any other contract. On the first trick East plays the Queen of clubs. It would be foolish to hold up and expose my weakness, so I win with the Ace.

There are eight tricks on top but the clubs are wide open. What are my chances of slipping through a heart, supposing that West has the Ace? It would work against some players because West cannot tell that my Jack of clubs is now single. But this West has played the game before and he will be suspicious if I play on hearts instead of on diamonds. He is quite good enough to go up with the Ace of hearts and lay down the King of clubs. It would be less suspicious if I played a couple of rounds of diamonds without showing that the suit was solid.

That must be the best plan. I lead the 8 of diamonds to dummy's Queen and return a low diamond to the King. On the second diamond West shows void, discarding a small spade. That's just as well. Having a singleton West may well conclude that his partner holds four to the Jack. Now I must try the heart. I lead the 5, West plays the 4 and dummy's King holds the trick.

That has passed off well. I have nine tricks now. When I play off the remaining diamonds West discards another low spade, the 9 of hearts and the 10 of spades. After the fifth diamond the following cards are left:

♠ A 8 4
♡ 10 7
◇ —
♣ 8

♠ K 9 6
♡ J 8
◇ —
♣ J

On the Ace of spades West drops the Queen. Goodness me! I'm going to make an overtrick. It must be completely safe to finesse the 9 of spades. And so it is, the full hand being:

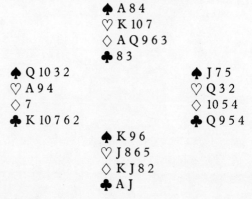

♠ A 8 4
♡ K 10 7
◇ A Q 9 6 3
♣ 8 3

♠ Q 10 3 2   ♠ J 7 5
♡ A 9 4   ♡ Q 3 2
◇ 7   ◇ 10 5 4
♣ K 10 7 6 2   ♣ Q 9 5 4

♠ K 9 6
♡ J 8 6 5
◇ K J 8 2
♣ A J

Post-mortem

There are a number of points worth noting in this hand:

It would not be good play to hold up the Ace of clubs on the first trick, thus exposing the weakness in clubs.

It would be poor play to run off the five diamonds, giving the defense a chance to signal to one another and to realize that they have to win four club tricks.

If South plays a low heart at trick 2 an expert West might well go up with the Ace of hearts and lay down the King of clubs. From the failure to play on diamonds he would judge that declarer was trying to slip through a ninth trick.

That is why South had to introduce a diversion by playing the diamonds in a way that gave West the impression that his partner controlled the fourth round. The same sort of technique can be applied to almost all suit combinations when the honors are divided.

26. Full Stretch

Playing a team-of-four match against first-class opponents, I hold the following third in hand:

♠ Q   ♡ K Q 10 6 4 2   ◇ A Q 9 6   ♣ J 7

We are vulnerable and they not. After two passes I open **one heart** and West overcalls with **one spade**. Partner bids **1NT** and East **two spades**.

My hand is really not worth more than three hearts now, but at this vulnerability it is sound tactics to overbid a little. They are almost sure to sacrifice in four spades if I bid four hearts with confidence. Partner having bid 1NT freely, we should be able to beat four spades by a trick or two. So I jump to **four hearts**.

West, as expected, defends with **four spades** but partner now surprises me by going to **five hearts**. That is passed out, so the bidding has been:

South	West	North	East
—	—	pass	pass
1♡	1♠	1NT	2♠
4♡	4♠	5♡	pass
pass	pass		

West leads the 8 of diamonds and partner puts down:

♠ A 10 5
♡ J 7
◇ J 4 3 2
♣ A 10 5 3

◇ 8 led

♠ Q
♡ K Q 10 6 4 2
◇ A Q 9 6
♣ J 7

At total-point scoring North would no doubt have doubled four spades, taking the certain penalty. At the international match-point scoring that we use in these matches, to accept a penalty of 500 instead of making 650 means a loss of 3 I.M.P. Not knowing that my four hearts was a bit of a push, partner has decided to play for the vulnerable game instead of taking a penalty. For my part, I would rather be collecting a safe 500 or so from four spades doubled.

Now what are the prospects in five hearts? At least one club and one heart to lose. That diamond lead could be a singleton. They have bid up to four spades on such moderate values, I'm sure West has a singleton somewhere. If I am going to play on that assumption I must cover with the Jack of diamonds to create a finesse position. East covers the Jack with the King and I win with the Ace.

Before I take any finesses in diamonds I have to draw trumps. I may be short of entries to the table but I'll have to see what develops. On the 2 of hearts West plays the 5 and dummy's Jack holds the trick. A heart is returned from the table and both follow, West winning with the Ace. Perhaps West will simplify matters for me by leading a low club or a low spade away from the King. Even a trump back won't do me any harm as I shall still have two entries left to dummy for diamond leads.

These hopes are vain, for West plays the only card I didn't want to see—the King of spades. It won't help me to duck, because they won't play another spade into the A 10. I win with the Ace and this is the position:

♠ 10 5
♡ —
♢ 4 3 2
♣ A 10 5 3

♠ —
♡ K 10 6 4
♢ Q 9 6
♣ J 7

I can take a deep finesse in diamonds now, but there is still a trump out and West very likely has it. Is there any other chance worth considering? Maybe I can do something with the clubs. Since East has so far shown only the King of diamonds he must have at least one club honor. In that case I think I can embarrass him in the end game. To begin with, I'm going to ruff a spade and draw the last trump.

West turns out to have the third trump, East discarding a spade. Now I lead the Jack of clubs and West covers with the Queen. I play the Ace from dummy and lead a low diamond, East following with the 5. Now have I any reason to change my original theory about the diamonds? West appears to have at least five spades headed by the K J, Ace of hearts and Queen of clubs. There is no certainty, but I think he is more likely to be 5 – 3 – 1 – 4 than 5 – 3 – 2 – 3.

Somewhat anxiously I put in the 6 of diamonds and it holds the trick. Now I am home, assuming that East has the King of clubs. I play off two more trumps, coming down to Q 9 of diamonds and 7 of clubs. At trick 11 I exit with a club and East has to play into my diamond tenace.

The full hand:

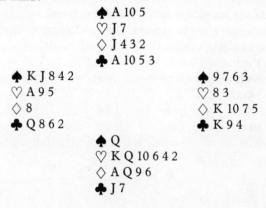

```
              ♠ A 10 5
              ♡ J 7
              ◇ J 4 3 2
              ♣ A 10 5 3
♠ K J 8 4 2                    ♠ 9 7 6 3
♡ A 9 5                        ♡ 8 3
◇ 8                           ◇ K 10 7 5
♣ Q 8 6 2                      ♣ K 9 4
              ♠ Q
              ♡ K Q 10 6 4 2
              ◇ A Q 9 6
              ♣ J 7
```

Post-mortem

West's lead of the singleton diamond was based on the hope that his partner would have a quick entry such as the Ace of spades. Most players would have done the same but my experience is that singleton leads by the side that is weaker in high cards lose a trick much more often than they gain one. A frequent result, as on the present hand, is that a finesse position is created which the declarer could scarcely have found for himself.

27. Deception Ended

Playing in a team-of-four match with a strong partner against average opposition, I hold the following as dealer:

♠ A 8 7 5 2   ♡ —   ◇ Q 2   ♣ K J 10 8 7 5

Neither side is vulnerable and I open **one club.** West overcalls with **three hearts** and my partner bids **3NT.** This is passed by East. I should think it is quite likely that partner has club support for me. In that case we ought to make five clubs. In any event I must take him out of 3NT and show my second suit. I bid **four spades.**

Partner raises this to **six spades.** I wasn't expecting anything like that. I hope he doesn't think I've got a good hand! Anyway, no one doubles, so the bidding has been:

South	West	North	East
1♣	3♡	3NT	pass
4♠	pass	6♠	pass
pass	pass		

West leads the 9 of diamonds and I await the dummy with some anxiety:

♠ K J 6 4
♡ K 8 5
◇ A J 6 3
♣ A 4

◇ 9 led

♠ A 8 7 5 2
♡ —
◇ Q 2
♣ K J 10 8 7 5

Partner has his bid, I suppose, but I don't like it much, especially on this lead. West is not the sort of player to underlead a King on this

94

bidding, so I must reckon the diamond finesse to be wrong. If East has a trump trick, which is also quite likely, I haven't much chance except, perhaps, to find West with a singleton Queen of clubs; then I might get rid of dummy's diamonds in time.

There's one other possibility. If I drop the Queen of diamonds East may think I have a singleton and try to make a trick in hearts instead of cashing his King of diamonds. It's worth trying, so I go up with the Ace of diamonds, East plays the 5 and I drop the Queen!

Now I play a low spade to the Ace, on which East rather surprisingly plays the Queen. That is good news in a way but it also suggests a bad break in clubs, for West appears to have three spades in addition to his long hearts. I must draw trumps and then consider the club position. On the second and third trumps East discards the 4 of diamonds and the 2 of hearts. That leaves the following situation:

♠ 6
♡ K 8 5
♢ J 6 3
♣ A 4

♠ 8 7
♡ —
♢ 2
♣ K J 10 8 7 5

The question at this point is whether the clubs are going to be 3 – 2 or 4 – 1. West appears to have at least ten cards in the major suits and I want to find out whether he has a doubleton or singleton diamond. I think the time has come to undo my small deception in that suit.

A low diamond from dummy is won by East's 8, West playing the 7. East now leads a heart which I ruff. I play a club to the Ace and West plays the 6. It seems certain now that West's distribution is 3 – 7 – 2 – 1. I finesse the Jack of clubs and when that holds the hand is over. After a low club has been ruffed in dummy my hand is high.

This was the full deal:

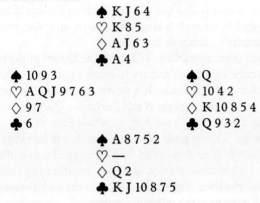

♠ K J 6 4
♡ K 8 5
◇ A J 6 3
♣ A 4

♠ 10 9 3   ♠ Q
♡ A Q J 9 7 6 3   ♡ 10 4 2
◇ 9 7   ◇ K 10 8 5 4
♣ 6   ♣ Q 9 3 2

♠ A 8 7 5 2
♡ —
◇ Q 2
♣ K J 10 8 7 5

Post-mortem

The main interest of the play lies in the handling of the diamonds.
First there was the drop of the Queen of diamonds under the Ace.
Had the hand been different this might have dissuaded East from laying
down the King of diamonds when he was in. Next, there was the play
of the second diamond after West had turned up with three trumps.
This was a simple enough maneuver but of a sort that players sometimes overlook.

28. Reward for Sacrifice

Playing in a pairs event against moderate opposition, I hold:

♠ K 8   ♡ 10 7 5 2   ◇ Q J 10 8 6 3   ♣ A

The opponents are vulnerable and we are not. East, on my right, deals and opens **one spade**. I overcall **two diamonds** and West bids **two spades**. Partner raises to **three diamonds** and East jumps to **four spades**.

I have some sort of defense against four spades. I can lead my Ace of clubs and perhaps put my partner in to give me a club ruff. After that I might still make the King of spades or some other trick. If the opposition were strong I might suspect them of trying to bounce me into five diamonds at the vulnerability. I don't think my present opponents are up to that strategy, but if the bidding goes this way at other tables South will generally sacrifice. So I will bid **five diamonds**. This is **doubled** by West and all pass. The bidding has been:

South	West	North	East
—	—	—	1♠
2◇	2♠	3◇	4♠
5◇	double	pass	pass
pass			

Knowing that his side has the balance of the high cards, West opens the trump 5. That looks to me like a good lead for the defense when dummy goes down with the following:

♠ 6 3
♡ 8 3
◇ A K 9
♣ Q 10 9 6 4 2

◇ 5 led

♠ K 8
♡ 10 7 5 2
◇ Q J 10 8 6 3
♣ A

I win this trick with the King of diamonds and East follows with the 2. If the trumps are 3 – 1, which is likely, they may keep me from ruffing any hearts at all. If I make only eight tricks, losing four hearts and a spade, that will surely be bad. I wonder if I can do anything with the clubs. If East has K J alone I can, but that's rather a slender chance. Suppose he has something like K x x. I can lead a club to the Ace, return to the King of diamonds and lead the Queen of clubs. But that's no good, as I'm short of an entry to dummy.

I might try leading the Queen of clubs from dummy. Yes, that's worth considering. If East has the King he may cover, and that should save me a trick or two. If I am going to make that play I had better do it quickly, so I call for the Queen of clubs. East looks at this for a moment, then covers with the King. The Ace wins and West plays the 3. I enter dummy with a diamond, on which East discards a spade. (I'm glad to see that because if the diamonds had been 2 – 2 we would have had a sure defense against four spades.)

Now if East's clubs are the K J alone I can make the contract by leading a low club from dummy, but if he has K J x I have to lead the 10. I think that must be the better play for two reasons. East's slight hesitation before covering the Queen of clubs suggests that he had K J x rather than K J alone. Secondly, if I lead the 10 I shall set up a trick for the 9 whatever happens. That will save me from going more than two down.

When I lead the 10 of clubs from table East again looks worried. Finally he puts on the Jack. I ruff and enter dummy with a third round of trumps. When both opponents follow to the 9 of clubs I am able to discard four hearts. The Ace of spades is right, so I finish up with a most unexpected overtrick.

East's play in covering the Queen of clubs made a difference of four tricks, as the full hand will show:

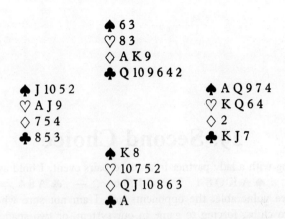

♠ 6 3
♡ 8 3
◇ A K 9
♣ Q 10 9 6 4 2

♠ J 10 5 2   ♠ A Q 9 7 4
♡ A J 9   ♡ K Q 6 4
◇ 7 5 4   ◇ 2
♣ 8 5 3   ♣ K J 7

♠ K 8
♡ 10 7 5 2
◇ Q J 10 8 6 3
♣ A

Post-mortem

This type of play—the lead of the Queen of clubs towards the singleton Ace—is not exploited as much as it could be. The same sort of play can be made with J 9 8 x x x opposite a singleton Ace or J 9 8 x x opposite doubleton A K or A Q. There are many similar situations.

It was not so easy for the defense to judge the right play. If declarer had had A x in clubs he might have made the same play of the Queen from dummy and then it would have been fatal for East not to cover!

29. Second Choice

Playing with a lady partner in a mixed pairs event, I hold as dealer:

♠ A K Q 8 4   ♡ A Q J 10 6   ◇ —   ♣ A 8 4

We are vulnerable, the opponents not. I am not sure whether to open two clubs, forcing to game in our system, or two spades which shows a strong hand and is forcing for one round. The hand is good enough for two clubs but at this vulnerability I think it is better to name one of my suits on the first round. If I open with a conventional two clubs they may be able to pre-empt in diamonds before I have had a chance to show either suit, so I open **two spades.**

The opponents are silent and partner makes the negative response of **2NT.** To show my extra strength I jump to **four hearts.** Partner gives that some consideration and eventually bids **five spades.** That makes the bidding up to now:

South	West	North	East
2♠	pass	2NT	pass
4♡	pass	5♠	pass
?			

I wonder what she has! Something like King of hearts and J x x of spades, I should think, or perhaps a singleton heart and four spades. I'm certainly going six and I just wonder whether I can invite seven. At best she could have three spades, King of hearts and King of clubs, but even then the third round of clubs is unaccounted for. I must be content with **six spades.** That makes the complete auction:

South	West	North	East
2♠	pass	2NT	pass
4♡	pass	5♠	pass
6♠	pass	pass	pass

West leads the Queen of diamonds and I observe that we are quite high enough when partner puts down:

♠ 7 5 2
♡ K
◇ K 9 7 6 3
♣ J 9 7 3

◇ Q led

♠ A K Q 8 4
♡ A Q J 10 6
◇ —
♣ A 8 4

Assuming that the spades break, I can see eleven tricks on top.
Somehow I've got to negotiate a club ruff. Before thinking it out I'll
see what happens to the first trick.

Is there any possibility that West has underled the Ace of diamonds?
Not really, and the King of diamonds may come in useful if the hand
breaks badly. So I play a low diamond from dummy, East plays the 5
and I ruff with the 4 of spades.

Now I could play a heart to the King, draw two rounds of trumps
and discard three clubs from dummy on A Q J of hearts. If no one
ruffed I could then trump a club and make my twelfth trick that way.
For that play to succeed the spades have to be 3 – 2, the hearts 4 – 3,
and the hand with four hearts must have the three trumps. Not very
promising, but for the moment I don't see anything better.

At the second trick I lead the 6 of hearts to dummy's King. I come
back to hand with the Ace of spades and lead the Ace of hearts, discarding a club from table.

Suddenly something strikes me! Instead of trying to throw three
clubs from table on the high hearts, can't I duck a round of clubs and
then discard only twice from the table?

That's a better line, surely. Instead of having to find the same
opponent with three spades and four hearts I shall want the clubs to be
3 – 3 or, if they are 4 – 2, the same player to have four clubs and three
spades. But I mustn't play off two rounds of trumps immediately, for
then they may play a third trump when I duck the club. Also, I mustn't
play off a third heart too soon because they might lead a fourth heart
and bring about a trump promotion.

I shall duck the club immediately! On the lead of a low club from

101

hand West plays the 2, dummy the 9 and East the 10. East plays a trump and all follow. The position is now:

♠ 7
♡ —
◇ K 9 7 6
♣ J 9

♠ Q 8
♡ Q J 10
◇ —
♣ A 8

All follow to a third round of hearts, dummy discarding a club. When I play the Ace of clubs and ruff a club the clubs turn out to be 3 – 3. I come back to hand by ruffing a diamond, draw the last trump and make the remaining hearts.

This was the full deal:

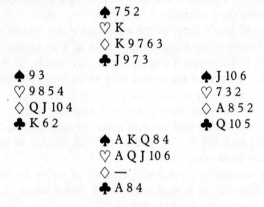

♠ 7 5 2
♡ K
◇ K 9 7 6 3
♣ J 9 7 3

♠ 9 3
♡ 9 8 5 4
◇ Q J 10 4
♣ K 6 2

♠ J 10 6
♡ 7 3 2
◇ A 8 5 2
♣ Q 10 5

♠ A K Q 8 4
♡ A Q J 10 6
◇ —
♣ A 8 4

Post-mortem

The line of play that I first thought of would have been no good. If I had drawn two trumps and tried to discard three clubs on the high hearts, East would have ruffed the fourth round of hearts, leaving me a trick short.

The play of ducking a club early is for some reason not easy to see. Most players, when shown the hand, tend to miss it.

The deal also presents an interesting defensive point. If West happens to lead the 2 of clubs originally and East plays the 10 declarer ducks with the same result. But suppose East puts in the Queen ? Then declarer will surely win with the Ace and rely on a finesse of the 9 of clubs for his twelfth trick.

That's one to remember.

30. Two Doubtful Doubles

Playing in a team event with a reliable partner, I hold:

♠ 4 ♡ A K J 8 4 ◇ A 8 6 ♣ K Q J 3

Neither side is vulnerable and I am fourth hand. After two passes East, on my right, opens **one diamond.**

This is a familiar situation in which there is no good bid. The objection to a double is that partner will probably respond in spades. A jump overcall of two hearts would be strength-showing in my system but would suggest more of a one-suited hand. Some players would favor a simple one heart on the grounds that this would be more likely to attract further bidding than a higher call.

In my opinion the disadvantage of a double in this sort of situation is usually exaggerated. If partner does bid spades the roof won't fall down! I can bid two hearts over one spade and consider the matter again over two spades. At any rate I decide to **double** and see what happens.

West passes and partner makes the strength-showing response of **two diamonds.** I didn't expect that. We play that response in the enemy suit as forcing to game, so when East passes I simply bid **two hearts.**

Another surprise! Partner raises to **four hearts.** That makes the bidding to date:

South	West	North	East
—	pass	pass	1◇
double	pass	2◇	pass
2♡	pass	4♡	pass
?			

He can't have less than one Ace and a singleton diamond or equivalent values. A small slam looks certain. What about a grand? East opened third in hand and may be psychic. It is possible for partner to have two Aces, second round control of diamonds and Queen of hearts. I think I'll bid 4NT (we are playing the Culbertson 4NT showing two Aces and the King of a bid suit) and if he responds 5NT (showing two Aces) I will make a grand slam suggestion by bidding six diamonds.

In response to **4NT** partner bids **five hearts.** Technically, that is a sign off, being a bid of the lowest valued suit bid by the partnership. No doubt he is missing the Ace of clubs but I am sure he must have **the** Ace of spades. Without it he would not have jumped to four hearts over two hearts. I am not going to stop short of **six hearts. Double,** says West. Perhaps I have done the wrong thing. We shall see.

The full bidding:

South	West	North	East
—	pass	pass	1♢
double	pass	2♢	pass
2♡	pass	4♡	pass
4NT	pass	5♡	pass
6♡	double	pass	pass
pass			

West leads the 2 of diamonds and partner displays the following:

♠ A Q 9 8
♡ Q 10 9 2
♢ K 10 4
♣ 10 8

♢ 2 led

♠ 4
♡ A K J 8 4
♢ A 8 6
♣ K Q J 3

The dummy is about what I expected. He thought he had done enough and wasn't going to carry the bidding beyond five hearts.

So far as I can see, this is going to be a lay-down unless the hearts are 4 – 0. I play the 4 of diamonds on the first trick, East plays the 9 and I win with the Ace. I lay down the Ace of hearts and East discards a diamond. Disappointing but not surprising.

There are eleven tricks on top—five hearts, three clubs, two diamonds and one spade. The spade finesse would make twelve. What about a squeeze if East has the King of spades and the long diamonds? Can I maneuver an ending in which my last two cards are a spade and a diamond while dummy has the A Q of spades?

No, I can see two objections to that plan. West must have one of the high cards, probably the Ace of clubs, and when he comes in he will lead a spade through the dummy. Furthermore, even if East had the Ace of clubs, he could hold it up for one round and put me back in dummy, so that's no good.

I'd like to discover who has the Ace of clubs, but if I play a club early on I shall be exposed to a ruff should East have the Ace of clubs and West a singleton diamond. But there's West's double to be accounted for. He wouldn't double a slam on the strength of his partner's third-hand opening unless he had at least one sure trick. I'm definitely inclined to place him with the Ace of clubs. If so, I wonder whether I can throw two diamonds from dummy on my good clubs and then play some sort of cross-ruff. I must examine that. If West follows to four rounds of clubs that play can't go wrong.

If I am going to play for this cross-ruff I don't want to draw any more trumps now. I am going to put these clubs to the test. I play the 3 of clubs to dummy's 10, which holds. A club is led back and West wins with the Ace. After studying the position West leads the 6 of spades. I win this in dummy and the position is then as follows:

♠ Q 9 8
♡ Q 10 9
◇ K 10
♣ —

♠ —
♡ K J 8 4
◇ 8 6
♣ K J

I ruff a spade and lead the King of clubs, throwing a diamond from dummy. When West follows to the Jack of clubs I discard another diamond and make the rest of the tricks by a cross-ruff.

The full hand turns out to be:

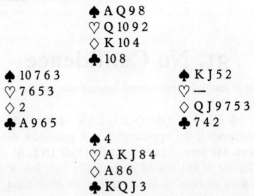

♠ A Q 9 8
♡ Q 10 9 2
◇ K 10 4
♣ 10 8

♠ 10 7 6 3　　　　　　　　♠ K J 5 2
♡ 7 6 5 3　　　　　　　　♡ —
◇ 2　　　　　　　　　　　◇ Q J 9 7 5 3
♣ A 9 6 5　　　　　　　　♣ 7 4 2

♠ 4
♡ A K J 8 4
◇ A 8 6
♣ K Q J 3

Post-mortem

It seemed during the play that it was essential that West should follow to four rounds of clubs. Actually that is not so, for if West had had a club less and a spade more it would have been possible to ruff out East's King of spades.

One lesson from the hand is the old one that it does not pay to double slam contracts when the double can give any information. This contract would surely have failed had declarer not been able to place West with the Ace of clubs.

31. No Confidence

Playing in a multiple team event against one of the weaker teams, I deal and hold:

♠ A 10 7   ♡ 8   ◇ A Q 8 5 4   ♣ A Q J 5

We are vulnerable, the opponents not. I open **one diamond** and West **doubles**. My partner passes and East bids **1NT**. At the score it's dangerous for me to bid now. I could easily walk into a 200 or even 500 penalty with nothing on for them. On the other hand, (a) if I bid two clubs it is possible that partner will have some distribution and will be able to contest with three clubs against, say, two hearts; and (b) the present opponents are not champions and if I do walk into trouble much the same thing is likely to happen at the other table. So I bid a slightly unsound **two clubs**.

West **doubles** and my partner puts me back to **two diamonds**. This is **doubled** by East and all pass.

The bidding has been:

South	West	North	East
1◇	double	pass	1NT
2♣	double	2◇	double
pass	pass	pass	

West opens the King of hearts and partner makes his contribution:

♠ 8 5 4
♡ 6 5 4 3 2
◇ 7 3 2
♣ 4 2

♡ K led

♠ A 10 7
♡ 8
◇ A Q 8 5 4
♣ A Q J 5

The appearance of the dummy is greeted with some hilarity. On the first round of hearts East plays the 7. I may have some chance if West doesn't attack spades right away. Better! He follows with the Ace of hearts, East plays the 10 and I ruff. Shall I try the Queen of clubs now or the Jack? I don't suppose I have much chance of slipping through either card. As the Jack is the card that most players would try from this combination, I will see if I can create any confusion by leading the Queen. No, West takes the King and now switches to a low spade. East plays the Jack and I win with the Ace. All follow to the Ace and Jack of clubs and I discard a spade from table. The position is now:

♠ 8
♡ 6 5 4
♢ 7 3 2
♣ —

♠ 10 7
♡ —
♢ A Q 8 5
♣ 5

When I lead the last club West follows with the 10. It is obviously better to discard the loser than to be over-ruffed, so I throw the third spade from table. East also discards a spade.

West battles on with a third round of hearts, which again does me no harm. I ruff this with the 5 of diamonds and ruff a spade in dummy with the 2. Now I have the 10 of spades and A Q 8 of diamonds left in hand. I have only lost three tricks, so the contract is completely safe. I am wondering whether there is any chance of an overtrick. East's last four cards are all diamonds, probably K J 10 9 but possibly K J 10 x. I can see a chance if West has the singleton 9 and the defense makes another mistake. I lead the 3 of diamonds from dummy, East plays the 10 and I win with the Queen. West, with an irritable glance at his partner, drops the 9. Now I ruff my spade with the 7 of diamonds, East over-ruffs and I make the last two tricks with the A 8 of diamonds.

The defense has missed its way on two or three occasions, for this is the full hand:

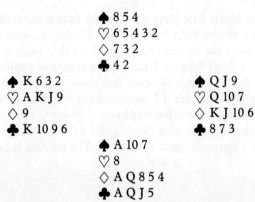

```
              ♠ 8 5 4
              ♡ 6 5 4 3 2
              ◇ 7 3 2
              ♣ 4 2
♠ K 6 3 2              ♠ Q J 9
♡ A K J 9              ♡ Q 10 7
◇ 9                    ◇ K J 10 6
♣ K 10 9 6            ♣ 8 7 3
              ♠ A 10 7
              ♡ 8
              ◇ A Q 8 5 4
              ♣ A Q J 5
```

We enter 380 for two diamonds doubled with an overtrick and partner apologizes for lack of confidence.

Post-mortem

As the play went, declarer did not need to display any special skill. It is clear that the defense can take six tricks if they play on spades early, but at the other table East-West had to work hard after a trump opening against the same contract.

Winning the first diamond, South played Ace and Jack of clubs. West now switched to a low spade and East's Jack was headed by the Ace. South continued with Queen of clubs, discarding a spade, and a fourth club, discarding another spade. West was in and again had to avoid the mistake of laying down the King of hearts. He played a small spade which dummy ruffed. When declarer came off table with a small heart East went up with the Queen and led the King of diamonds. That stopped South from ruffing more than once in dummy and he was one down. This was a finely played defense.

32. Counted Out

In a game of rubber bridge against resourceful opponents I deal myself the following:

♠ Q 7   ♡ A K 9 6 5   ◇ A Q J 2   ♣ Q 6

Both sides are vulnerable and I open **one heart.** The opponents are silent and my partner raises to **two hearts.** I may not make it but I must go to **four hearts.** That concludes a simple auction:

South	West	North	East
1♡	pass	2♡	pass
4♡	pass	pass	pass

West leads the King of clubs and with suitable apologies partner puts down:

♠ A 6 4
♡ J 10 8 4
◇ 7 6
♣ 9 5 4 3

♣ K led

♠ Q 7
♡ A K 9 6 5
◇ A Q J 2
♣ Q 6

East plays the 2 of clubs on the first lead and the 8 of clubs when West continues with the Ace. West then switches to the 2 of spades. He can hardly be leading away from the King but it costs me nothing to let it run. East, as expected, plays the King and returns the 3 of spades.

Now I have to find the diamond finesse and not lose a trick in hearts. The diamond finesse may be right or wrong—there's nothing I can do about that. As to the hearts, I'd like to get a count of the hand if I can. If the hearts are 2 – 2 I won't need the Ace of spades as an entry

111

and equally I can do without the discard. I overtake the Queen of spades with the Ace and finesse the Queen of diamonds.

The diamond finesse wins. I cash the Ace of hearts but nothing appears. Now I'd like to play the Ace of diamonds and ruff a diamond to get a further count but I pause to consider if there is any danger in that. I don't think so. West appears to have four spades and four clubs, so if he's going to ruff a third round of diamonds it will be from Q x x in hearts.

All follow to the Ace of diamonds and on the 2 of diamonds West plays the 9, dummy ruffs and the King comes down from East. The position is now:

♠ 6
♡ J 10
◇ —
♣ 9 5

♠ —
♡ K 9 6 5
◇ J
♣ —

I think I have a complete picture now. Unless both opponents were false-carding in spades they are 4 – 4. As to the clubs, my original impression was that they were 4 – 3 but let me check that. West led the King and East played the 2. Then West continued with the Ace and East played the 8. West wouldn't have played a second round from A K x in case he were setting up the Queen. So that marks East with three clubs, and, to judge from the fall of the King of diamonds, three diamonds. In short, he seems to be 4 – 3 – 3 – 3. If East plays low on the Jack of hearts I'm going to finesse.

Misery! West wins with the Queen of hearts and I am one down.

"Then you had five spades?" I say to East.

"No, only four," he answers. "But I've got another diamond tucked away somewhere."

Yes, he has fooled me, for this is the full hand:

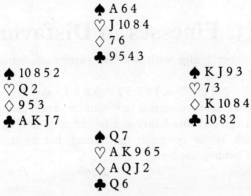

                    ♠ A 6 4
                    ♡ J 10 8 4
                    ◇ 7 6
                    ♣ 9 5 4 3

♠ 10 8 5 2   ♠ K J 9 3
♡ Q 2   ♡ 7 3
◇ 9 5 3   ◇ K 10 8 4
♣ A K J 7   ♣ 10 8 2

                    ♠ Q 7
                    ♡ A K 9 6 5
                    ◇ A Q J 2
                    ♣ Q 6

Post-mortem

All one can say of this hand is that it is mistake to underestimate one's opponents. The declarer's maneuvers to obtain a count were sound enough in themselves but were easily read by the defense. In this company no reliance should have been placed on the fall of the King of diamonds.

33. Finesses in Disfavor

Playing rubber bridge with a sound partner against experienced opponents I pick up:

♠ J 2 ♡ K J 8 7 5 2 ◇ 8 7 3 ♣ J 9

With neither side vulnerable my partner deals and opens **one diamond**. I respond **one heart** and he jumps to **2NT**. I bid **three hearts**, which in our system is not forcing, but he raises to **four hearts**. The bidding has been:

South	West	North	East
—	—	1◇	pass
1♡	pass	2NT	pass
3♡	pass	4♡	pass
pass	pass		

West opens the 5 of clubs and partner goes down with a strong hand:

♠ A 7 4
♡ A 6
◇ A K J 5 2
♣ K 6 3

♣ 5 led

♠ J 2
♡ K J 8 7 5 2
◇ 8 7 3
♣ J 9

The normal thing with this club combination is to play low from dummy but I am not sure that is right here. If East has the Queen he will probably switch to spades. That will set up three quick tricks for the defense and I shall have to find the trumps well placed.

It's quite possible that West has underled the Ace of clubs, knowing that the dummy is strong. In fact, he's as likely to underlead an Ace as a Queen. If I could hold that first trick with the King of clubs I wouldn't be so dependent on finesses. It may be wrong but I am going to put up the King.

As I rather expected, the King holds. Now the game is to get the

diamonds going before they have a chance to knock out the Ace of
spades. All follow to the Ace and King of hearts but the Queen does
not drop. No matter, so long as the diamonds are 3 – 2.

Before I play the diamonds I'll just check up on the possibilities. It
would pay to finesse if West had Q x x x. But if the finesse loses East
will attack spades and then I shall be dependent on the player with the
Queen of hearts having three diamonds. It must be better, as I thought,
to play off Ace and King.

When these two cards stand up the contract is safe, for these are the
remaining cards:

♠ A 7 4
♡ —
◇ J 5 2
♣ 6 3

♠ J 2
♡ J 8 7 5
◇ 8
♣ J

The next round of diamonds is won by East. The defenders cash a
club and then attack spades. I go up with the Ace, throw the Jack of
spades on an established diamond and lose only to the Queen of hearts.

As it happens, both finesses would have been wrong, the full hand
being:

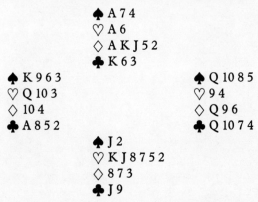

♠ A 7 4
♡ A 6
◇ A K J 5 2
♣ K 6 3

♠ K 9 6 3   ♠ Q 10 8 5
♡ Q 10 3   ♡ 9 4
◇ 10 4   ◇ Q 9 6
♣ A 8 5 2   ♣ Q 10 7 4

♠ J 2
♡ K J 8 7 5 2
◇ 8 7 3
♣ J 9

Post-mortem

The critical play on this hand was on the first trick. Declarer had to look ahead and realize that while he could establish a sure trick by playing low that trick would come too late. Having appreciated that point declarer still had to make the right guess. Most players, when defending, will readily underlead an Ace through a strong dummy but when playing the hand they tend to forget that other defenders are liable to do the same. A further consideration on this hand was that if the King won South would gain a tempo and would not need to finesse in either red suit.

34. Lucky Pin

In a rubber bridge game of average standard I hold the following in last position:

♠ 9 6 5   ♡ A K J 8 4   ◇ K J 8   ♣ A 10

West, on my left, deals and opens **one spade.** This is followed by two passes. I am too strong for a simple overcall of two hearts in the protective position, so I **double.** West passes and my partner responds **two clubs.** Now I introduce **two hearts** and partner raises to **three hearts.** My three small spades are unattractive but I don't like to languish in three when there is a fair chance of a vulnerable game. I bid **four hearts** and all pass. The bidding has been:

South	West	North	East
—	1♠	pass	pass
double	pass	2♣	pass
2♡	pass	3♡	pass
4♡	pass	pass	pass

West opens the King of spades and partner puts down:

♠ 8 3 2
♡ Q 10 2
◇ A 5 2
♣ K 7 5 3

♠ K led

♠ 9 6 5
♡ A K J 8 4
◇ K J 8
♣ A 10

At first sight it looks as though I shall have to find the diamond finesse or perhaps squeeze West should he have four clubs and the Queen of diamonds. On the King of spades East plays the 7. West continues with the Ace, dropping his partner's Queen, then Jack of spades, on which East discards the 2 of clubs.

117

West exits with a trump and I draw three rounds. On the third round East discards the 4 of diamonds. The cards are now as follows:

♠ —
♡ —
◇ A 5 2
♣ K 7 5 3

♠ —
♡ K J
◇ K J 8
♣ A 10

Since West has turned up with five spades and three trumps any idea of squeezing him in diamonds and clubs is out as there is not room for him to have the guarded Queen of diamonds and four clubs. Unless he has opened semi-psychic he should have both the minor suit Queens. Could the Queen of diamonds be doubleton? To judge from the discarding, I think not. If East had had only four clubs he would not have let one go so early, seeing the four clubs on the table. I am certainly inclined to place East with four diamonds and five clubs.

If West has Q 9 x or Q 10 x of diamonds there is nothing I can do against best defense, though it is possible that if I were to lead the Jack he might not cover from Q 9 x. But if West has Q x x and East 10 9 x I may be able to bring some pressure to bear on East. At any rate it cannot lose at this point to lead a trump and discard the 2 of diamonds from dummy.

On this trick West discards a spade and East another diamond. It is obvious that East began with five clubs and cannot let another one go. I am going to lead the Jack of diamonds in the hope that his two remaining diamonds are the 10 9.

West plays low on the Jack of diamonds. Having taken this view of the diamonds I must let the Jack run. If it loses to the Queen I shall look foolish, not for the first or last time. But all is well. East plays the 9 and I make the rest of the tricks, the full hand being:

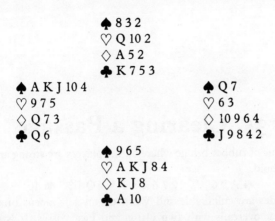

```
                ♠ 8 3 2
                ♡ Q 10 2
                ◇ A 5 2
                ♣ K 7 5 3
♠ A K J 10 4              ♠ Q 7
♡ 9 7 5                   ♡ 6 3
◇ Q 7 3                   ◇ 10 9 6 4
♣ Q 6                     ♣ J 9 8 4 2
                ♠ 9 6 5
                ♡ A K J 8 4
                ◇ K J 8
                ♣ A 10
```

Post-mortem

Like most hands, this one was easy enough to play once declarer made the right inferences, all simple enough in themselves. When it became apparent that West had five spades and three hearts it followed that he could not be squeezed in clubs and diamonds.

The fact that East had discarded a club at the first opportunity was evidence that he had five. That meant that West could have only two clubs and therefore must have at least three diamonds. That these most likely included the Queen could be inferred from the fact that West had opened the bidding and East had passed the opening bid. (Remember that East had already turned up with the Queen of spades.) Thus it became clear that the only hope was to exert pressure on East in the minor suits.

To play such hands correctly it is not necessary to be a master of squeeze technique. The important thing, as always, is to keep alive as to what is going on.

35. Clearing a Passage

In a game of rubber bridge where all the players are strong and enterprising I hold:

♠ A 9 6   ♡ 10 7 6 4 3 2   ◇ Q J 3   ♣ 10

Both sides are vulnerable and West, on my left, opens **one spade**. My partner overcalls with **two clubs** and East passes. It is doubtful whether I ought to say anything on my hand but this is the sort of game where everyone likes to be in the bidding, so I introduce **two hearts**. West passes and my partner raises to **three hearts**. Again I feel that I ought to pass but perhaps the heart honors are well placed. Anyway, I bid a prompt **four hearts** and nobody doubles. The bidding has been:

South	West	North	East
—	1♠	2♣	pass
2♡	pass	3♡	pass
4♡	pass	pass	pass

West leads the Jack of spades and partner's hand is no better than I deserve:

♠ K Q
♡ Q 5
◇ A 10 7
♣ Q 9 7 6 4 2

♠ J led

♠ A 9 6
♡ 10 7 6 4 3 2
◇ Q J 3
♣ 10

The diamond finesse is probably right, but how am I going to avoid losing three trumps and a club? It's no use leading a low heart from

120

dummy hoping to slip past the Jack, because I am missing both 8 and 9. I can keep the trump losers to two if West has precisely A J or K J, or if he has A K x and East has J x.

At any rate, I have to lead hearts from hand. The only way I can conveniently come to hand is by ruffing clubs, so to the second trick I play the 2 of clubs from table. East studies this for a while, then goes in with the Jack of clubs and leads the 9 of diamonds. I put on the Queen and this holds the trick.

It looks as though East went up with the Jack of clubs so that he could lead a diamond to a possible K J in his partner's hand. I still think West has the King of diamonds even though he played low. In my own hand after the Queen of diamonds I lead a low heart. West plays the Ace and East the 9. West exits with the Ace of clubs, which I ruff. That leaves the following cards:

♠ K
♡ Q
♢ A 10
♣ Q 9 7 6

♠ A 9
♡ 10 7 6 4
♢ J 3
♣ —

My finger is on a small heart when I foresee a possible difficulty. West won the first trick with the Ace of hearts but it is quite likely that his holding is A K 8. At least, that is one of the chances I am playing for. If he takes this next heart and plays a spade how do I get back to hand? I can't afford to overtake King of spades with the Ace and a club would be dangerous because I am not sure that West has any more.

Well, I can get around that. All I have to do is cross to dummy's King of spades before leading the Queen of hearts. Then if West plays a third spade the line will be clear up to my hand. All follow to the second spade and on the Queen of hearts there is the welcome sight of East's Jack. West wins and plays a third spade which runs up to my Ace. I draw the last trump and when the diamond finesse wins I make the rest, having lost only two hearts and one club.

This was the full hand:

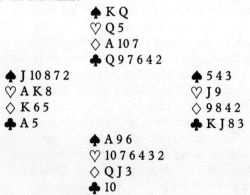

♠ K Q
♥ Q 5
♦ A 10 7
♣ Q 9 7 6 4 2

♠ J 10 8 7 2
♥ A K 8
♦ K 6 5
♣ A 5

♠ 5 4 3
♥ J 9
♦ 9 8 4 2
♣ K J 8 3

♠ A 9 6
♥ 10 7 6 4 3 2
♦ Q J 3
♣ 10

"Six to the 10 spot! I've never seen such a lucky hand!" exclaims West, exaggerating a little.

Post-mortem

The bidding of this hand can well be forgotten. There are two points to remember in the play: the advantage of leading towards the Q x on the first round of trumps and the later play of the King of spades so as not to be stranded in dummy.

It may seem that if declarer fails to play off the King of spades he can still recover by overtaking with the Ace, drawing the last trump and finessing the 10 of diamonds. Then the Queen of clubs can be led through East's King and South returns to dummy with the Ace of diamonds to discard his spade on the 9 of clubs. But West can defeat that plan by playing the King of diamonds on the second round so that declarer will be short of an entry to dummy.

36. What Must Be, Must Be

Playing rubber bridge with a partner who knows the game but is not over-scientific, I pick up as dealer:

♠ A 8 6 4   ♡ A 9   ◇ A 8 7 5 2   ♣ K 10

We are not vulnerable and I open **one diamond**. With the opponents silent, partner forces with **two hearts**. That doesn't mean the earth in present company but with my three Aces and a King there must be a good chance of a slam. For the moment I bid **two spades** to see what develops. Partner bids **three diamonds** and I give him delayed support to **three hearts**. Over that he goes to **four hearts**.

As he can have only one Ace it's not surprising that he has bid quietly after his original force. Even so, he may have a fair suit of hearts, diamond support and Ace of clubs. There should be a play for six and the only question is whether diamonds or hearts will be better. I can bid five clubs to see whether he can repeat his support for diamonds. No, that might confuse him. As I haven't rebid the diamonds I am going to bid **six diamonds**. He knows I've got the Ace of hearts and if he wants to go back to hearts he can.

Six diamonds is passed out, so the bidding has been:

South	West	North	East
1◇	pass	2♡	pass
2♠	pass	3◇	pass
3♡	pass	4♡	pass
6◇	pass	pass	pass

West leads the 5 of spades and observing that he is not proud of his force partner puts down:

♠ Q 10
♡ K Q 10 6 4
♢ K 9 4 3
♣ A 3

♠ 5 led

♠ A 8 6 4
♡ A 9
♢ A 8 7 5 2
♣ K 10

He needn't apologize to me for forcing. I fully approve, although such bids are not the fashion. This sort of slam is frequently missed when the bidding begins one diamond – one heart – one spade.

However, we haven't made it yet. Players lead from Kings more often than from Jacks against a small slam, they tell me. I put on the Queen, with little hope. Sure enough, the King is played by East and I have to win with the Ace.

There will be no difficulty if the diamonds are 2 – 2, so I have to assume they will be 3 – 1. The situation's rather worse than I thought at first glance. Even a 3 – 3 break in hearts won't help if the diamonds are 3 – 1. I can discard one spade but the player with the long trump will ruff the fourth heart and cash the Jack of spades.

This may be one of those hands where I have to play for the same opponent to have four hearts and three diamonds. That will mean finessing in hearts because the Jack is more likely to be in the hand that has the length. I can play either opponent for J x x x but I must look at the entry position. If I play a small diamond to the King and back to the Ace, and East turns up with three diamonds, I shall be short of an entry to dummy. So I must play diamonds the other way.

At trick 2, then, I play Ace of diamonds. All follow and I cross to the King, West showing out. That's the situation I was thinking of. Now I just have to assume that East has four hearts as well as three trumps. Playing East for J x x x in hearts I finesse the 9. It wins and I cash the Ace, then back to the Ace of clubs in the following position:

♠ 10
♡ K Q 10
◇ 9 4
♣ 3

♠ 8 6 4
♡ —
◇ 8 7 5
♣ K

When East follows to the King of hearts and West shows out, the contract is safe. East ruffs the fifth round of hearts but meanwhile my three spades go away.

After all this I find that I could have made the slam without any difficulty by playing the 10 of spades at the first trick, the full hand being:

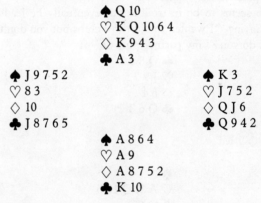

♠ Q 10
♡ K Q 10 6 4
◇ K 9 4 3
♣ A 3

♠ J 9 7 5 2   ♠ K 3
♡ 8 3   ♡ J 7 5 2
◇ 10   ◇ Q J 6
♣ J 8 7 6 5   ♣ Q 9 4 2

♠ A 8 6 4
♡ A 9
◇ A 8 7 5 2
♣ K 10

Post-mortem

This is a trappy hand because it is very easy for declarer to say to himself, "If the diamonds are 2 – 2 I don't have to worry. If they are 3 – 1 I'll reconsider after playing the King and Ace." But then, with this distribution, it is too late. If South is in his own hand after drawing the top trumps he cannot cross to dummy for the finesse of the 9 of hearts and enter dummy again to make the good hearts.

The only moral to be drawn is the old one that so far as possible the difficulties should be studied at the first trick.

37. Convention Not Missed

Playing rubber bridge with a lady partner who has a studious approach to the game, I deal myself the following:

♠ A 7 4   ♡ A K Q 10 6   ◇ Q 8 5   ♣ A 9

The orthodox opening on such a hand is one heart but especially when the five-card suit is reasonably solid I prefer **2NT**. This good news does not seem to please my partner. After some agonized reflection, she eventually gives me **3NT**. All pass, so the bidding has been simple:

South	West	North	East
2NT	pass	3NT	pass
pass	pass		

West also seems to be in trouble but eventually he leads the 7 of diamonds. Saying, "I wanted to bid three clubs but you don't play that convention, do you?" my partner puts down:

♠ Q 8 6 2
♡ J 9 7 5
◇ 6 4
♣ Q 6 3

◇ 7 led

♠ A 7 4
♡ A K Q 10 6
◇ Q 8 5
♣ A 9

Partner wanted to steer me into a major suit by responding with an artificial three clubs. If I go down badly in 3NT I shall never hear the end of it.

Prospects improve when East plays the Jack of diamonds on the first trick and I win with the Queen. Evidently West had something like A K 10 x x and wasn't sure whether to lead the King or a small one. I have eight tricks on top now and all I can do is play off the hearts and see what develops. Both opponents follow to two rounds of hearts.

On the third and fourth rounds West discards two clubs, East a spade and a club. On the last heart West discards another club, dummy a spade and East a diamond.

I am rather pleased to see that diamond from East because it suggests that the suit is divided 5 – 3 rather than 6 – 2. It also means that if I exit in diamonds, as I am intending to do, West will have to cash his winners or abandon the suit. By throwing a diamond East has limited the communication between the two hands.

When I exit with a diamond West takes the 10, then the King and Ace. East discards one more spade and one more club. The following cards are left:

♠ Q 8
♡ —
♢ —
♣ Q 6

♠ A 7
♡ —
♢ —
♣ A 9

West has one more diamond left and East, I suspect, has two guarded Kings. West thinks for a long while before deciding whether or not to cash his last diamond. If my picture of the hand is right it doesn't make any difference. If he exits with a club or a spade now I can throw East back with the same suit.

Eventually West plays his last diamond. Now I must throw a club from dummy because West has only one club left. My A 9 will be a sufficient threat against East. When East discards the Jack of spades I throw my club, keeping the two spades. West exits with the 3 of spades, I play low from table, East plays the King and I make the last three tricks.

East was squeezed on the diamonds as can be seen from the full diagram:

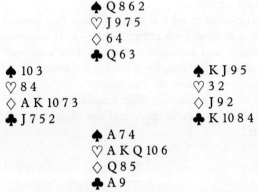

```
              ♠ Q 8 6 2
              ♡ J 9 7 5
              ◇ 6 4
              ♣ Q 6 3
♠ 10 3                        ♠ K J 9 5
♡ 8 4                         ♡ 3 2
◇ A K 10 7 3                  ◇ J 9 2
♣ J 7 5 2                     ♣ K 10 8 4
              ♠ A 7 4
              ♡ A K Q 10 6
              ◇ Q 8 5
              ♣ A 9
```

"That was hard work," remarked my partner. I forbore to point out that if I had been playing her convention and had had to play in four hearts it would have been still harder.

Post-mortem

While East had no sound defense at the finish he made a very common mistake earlier when he let go one of his diamonds on the fifth heart. He had to assume that his partner had tricks to make in diamonds and he could have afforded to throw a second spade or club. Say that he throws a club and that South, as before, exits in diamonds. Realizing the danger of running off the diamonds, West, who still has two spades left, leads the 10 of spades. That leaves declarer with no resource, for if he wins with the Ace and plays a spade back East will still have a diamond to lead to his partner.

Of course, South was lucky to make 3NT. The lead was favorable and the defense imperfect. It is often so and that is why one should not underestimate the advantage of playing borderline hands in no-trump. Many more contracts that could be defeated by perfect defense are made at no-trump than in a suit.

38. Major Road

Playing in a team event against strong opposition I pick up this powerful two-suiter:

♠ A K 7 6 4 2 ♡ A K J 8 5 3 ◇ A ♣ —

Both sides are vulnerable and I am first to speak. I like to make a start with my suits on this type of hand in preference to bidding an artificial two clubs, so I open **two spades**, forcing for one round in our system. If partner gives me a negative response I can always jump to four hearts. On this occasion West overcalls with three diamonds, North passes and so does East. I jump to **four hearts**, as planned, but this does not silence West. He bids **five clubs.**

Now my partner supports to **five spades** and East bids **six clubs.** I could bid six diamonds now to suggest the possibility of a grand slam to my partner. However, I think I ought to be content to play this hand in six if they will let me. The suits are sure to break badly. So I am content with **six spades** and the opponents compete no further. This has been the adventurous auction:

South	West	North	East
2♠	3◇	pass	pass
4♡	5♣	5♠	6♣
6♠	pass	pass	pass

West opens the King of diamonds and I see that my partner's five spades was imaginative:

♠ J 10 5 3
♡ 10 6 2
◇ 5 4 2
♣ 6 4 3

◇ K led

♠ A K 7 6 4 2
♡ A K J 8 5 3
◇ A
♣ —

After winning the first trick with the Ace of diamonds I lay down the Ace of spades. West discards a diamond, which is sad but not surprising.

Now how am I going to encompass these major suits? I can give up a trick to the Queen of spades and then enter dummy with the Jack, but I am not yet sure whether or not I want to finesse in hearts. West could be 0 – 1 – 6 – 6 but I suppose he could also be 0 – 2 – 6 – 5.

Another way would be to give up a trick to the Queen of hearts and enter dummy with the 10 of hearts to take the marked finesse in spades. I can lay down Ace of hearts and then play the Jack. No, what am I thinking of? That will be all right if East has Q x x but calamitous if either defender has Q x.

Having formed two rather poor plans I now consider the possibility of leading the Jack of hearts first. That would lose only if West had Q x x in hearts. Then he would have to be 0 – 3 – 5 – 5 and East, with a singleton heart and four diamonds, would probably have raised the diamonds on the first round of bidding.

This hand is driving me mad. If West has Q x x in hearts I can't make the contract whatever I do. It is only if East has singleton Queen of hearts that the lead of the Jack will be a disaster.

At the end of these confused reflections I decide to lead the Jack of hearts. West stares at this card for some while, as well he may. Eventually he puts on the Queen of hearts and leads the Ace of clubs. I ruff, enter dummy with the 10 of hearts, both defenders following, and claim the remainder with the aid of the spade finesse. This was the full hand:

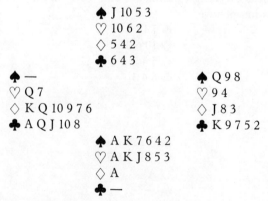

Post-mortem

The reader may well have been ahead of me on this hand. The lead of the Jack of hearts at trick 3 is obvious when one thinks of it, but I was very close to committing the folly of establishing entry to dummy in spades and finessing the Jack of hearts.

39. Making the Minimum

Playing rubber bridge with a partner who is not especially strong, I hold:

$$\spadesuit K\,7\,6\,2 \quad \heartsuit K\,7 \quad \diamondsuit 10\,8\,4 \quad \clubsuit K\,Q\,J\,8$$

Neither side is vulnerable and my partner, sitting North, deals and opens **one heart**. After a pass by East I have to choose between the responses of one spade and two clubs. In general, I dislike bidding weak major suits but there may be some advantage in averting an eventual spade lead. So I respond **one spade** and partner rebids **two hearts**. I won't bid three clubs now in case he gives me preference to three spades or, even worse, four spades. Technically, my right bid is probably three hearts. However, his dummy play is rather poor, so I am going to take a chance on the diamonds and introduce **2NT**. This is raised to **3NT**. Thus the full bidding, not very elegant on my part, has been:

South	West	North	East
—	—	1♡	pass
1♠	pass	2♡	pass
2NT	pass	3NT	pass
pass	pass		

West leads the 10 of clubs, which is a pleasant sight especially when the dummy goes down as follows:

$$\spadesuit 10\,5$$
$$\heartsuit A\,Q\,10\,9\,6\,3$$
$$\diamondsuit A\,K\,3$$
$$\clubsuit 5\,2$$

♣ 10 led

$$\spadesuit K\,7\,6\,2$$
$$\heartsuit K\,7$$
$$\diamondsuit 10\,8\,4$$
$$\clubsuit K\,Q\,J\,8$$

We seem to have ended up in the best spot, after all. East plays the Ace of clubs on the first trick and as I would like to see them continue clubs rather than perhaps lead a spade through my King, I play the Jack. However, East does not return a club. He switches to the Queen of diamonds. West plays the 2 and dummy wins.

Now I wonder whether, for safety, I ought to run the 9 of hearts from table. That Ace of clubs must have been a singleton, so East is most likely to have length in hearts. If I have to give up a heart to East and a spade comes through I may go down, so I finesse the 9 of hearts. West wins with the Jack and plays the 7 of diamonds. I take this in dummy and play off four rounds of hearts. That leaves the cards as follows:

♠ 10 5
♡ 3
♢ 3
♣ 5

♠ K 7
♡ —
♢ —
♣ K Q 8

West followed to the second heart and then threw two clubs, confirming my diagnosis that he began with six. His next discard was the Jack of spades. East threw two spades. On the last heart East threw the 9 of diamonds, I discarded a spade and West the 5 of diamonds.

Now I play a club from the table, East throws the Jack of diamonds and I win with the club Queen. I have the K 8 of clubs and the King of spades left. Despite my ill-starred maneuver in the heart suit the contract is safe, for the King of clubs is a ninth trick. However, it is obvious for several reasons that West has the Ace of spades and a minor tenace in clubs. (With five spades to the Ace and the Ace of clubs East would probably have overcalled with one spade; even more conclusive is that if East had had Ace of spades he would not have thrown his winning diamonds.) So in some attempt to regain prestige I exit with the King of spades and make the last two tricks when West has to play up to my K 8 of clubs. This was the full deal:

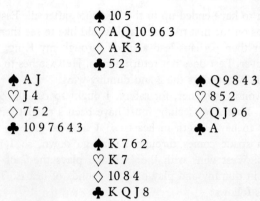

```
                    ♠ 10 5
                    ♡ A Q 10 9 6 3
                    ◇ A K 3
                    ♣ 5 2
    ♠ A J                           ♠ Q 9 8 4 3
    ♡ J 4                           ♡ 8 5 2
    ◇ 7 5 2                         ◇ Q J 9 6
    ♣ 10 9 7 6 4 3                  ♣ A
                    ♠ K 7 6 2
                    ♡ K 7
                    ◇ 10 8 4
                    ♣ K Q J 8
```

"You could have made another trick, couldn't you?" asks my partner. I have to agree.

Post-mortem

The Jack of clubs was perhaps an unnecessary offering, for if East had had a second club he would probably have returned it in any event. Possibly not, however, if he had had Q J 9 8 or some such holding in spades. The finesse of the 9 of hearts, though unsuccessful, was sound play at that point.

40. Proper Respect

Playing in a team-of-four match against capable opposition, I hold as dealer:

♠ Q 9   ♡ A 8 3   ◇ A K 10 9 4   ♣ J 9 7

Both sides are vulnerable and I open **one diamond**. West passes and my partner responds **one spade**. Having fair scattered values I rebid **1NT** rather than two diamonds. My partner raises to **3NT** and all pass. The bidding has been:

South	West	North	East
1◇	pass	1♠	pass
1NT	pass	3NT	pass
pass	pass		

West leads the 4 of clubs and this dummy goes down:

♠ K 10 7 4 3
♡ K 10 2
◇ Q J 5
♣ K 3

♣ 4 led

♠ Q 9
♡ A 8 3
◇ A K 10 9 4
♣ J 9 7

A club trick is certain after the lead, so there are eight tricks on top. A ninth can be established in spades but meanwhile they may set up four club tricks and the Ace of spades. Well, I must play low from table and see what develops.

East plays the Ace of clubs on the first trick and returns the 6. When I play the 9 West puts on the 10 but I don't suppose that's from Q 10 x. More likely he has Q 10 x x x and is trying to convey to his partner that he controls the rest of the suit.

If the clubs are 4 – 4 (or 6 – 2, East having the Ace of spades) I am in no danger. The question is how to play if they are 5 – 3. I can run my diamonds and see what they discard or I can try to slip through a spade. Obviously I shan't be able to do that if West has the Ace of spades and three good clubs, but if East has the Ace of spades will he play it when I lead a low spade from table? I think so. He is quite a good player and, moreover, my failure to play diamonds would be suspicious. I am not going to insult him. I'll play off the diamonds and see if anything turns up.

West has to discard three times on the diamonds. He lets go, in order, 5 of hearts, 6 of spades and Jack of spades. East signals in spades, playing the 8 and then the 2. After the five diamonds the following cards are left:

♠ K 10 7
♡ K 10 2
◇ —
♣ —

♠ Q 9
♡ A 8 3
◇ —
♣ J

Neither player has discarded a club. That confirms my original impression that they were 5 – 3. So West has three clubs left and either three hearts or two hearts and a spade. If two hearts and a spade there is nothing I can do (unless the hearts are Q J alone). But the Jack of spades may have been his last spade; maybe he couldn't let go another heart or thought he couldn't. I think I'll make the favorable assumption that he began with Q J x x in hearts and has been under pressure. I'd like to play off one round of hearts to see if the Queen or Jack falls, but if I do that I give up my tenace position. It's possible that he has discarded too well and has come down to Q J of hearts alone. But I'm going to play for what I think is the best chance and exit with the Jack of clubs.

West takes the Queen and plays off two more rounds of clubs. Since I can't afford to lose another trick and am hoping that West has no spade left I discard three spades from dummy and two from my own hand. That leaves me with K 10 2 of hearts on the table and A 8 3 in hand. At trick 11 West, as I was hoping, leads the 6 of hearts.

The only question now is whether that lead is from Q 9 x (or J 9 x) or from Q J x. I must assume from Q J x because with an original holding of Q 9 x x or J 9 x x he could have let go another heart and kept a spade. When I play the 10 from dummy it holds the trick, so I make the contract. The full hand:

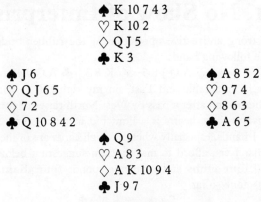

```
                    ♠ K 10 7 4 3
                    ♡ K 10 2
                    ◇ Q J 5
                    ♣ K 3
      ♠ J 6                           ♠ A 8 5 2
      ♡ Q J 6 5                       ♡ 9 7 4
      ◇ 7 2                           ◇ 8 6 3
      ♣ Q 10 8 4 2                    ♣ A 6 5
                    ♠ Q 9
                    ♡ A 8 3
                    ◇ A K 10 9 4
                    ♣ J 9 7
```

Post-mortem

The main point of this hand is to stress the advisability of playing off the long suit. Players often underestimate the advantage of that procedure. On a hand of this sort they say, "There can't be any squeeze unless West has all the clubs and all the hearts plus the Ace of spades. It must be a better chance to try to slip a round of spades past East."

Actually, as we saw, West was under pressure even though he did not have the Ace of spades. A further practical consideration is that defenders often make a mistake when a long suit is led against them. Sometimes both players unguard the same suit; sometimes the player with the long suit lets one go when he should not. It's not necessary to see around corners. When there is no good alternative declarer should play off his long suit even when there seems no likelihood of a squeeze, pseudo or otherwise.

41. No Show of Enterprise

Facing strong and active opposition at the rubber bridge table, I pick up the following hand:

♠ 6   ♡ A Q J 6 5   ♢ K 8 5   ♣ A Q 9 4

My side is vulnerable and East, on my right, deals and passes. I open **one heart** and after a pass by West North raises to **three hearts**.

That raise to three hearts is a limit bid in our system. Still, I like 5 – 4 – 3 – 1 hands, especially when the high cards are in the long suits. I reckon that I can afford to make a slam suggestion below the game level. I bid **four clubs** and partner responds **four diamonds**. Our bidding has gone so far:

South	North
1♡	3♡
4♣	4♢
?	

This bid of four diamonds suits my hand well enough, but we are still some way from a slam. In addition to Ace of diamonds, I want partner to hold either Ace of spades or King of hearts and second round control of clubs. Having made one slam try, I must leave it to partner to make the next move. Therefore, I bid **four hearts**.

After a pass from West, partner bids **five clubs**.

That's different! Either he has the King, or a singleton with very good trumps. Either way it looks as though a spade should be the only loser. I go to **six hearts** and all pass.

The full bidding:

South	West	North	East
—	—	—	pass
1♡	pass	3♡	pass
4♣	pass	4♢	pass
4♡	pass	5♣	pass
6♡	pass	pass	pass

West leads the 4 of spades and this suitable dummy goes down:

♠ 9 5 3
♡ K 10 8 3
◇ A 6
♣ K 8 7 2

♠ 4 led

♠ 6
♡ A Q J 6 5
◇ K 8 5
♣ A Q 9 4

Rather well bid by us! Only a bad break in clubs will beat it.

East goes up with the King of spades and follows with the Ace, which I ruff. All follow to two rounds of trumps. I want to get as good a count as I can, so I ruff a third spade, East putting in the 10 and West the Queen. That leaves:

♠ —
♡ K 8
◇ A 6
♣ K 8 7 2

♠ —
♡ Q
◇ K 8 5
♣ A Q 9 4

I could play off the two hearts now, and discard a club. But is there any possibility of a squeeze? The same hand would have to have six diamonds and four clubs, and that is quite impossible in view of the play up to date. It is better not to weaken the club holding in any respect. I will play three rounds of diamonds and see if that produces any information.

It does! East plays the 9 and Jack, and when I ruff the third round in dummy he discards the Jack of spades.

So East has a doubleton heart and a doubleton diamond. If anyone has long clubs, it must be East. I can play off the King of clubs. If that brings down the Jack or 10 from West I shall be home for certain.

But the King of clubs produces the 5 from East and the 3 from West.

I follow with the 2 of clubs from table and East plays the 6. Now I've got to think. Has East got four clubs? I know he has only four red cards. Did he start with five spades or six? I must go back over the play of the spades.

West led the 4 and East played the King and Ace on the first two tricks. Later he showed up with the 10 and Jack. West has shown the 4, 7 and Queen. The missing cards are the 8 and the 2. They have both discarded well. For example, if West had not dropped the Queen I would have known that he still had it and could have been sure on that account that East had only five.

So far as the play of the spade suit goes, I don't see that I have any strong indication. What about the bidding, though? East could have A K J 10 x, but could he have A K J 10 x x? He passed as dealer against vulnerable opponents. True, he has at most a couple of Jacks outside, but with such a strong suit, especially spades, wouldn't he have put up some show of enterprise?

At the risk of looking foolish I am going to take the deep finesse of the 9 of clubs, expecting the full hand to be:

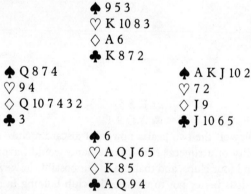

```
              ♠ 9 5 3
              ♡ K 10 8 3
              ◇ A 6
              ♣ K 8 7 2
♠ Q 8 7 4                    ♠ A K J 10 2
♡ 9 4                        ♡ 7 2
◇ Q 10 7 4 3 2               ◇ J 9
♣ 3                          ♣ J 10 6 5
              ♠ 6
              ♡ A Q J 6 5
              ◇ K 8 5
              ♣ A Q 9 4
```

And so it was.

Post-mortem

It was lucky to find the diamonds 6 – 2 and so to gain this un-expected clue to the distribution. You often reap such a windfall if you follow the principle of discovering everything you can about the hand before testing the critical suit (in this case clubs).

Note, also, that a master heart had to be kept in dummy, for other-wise East could have defeated the hand by splitting his honors in clubs.

42. Lifeless Knave

Playing rubber bridge against opponents of average strength I deal and hold:

♠ A 10 9 8 6 4   ♡ Q 5   ◇ 8 6   ♣ A 10 4

As we are not vulnerable and they are, I make a light opening of **one spade.** West **doubles,** my partner **redoubles,** and East passes. Some players in my position would bid two spades to signify a good suit but a weakish hand. According to my old-fashioned notions the way to show weakness is to pass. West rescues himself into **two clubs.** This is passed by North and East. My partner expects me to say something, I know, and as I don't fancy a double of two clubs I bid **two spades.** Partner raises to **four spades** and all pass. The bidding has been:

South	West	North	East
1♠	double	redouble	pass
pass	2♣	pass	pass
2♠	pass	4♠	pass
pass	pass		

West leads the King of clubs. Remarking that he had hoped I would be able to double two clubs, partner puts down:

♠ K 3
♡ K 10 6 4 3
◇ A Q 10 2
♣ 8 7

♣ K led

♠ A 10 9 8 6 4
♡ Q 5
◇ 8 6
♣ A 10 4

Prospects seem reasonable. Assuming the diamond finesse to be right I should lose at most a spade, a heart and a club. On the first trick East plays the 2 of clubs and I let the King hold. West switches to the 5 of diamonds. I play dummy's Queen with fair confidence but East puts on the King. That's an unexpected blow!

Now I can't afford to lose a trump trick. I must assume West has a singleton spade and project the play on the assumption that that singleton is the Queen or Jack.

After the King of diamonds East returns the 7 of hearts to his partner's Ace and West exits with the 3 of diamonds. This second finesse is probably right, but the question is, will it help me at all?

Suppose that the 10 of diamonds holds. I can then throw a club on the Ace of diamonds and ruff a diamond. Now cash Ace of clubs, lead a spade to the King and finesse the 8 on the way back; overtake Queen of hearts, ruff a heart—and I'm still in the wrong hand at trick 12, unable to lead trumps through East.

This has got to be managed in a different way. If I'm going to play West for a singleton trump honor I need every possible entry to dummy, including the ruff of the third club. I think it can just be done. At any rate there is no point in finessing the diamond so I go up with the Ace and ruff a diamond, East following suit. I overtake the Queen of hearts and ruff a heart. The hearts break 3 – 3 and this is now the situation:

♠ K 3
♡ 10 6
◇ 10
♣ 8

♠ A 10 9 8
♡ —
◇ —
♣ A 10

After cashing the Ace of clubs I ruff my last club with dummy's 3 and lead the 10 of diamonds. East, who is evidently down to four trumps, ruffs with the 2 of spades and I over-ruff with the 8. Now the 9 of spades brings the Queen from West. Dummy's King wins and I make the last two tricks with the A 10 over East's J 7, the full hand being:

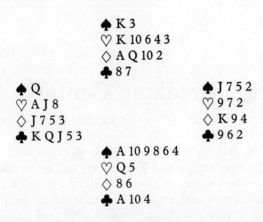

♠ K 3
♡ K 10 6 4 3
♢ A Q 10 2
♣ 8 7

♠ Q
♡ A J 8
♢ J 7 5 3
♣ K Q J 5 3

♠ J 7 5 2
♡ 9 7 2
♢ K 9 4
♣ 9 6 2

♠ A 10 9 8 6 4
♡ Q 5
♢ 8 6
♣ A 10 4

Post-mortem

Dummy's singleton King of trumps opposite the A 10 9 8 proved a
very powerful combination in the end-game. Note that the contract
cannot be made if South uses dummy's 3 of spades for a finesse of the 8.
The basic reason for this is that the small trump on the table is required
as an extra entry. At the twelfth trick South picks up East's J 7 of spades
by means of a trump coup.

43. Breaking Contact

Playing in a pairs event, with a high standard all round the table, I hold in fourth position:

♠ A Q 6   ♡ Q 8 4   ◇ Q 8 5   ♣ A Q 9 5

Neither side is vulnerable and West, on my left, opens **one spade**. This is followed by two passes. This is a situation I never care for. The natural action on my hand is to bid no-trump but in this protective position there is such a wide gap between 1NT and 2NT! Players generally reopen with 1NT on about 11 to 13 points. Here I have a not very good 16 but I can hardly bid 2NT on it. Nor is it altogether satisfactory to double and then bid 2NT over a minimum response. Nevertheless, that is what I may have to do. For the moment, I **double.**

West passes and North bids **two diamonds**. East passes again. Technically I ought to pass now, but at match-point scoring I am not going to let him play in two diamonds. It's an overbid in a sense but I'm going to bid **2NT.** I only hope he doesn't take me too seriously and raise on about 5 or 6 points. No, all pass, so the bidding has been:

South	West	North	East
—	1♠	pass	pass
double	pass	2◇	pass
2NT	pass	pass	pass

West leads the Jack of spades and partner puts down:

♠ 9 8 5 3
♡ 10 3 2
◇ J 9 7 2
♣ K 3

♠ J led

♠ A Q 6
♡ Q 8 4
◇ Q 8 5
♣ A Q 9 5

I wish I'd followed my instinct and re-opened with 1NT on the South hand. Next time I shall. It's not going to be easy to make 2NT but at least that's better than playing in two diamonds.

East plays the 2 of spades on the first trick and I win with the Queen. To make any tricks at all I've got to find the 10 of diamonds. It's more convenient to play West for that card than East, so to the second trick I lead the 5 of diamonds. West plays the 6 and I put in dummy's 7, which holds the trick. That's slightly better. I return the 2 of diamonds to the Queen and West wins with the King.

West now studies the matter at some length and finally exits with the 7 of spades. I put in the 8 from dummy and that holds the trick, East discarding the 2 of clubs. West has played a low spade because, from his point of view, I might have had A Q alone. Now I am on the table and this is the position:

♠ 9 5
♡ 10 3 2
◇ J 9
♣ K 3

♠ A
♡ Q 8 4
◇ 8
♣ A Q 9 5

The general lie of the cards is fairly plain. West began with K J 10 x x in spades and, according to all indications, A K 10 x in diamonds. He could have A x x in hearts and a singleton club or, perhaps more likely, A x in hearts and a doubleton club. I have made three tricks and can see four more but that is still one short. The trouble is that I cannot conveniently enjoy a second trick in diamonds. If I come to hand with the Ace of spades the defense will make too many tricks, and if I play a club to the Queen in order to lead a diamond the clubs will be blocked.

I wonder whether I can make a fourth trick out of the clubs. If West has something like J x or 10 x, which is not unlikely, I can establish a major tenace over East. But can I throw him in?

Now I think I'm getting somewhere. If West has a doubleton A x or K x of hearts I may be able to cut the communications between the defending hands and eventually throw East in on the third round of hearts. To do that I have got to find West with only one entry in hearts (for otherwise he will get his spades going). I can't do it if he has A J. But he may have A 9 and to take care of that I must lead the 10 from dummy. On the 10 of hearts East plays the Jack, I play low and West follows with the 6. East exits with a heart to his partner's Ace. The hand is developing favorably, for West cannot cash his high diamond while I still have a club entry to table. West therefore exits with a spade to the Ace, and on this trick East has to throw a heart in order to keep his clubs. Now there are six cards left:

♠ 9
♡ 3
◇ J 9
♣ K 3

♠ —
♡ Q
◇ 8
♣ A Q 9 5

Prospects have improved but there is still a view to take in clubs. I play a club to the King, West following with the 6, and return a club on which East plays the 7. Now if East began with J 10 x x x I have to finesse the 9. However, he would then have been close to a response to the opening bid of one spade. Apart from that, I cannot resist the more artistic ending. So I put in the Queen, West drops the Jack and now I have them for sure! I exit with the Queen of hearts and after making two heart tricks East has to lead a club into my A 9.

This was the full deal:

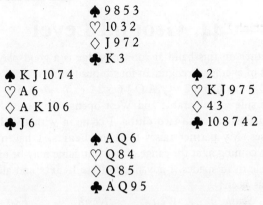

```
              ♠ 9 8 5 3
              ♡ 10 3 2
              ◇ J 9 7 2
              ♣ K 3
♠ K J 10 7 4                    ♠ 2
♡ A 6                           ♡ K J 9 7 5
◇ A K 10 6                      ◇ 4 3
♣ J 6                           ♣ 10 8 7 4 2
              ♠ A Q 6
              ♡ Q 8 4
              ◇ Q 8 5
              ♣ A Q 9 5
```

Post-mortem

While East was making his heart tricks at the finish West was sitting with two good spades and the Ace of diamonds. The two rounds of hearts had put the defending hands out of touch with one another.

The same sort of result can sometimes be effected by a deceptive play in a position such as the following:

```
                   ◇ 9 7 3
◇ A Q J 10 4                    ◇ K
                   ◇ 8 6 5 2
```

Playing either in a suit or at no-trump, South knows that West, although he has not led diamonds, has a five-card suit. Obviously if East gains the lead at any point he will lead his King and West will overtake. If West has no side entry, however, a low diamond from hand may trick him into playing the 10 and so losing contact with his partner.

44. Ground Level

My partner on this hand at rubber bridge is a good player and the opponents of average strength. In fourth position I hold:

♠ Q 5 3 2　♡ A Q J 6 5 2　♢ 7　♣ A 6

Neither side is vulnerable and West opens **one club.** My partner passes and East raises to **two clubs.** I come in with **two hearts** and West passes. My partner raises to **three hearts.** I haven't much to spare after coming in at the range of two but game may be on if there is a reasonable fit in spades. I advance to **four hearts** and all pass. The bidding has been:

South	West	North	East
—	1♣	pass	2♣
2♡	pass	3♡	pass
4♡	pass	pass	pass

West opens the King of clubs and I see that partner also has been pressing a little:

```
          ♠ K 10 6
          ♡ 9 7 3
          ♢ A J 5 2
          ♣ 7 4 2


♣ K led


          ♠ Q 5 3 2
          ♡ A Q J 6 5 2
          ♢ 7
          ♣ A 6
```

The contract is going to depend on a number of factors—the finesses in the major suits and the break in spades. I have to consider whether or not to win the first club and whether to finesse the 10 of spades early or to cross to dummy and finesse the trumps first.

If the heart finesse is wrong I'll need three spade tricks, but if it's right I can afford to lose two spade tricks. That may have some bearing on how I play the suit so I'm inclined to think I should settle the heart position before I play on spades.

Now can it make any difference whether or not I take the Ace of clubs at once? I don't really want an early switch to spades, threatening a ruff and making it dangerous to finesse in trumps. Taking the Ace at once will establish an entry for East, but that is unlikely to matter.

So I take the Ace of clubs, cross to the Ace of diamonds and finesse the Queen of hearts. This holds, West dropping the 10. I don't think it's likely that he is holding off from K 10 x—he is not that sort of player. The question now is how to tackle the spades on the assumption that the heart finesse is right. I don't want to finesse the 10 of spades, lose to the Jack and run into a spade ruff. If West's 10 of hearts is a singleton the spades are probably 4 – 2. As the clubs were supported and no one mentioned diamonds, West's most likely distribution is 4 – 1 – 4 – 4.

Now suppose West has A J x x in spades. I don't need to finesse the 10. If I lead low to the King, draw trumps and then lead a low spade towards the 10 6, that will be good enough. Of course East may have J x, but I can think about that later.

For the moment I'm going to play a low spade to dummy's King. That wins and I return a trump. (A spade would not be safe because if West had A J x left he would make the Jack and Ace and give his partner a ruff.) The second heart finesse wins, West discarding a club. On the Ace of hearts West discards a diamond. The following cards are left:

♠ 10 6
♡ —
♢ J 5 2
♣ 7 4

♠ Q 5 3
♡ 6 5 2
♢ —
♣ 6

I lead a low spade towards the dummy and West plays the 7. Now I'm sure the spades are 4 – 2, but if West had A J 7 x wouldn't he at any rate consider going up with the Jack in front of dummy's 10 x? It might not be right play but he would still think about it. I'm fairly confident that East has the bare Jack left. I'm going to stay close to the ground and play the 6 from dummy.

That turns out to be right, for East plays the Jack. That leaves the Queen and 10 of spades equals against West's Ace and I make the contract, having lost a club and two spades. The full hand was as follows:

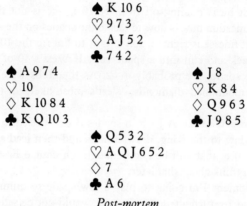

♠ K 10 6
♡ 9 7 3
◇ A J 5 2
♣ 7 4 2

♠ A 9 7 4
♡ 10
◇ K 10 8 4
♣ K Q 10 3

♠ J 8
♡ K 8 4
◇ Q 9 6 3
♣ J 9 8 5

♠ Q 5 3 2
♡ A Q J 6 5 2
◇ 7
♣ A 6

Post-mortem

Whenever a hand seems to call for two or more finesses it's important to decide on the priority. Sometimes one successful finesse will obviate the other, but not vice versa. In this hand the first play had to be the trump finesse because the management of the spades was going to depend to some extent on whether the heart finesse succeeded.

When West's 10 of hearts fell on the first round his distribution could be assessed with fair certainty. The clubs were likely to be 4 – 4 since they had been supported. The diamonds were sure to be 4 – 4 since neither defender had mentioned them. The 10 of hearts appeared to be a singleton, so West was marked with four spades.

Having reached that conclusion, South had to appreciate that it was not necessary to finesse the 10 of spades before drawing trumps. If West had A J x x it would be safe to win with the King and later lead towards the 10 x.

The next point was the psychological one that when West played the 7 of spades in front of dummy's 10 x it was unlikely that he had the A J. However, it is interesting to reflect that if West had in fact held something like A J 9 x it would have been a brilliant defense to play the 9 when declarer led low towards the table.

45. "Flight Square"

Playing a team-of-four match against opponents of average strength, I hold as dealer:

♠ A Q 10 9 6 4   ♡ 8 2   ◇ 9 7   ♣ A J 4

Neither side is vulnerable and I open **one spade**. West passes and my partner responds **two diamonds**. East comes in with **two hearts**. Although I have a minimum opening in terms of high cards I am not going to be deterred from rebidding my good suit so I say **two spades**.

My partner now bids their suit, **three hearts**. That means he wants to play in game at some denomination and, as we play that bid, he should have a heart control. Having a fair guard in clubs I could bid 3NT, but my spades are broken and I have no high card in his suit. I think that **three spades** is more prudent. This he raises to **four spades** and all pass. The bidding has been:

South	West	North	East
1♠	pass	2◇	2♡
2♠	pass	3♡	pass
3♠	pass	4♠	pass
pass	pass		

West leads the King of hearts and I see that partner had in fact a difficult bid over two spades, his hand being:

♠ 7 3
♡ A 10
◇ A K 10 6 5 4 2
♣ Q 9

♡ K led

♠ A Q 10 9 6 4
♡ 8 2
◇ 9 7
♣ A J 4

I dare say we are as well off in four spades as 3NT, which would be an anxious affair after a heart lead.

As most players lead low from K x x this lead of the King may be from a doubleton. I am going to duck and if they switch to diamonds I can study the position again. East plays the 7 and West continues with another heart, taking out dummy's Ace.

I can't rely on the diamonds breaking, especially as there was an intervening bid. I must test the clubs, as I may want to ruff the third round. East covers the Queen with the King. I cash the Ace and Jack and when I ruff a third round with dummy's 7 I get my first surprise. East throws a spade. That leaves the cards as follows:

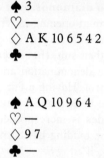

♠ 3
♡ —
◇ A K 10 6 5 4 2
♣ —

♠ A Q 10 9 6 4
♡ —
◇ 9 7
♣ —

I have only lost one trick but I'm not all that happy about the hand. Unless East is playing a remarkably deep game he couldn't over-ruff the 7. That means that West has K J 8 in trumps, but what if he has K J 8 x? I'll lose the second round to the King and West will put me back on the table with a diamond. Then how can I get back to draw trumps without promoting another trick for him?

Let me see if I can count the hand. West has six clubs, I know, and probably a doubleton heart. If he has three spades the contract is safe anyway for I'll lose only two trump tricks. But if West has four spades? Then he will have only one diamond and that's the situation I have to guard against. I must play off a top diamond so that West can't put me back on the table and promote an extra trump trick for himself.

All follow to the Ace of diamonds. Then I play Ace and Queen of spades. East shows void on the second round. West is in with the King but he hasn't got a diamond to play. He makes the Jack of trumps in due course but that is all.

So I am just home in four spades. Three no-trump wouldn't have been a success, as the full hand shows:

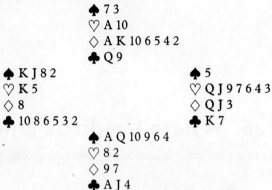

One must give credit to West for not doubling four spades.

Post-mortem

The play of the Ace of diamonds removed West's flight square, as the chess players call it. The play was by no means obvious because the count of West's hand was hypothetical, not inferential. There was danger only if West had four spades and the picture of the hand had to be built up on that premise.

46. Where Credit Is Due

Playing in a pairs event against strong and enterprising opponents, I pick up:

♠ 8 2   ♡ 9 5   ◇ 9 6 2   ♣ Q 10 7 6 4 2

Neither side is vulnerable and after a pass by West my partner opens **one diamond**. East overcalls with **one heart** and I pass. West raises to **two hearts** and my partner **doubles**. East pushes on to **three hearts**. The bidding so far has gone:

South	West	North	East
—	pass	1◇	1♡
pass	2♡	double	3♡
?			

Despite my six-card suit I am not making a free bid at the four level. I pass and so does West. Now my partner **doubles** again and East passes. This is a close decision. No doubt they are bidding defensively and probably we can set three hearts by one, possibly two, tricks. On the other hand, if we can make four clubs that is 130 and better than defeating them by one trick. I suppose I must make the natural call and bid **four clubs**. This I do and everyone passes, so the full bidding has been:

South	West	North	East
—	pass	1◇	1♡
pass	2♡	double	3♡
pass	pass	double	pass
4♣	pass	pass	pass

West leads the 2 of hearts and a not altogether welcome dummy goes down:

♠ A K 7 4
♡ 7 4
◇ A K 10 5
♣ A J 5

♡ 2 led

♠ 8 2
♡ 9 5
◇ 9 6 2
♣ Q 10 7 6 4 2

Very likely we could have collected 300 from three hearts doubled. It would have been better if my partner had bid two spades on the second round instead of doubling. Then if he later doubled three hearts I would have passed.

East takes the first trick with the King of hearts, cashes the Ace and leads the Jack of spades to dummy's King. I am not very hopeful of the club finesse but I suppose I must try it. I cash Ace of spades and ruff the third round, East playing the 10 and West the Queen. I run the 10 of clubs and it holds the trick, but on the next round West shows out, discarding the 10 of hearts. I put on the Ace and return the Jack to East's King. On this trick West discards the 3 of diamonds. Now East is on lead and the following cards are left:

♠ 7
♡ —
◇ A K 10 5
♣ —

♠ —
♡ —
◇ 9 6 2
♣ Q 7

East is giving the matter a lot of thought. He can't have the fourth spade or he would play that. If he plays a heart I think I may squeeze West. Yes, that seems certain, for East began with five hearts, three spades and three clubs that I know of. So if he plays a heart I shall ruff and lead out my last trump, which will squeeze West in spades and diamonds.

But East appears to have reached the same conclusion, for in the diagram position he leads the 4 of diamonds. West plays the Jack and dummy the King. Now the only way I can come to hand is by leading the last spade, destroying my threat card. East has played altogether too well: if he had taken the first club I would have been able to come to hand with a club now.

East throws a heart on the 7 of spades and I ruff. I lead a low diamond and West puts in the 7. Now do I finesse or not?

First I must consider whether there is any possibility that that diamond of East's was a singleton. So far as the bidding goes he could have had six hearts. That would make his three hearts an obvious bid. West's raise would be thin but valid. But what about the play? If East had had a singleton diamond wouldn't he have led it at trick 2? Holding the King of clubs twice guarded he would have planned to take the second round of trumps and put his partner in with the Queen of hearts. Yes, that seems certain: East's 4 of diamonds was not a singleton.

Then has he something like the 4 3 or has he made a masterly play from the Q 4? He is a good enough player to have foreseen the squeeze. The Queen of diamonds is not a particularly important card for his three heart bid.

What about West? Here, again, possession of the Queen of diamonds would not affect his bidding. Most players with Q J x under A K 10 would play the Queen, it's true, but that's not conclusive.

Unless I have missed something there is no good clue to the position of this Queen of diamonds. It becomes a matter of prestige. If East has made a clever play, as I think he has, I'm not going to be outwitted. I shall play the Ace of diamonds.

And I was right to give East credit! The Ace of diamonds brings down the Queen, the full hand being:

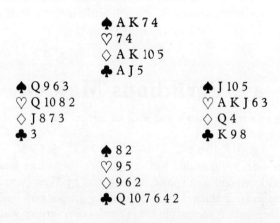

♠ A K 7 4
♡ 7 4
◇ A K 10 5
♣ A J 5

♠ Q 9 6 3   ♠ J 10 5
♡ Q 10 8 2   ♡ A K J 6 3
◇ J 8 7 3   ◇ Q 4
♣ 3   ♣ K 9 8

♠ 8 2
♡ 9 5
◇ 9 6 2
♣ Q 10 7 6 4 2

Post-mortem

East's bid of three hearts was daring and well-timed. Had he passed over the double of two hearts South would have bid three clubs and then, if East-West bid three hearts, North would double and South pass. North-South have only to find the spade ruff to take 300 from three hearts doubled.

In four clubs, this was the situation when East was in after the third round of trumps:

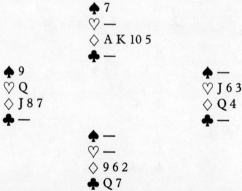

♠ 7
♡ —
◇ A K 10 5
♣ —

♠ 9   ♠ —
♡ Q   ♡ J 6 3
◇ J 8 7   ◇ Q 4
♣ —   ♣ —

♠ —
♡ —
◇ 9 6 2
♣ Q 7

Looking at the four hands, it is apparent that if East makes the obvious lead of a heart declarer cannot miss the squeeze.

47. Perfidious Maiden

Playing in a mixed pairs event with an earnest but not over-talented partner I hold:

♠ A K 10 8 6 4   ♡ —   ◇ Q 7 5 2   ♣ J 9 6

Neither side is vulnerable and my partner opens **one heart**. East passes and I respond **one spade**. After a pass by West partner rebids **two diamonds**. I think I must repeat my spades now rather than support diamonds. A contract in either spades or no-trump will produce a better match-point score and apart from that I am not too keen for partner to be at the wheel in five diamonds. I jump to **three spades** and partner brightly gives me **four spades**. This is passed out, so the bidding has been:

South	West	North	East
—	—	1♡	pass
1♠	pass	2◇	pass
3♠	pass	4♠	pass
pass	pass		

West leads the 9 of diamonds and partner's hand is slightly disappointing:

♠ J 3
♡ K Q 10 6 5
◇ A K 8 4
♣ 7 4

◇ 9 led

♠ A K 10 8 6 4
♡ —
◇ Q 7 5 2
♣ J 9 6

There are only eight tricks on top—five spades and three diamonds—but the diamonds may break and the spade finesse may be right. After this lead I won't be able to ruff a club. If I play clubs they will either lead trumps or, more likely, continue diamonds and come to a ruff there. But I can get rid of a club from my hand by setting up a heart trick so I take the King of diamonds and lead a heart at once.

East plays the Ace of hearts on the King and I ruff. (If East had played low I would, instead, have discarded a club.) Now I am home if the spades and diamonds break. I don't think I can afford to cross to dummy for a spade finesse because if that loses they may ruff a diamond. It must be better to play off the top spades.

On the Ace of spades West drops the Queen. That doesn't do me any harm. I cross to the Jack of spades, West throwing a club, and return by ruffing a low heart. I play off King and 10 of spades, West discarding two more clubs. That leaves the cards as follows:

$$\spadesuit \ —$$
$$\heartsuit \ Q\ 10$$
$$\diamondsuit \ A\ 8\ 4$$
$$\clubsuit \ 7$$

$$\spadesuit \ —$$
$$\heartsuit \ —$$
$$\diamondsuit \ Q\ 7\ 5$$
$$\clubsuit \ J\ 9\ 6$$

I am playing for overtricks now as I am certain of six spades, three diamonds and one heart. When I lead the Queen of diamonds West plays the 6 and East discards a heart. What's this? West has led the 9 of diamonds from J 10 9 x! The things these girls get up to! I play another diamond to the Ace and this time East discards the 10 of clubs.

Now I can take the Queen of hearts and run, but the way things have gone I think there is a chance to punish West for her chicanery in diamonds. West has discarded three clubs—actually the 3, 2 and 8 in that order. It's quite possible that she has the Ace left together with the winning diamond and J x of hearts. If I play a club now and the worst happens, East having the A K Q, he will still have to give me a heart at the finish. If East has something like A K x or A Q x left and goes up with the Ace he will drop his partner's honor and my Jack will control the third round. Yes, it seems safe enough: I play a club from dummy, East plays low and West wins with the Ace.

West cashes her diamond, East throwing the Queen of clubs. Now West leads the 8 of hearts into dummy's Q 10. Is it possible that East has Jack of hearts and King of clubs left? No, the evidence of the discards on both sides of the table is all against it. Anyway, one doesn't win mixed pairs events by playing for averages. I finesse the 10 and make the overtrick, the full hand being:

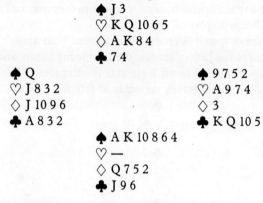

♠ J 3
♥ K Q 10 6 5
♦ A K 8 4
♣ 7 4

♠ Q
♥ J 8 3 2
♦ J 10 9 6
♣ A 8 3 2

♠ 9 7 5 2
♥ A 9 7 4
♦ 3
♣ K Q 10 5

♠ A K 10 8 6 4
♥ —
♦ Q 7 5 2
♣ J 9 6

Post-mortem

The finesse of the 10 of hearts at trick 12 was very safe if one studies the discards. Take West first. Would she have come down to Ace of clubs alone in order to keep two low hearts? Obviously not. And would East have bared the Jack of hearts when he could see the Q 10 in dummy and the probability was that declarer would lay down the Queen? Again most unlikely. Such inferences are constantly available and in a pairs contest especially, declarer must act on them.

48. The Light Was Bad

Playing rubber bridge against old rivals I hold the following in second position:

♠ 9 3　♡ A J　◇ K 9 7 2　♣ A J 10 8 6

Neither side is vulnerable and East, on my right, opens **one spade**. I can't very well make a take-out double on minimum values with a doubleton in the other major. It's not a particularly good overcall at the two level either, but I'm going to chance **two clubs**. West passes and my partner, a scientific player, bids **two spades**. Players seem to bid the enemy suit all the time nowadays with a variety of meanings. So far as I am concerned it is forcing to game and confirms clubs. He perhaps intends it as a directional asking bid and wants me to bid no-trump if I have an auxiliary guard in spades. For the moment I don't see what I can do but bid **three clubs**. Partner raises that to **four clubs**. I don't know what he's playing at, but I'm going **five clubs**. All pass, so the bidding has been:

South	West	North	East
—		—	1♠
2♣	pass	2♠	pass
3♣	pass	4♣	pass
5♣	pass	pass	pass

West leads the 5 of spades and I see that we are in the wrong contract when this dummy goes down:

♠ 7 6 4 2
♡ 8 2
◇ A Q 6 3
♣ K Q 2

♠ 5 led

♠ 9 3
♡ A J
◇ K 9 7 2
♣ A J 10 8 6

On this lead of a low spade I should think the spades are 4 – 3 and that we could have made 3NT. That's not easy to bid but five diamonds is a lay-down if the diamonds are 3 – 2. I suppose he'll tell me that I should have introduced diamonds on K x x x. I don't know why he couldn't bid them himself instead of making that meaningless, albeit fashionable, bid of two spades. If only players would bid what they've got instead of what they haven't got . . . .

I don't see how I'm going to make five clubs unless they give me a chance to develop a squeeze in the major suits and that's not at all likely. East wins the first trick with the King of spades and continues with the Ace on which his partner plays the 8. East then switches to the King of hearts. That's what I was afraid of; now there's no chance of a genuine squeeze.

Nevertheless I see a chance of putting East to the test. When I have ruffed a third round of spades he will have the master spade left and the master heart. If I come down to a spade and a diamond on the table at trick 12 and lead the diamond, East may not be sure which card to keep. I can manipulate the diamonds with a certain amount of cunning so that he won't be sure, unless he has been watching very carefully, whether the diamond on the table is a master or not.

To bring about the position I want, I have to conceal the 2 of diamonds. After three rounds of trumps I ruff the third spade in hand, lead the 7 of diamonds to the Queen and return the 6 to the King. I play off my last trump, discarding a heart, and play the 9 of diamonds to the Ace. For once it is appropriate to set out a two-card ending:

♠ 7
♡ —
◇ 3
♣ —

♠ —
♡ J
◇ 2
♣ —

East's last two cards are the Jack of spades and the Queen of hearts. When I lead the 3 of diamonds from the table East sits up. I can hear his brain working: "That's not the last diamond, is it? No, South still has one." After a short pause East throws his spade and the last trick is won by dummy's 7 of spades. This is the full hand:

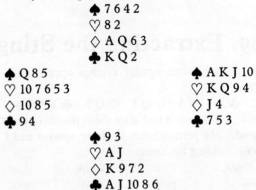

```
              ♠ 7 6 4 2
              ♡ 8 2
              ◇ A Q 6 3
              ♣ K Q 2
  ♠ Q 8 5                      ♠ A K J 10
  ♡ 10 7 6 5 3                 ♡ K Q 9 4
  ◇ 10 8 5                     ◇ J 4
  ♣ 9 4                        ♣ 7 5 3
              ♠ 9 3
              ♡ A J
              ◇ K 9 7 2
              ♣ A J 10 8 6
```

Before partner can begin his remonstrances about the bidding East is telling the old tale—he pulled the wrong card, he thought the spade had been led, the light was bad . . . .

Post-mortem

The type of pseudo-squeeze used on this hand is one of the least-known arts in the game. For it to have a chance of success, declarer needs to have two one-card threats against the right-hand opponent. There must be a side suit in which dummy and declarer have the same length. At trick 12 a card of this suit must be led from dummy which, from the point of view of an unobservant defender, may or may not be a winner.

49. Extracting the Sting

In a team-of-four match against average opposition I am last to speak and hold:

♠ A J 9 5 3   ♡ Q 3   ◇ Q 5   ♣ K Q J 6

Neither side is vulnerable and after three passes I open the bidding with **one spade**. My partner raises to **three spades** and I go to **four spades.** So the bidding has been:

South	West	North	East
—	pass	pass	pass
1♠	pass	3♠	pass
4♠	pass	pass	pass

West leads the four of diamonds and this dummy goes down:

```
              ♠ Q 8 6 4
              ♡ A 10 9 7 6
              ◇ K J
              ♣ 10 3

    ◇ 4 led

              ♠ A J 9 5 3
              ♡ Q 3
              ◇ Q 5
              ♣ K Q J 6
```

The hands don't fit too well. There are two Aces to lose and probably a heart unless they make me a present of some sort. It looks as though I can't afford to lose a trump trick.

On the first trick I play the Jack of diamonds from dummy. East wins with the Ace and returns a low club which I let run up to dummy's 10. If East has both minor suit Aces that makes prospects even worse for if he held the King of spades as well he would probably have opened the bidding third in hand. I am going to settle the club position before taking any finesse in spades. On a second round of clubs East does go up with the Ace, then exits with a diamond which runs to dummy's King.

Now, on the assumption that West has both major suit Kings, have I any play for the contract (other than dropping a singleton King of spades) if I refuse the spade finesse? Yes, if I can find him with exactly K x of spades and can eliminate the clubs before throwing him in. That's not such a remote chance and I'm going to play for it. I play a low spade and put on the Ace, East dropping the 7 and West the 2. All follow to a third round of clubs. The position is now:

♠ Q 8 6
♡ A 10 9 7
♡ —
♣ —

♠ J 9 5 3
♡ Q 3
◇ —
♣ Q

I don't know who has the last club but I can't lose by playing the Queen. If West has the fourth club I must play the Queen to extract his last card of exit. West does, in fact, follow to the fourth club. Since I am playing for West to have the King of spades and East the 10, I ruff with dummy's Queen of spades and return a trump. East follows, I duck and West wins with the King. Now if West leads a diamond I shall have a ruff and discard and if he plays a heart I can run it up to the Queen. He tries a heart and my Queen wins, the full hand being:

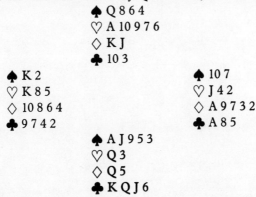

```
              ♠ Q 8 6 4
              ♡ A 10 9 7 6
              ◇ K J
              ♣ 10 3
♠ K 2                        ♠ 10 7
♡ K 8 5                      ♡ J 4 2
◇ 10 8 6 4                   ◇ A 9 7 3 2
♣ 9 7 4 2                    ♣ A 8 5
              ♠ A J 9 5 3
              ♡ Q 3
              ◇ Q 5
              ♣ K Q J 6
```

Post-mortem

A point not brought out in the narrative is that declarer's line of play will not necessarily fail if East has K x of spades. As the cards lie, giving East the King of spades instead of the 10, East will win the second round of trumps and a heart lead from his side also will be fatal to the defense. Declarer's line would fail, however, if East had K x of spades and West K J of hearts.

50. A Superfluous Nugget

It isn't my birthday but I pick up one of the best hands I have ever held:

♠ A K Q J 5 4　♡ A K Q　♢ A Q 9 4　♣ —

It is rubber bridge, too, and I am playing with a good partner. I am fourth to speak, with no one vulnerable. Not surprisingly, there are three passes, and I open **two clubs**, the conventional bid of the Acol system which my partner and I are playing. He responds **two diamonds** and, putting one of the system's rarer conventions to use, I bid **three spades**. That is a demand for Aces. Its advantage here is that on the next round I can ask for specific Kings.

Partner responds **3NT**, denying an Ace. I then bid **four diamonds**, according to plan. If he has the King of diamonds he will bid five diamonds while if he has a singleton diamond and some spade support he may jump to five spades, for my earlier bid of three spades set the suit.

None of these good things is forthcoming. He gives me just **four spades** but I am not going to give in. I shall bid **five spades**. Partner knows that the only side suit in which I am interested is diamonds and he will give me six if he has anything in his hand to suggest that I won't lose two diamond tricks. At last he comes to life with **six spades**.

Our auction has been:

South	West	North	East
—	pass	pass	pass
2♣	pass	2♢	pass
3♠	pass	3NT	pass
4♢	pass	4♠	pass
5♠	pass	6♠	pass
pass	pass		

West leads the 3 of spades and I contemplate the following dummy:

♠ 10 8 7
♡ J 10 7 6 3
◇ 6 2
♣ Q J 3

♠ 3 led

♠ A K Q J 5 4
♡ A K Q
◇ A Q 9 4
♣ —

We had to explain the various conventional bids to our opponents as we went along and while, in a technical way, I am quite proud of our auction it seems to have given them a clue to the best lead. On any other lead I could have ruffed a couple of diamonds. However, let us see what happens to the 7 of spades. East plays the 2 and I follow with the 4.

Now if I finesse a diamond and it loses they will play another trump. That won't matter if the trumps are 2 – 2 but if the trumps are 3 – 1 I won't be able to make the slam by ruffing diamonds. Can I do anything with the hearts? I could draw a second trump and play A K Q of hearts. If no one ruffed I would have enough tricks.

"What does it matter if the third round is ruffed?" did I hear you say? I thought that for a moment, but count the tricks again. Suppose that the trumps are 3 – 1 and that the third round of hearts is ruffed. Then when I enter dummy with the third spade there will be only two hearts left and I'll still have to take the diamond finesse.

I keep on getting so near, there must be some answer to this hand. If it weren't for that block in hearts there wouldn't be any difficulty. If I could bury that Queen of hearts, for example. Is that an idea? I believe it is! If I play a club and discard the Queen of hearts I should make six spades, five hearts (so long as the second round is not ruffed) and a diamond. Check? Check!

I play the 3 of clubs from dummy, East plays the Ace and I match it with the Ace of hearts. (The Ace looks sportier than the Queen!) East leads a diamond and I take with the Ace. Now I lead a second round of spades, for if the spades are 2 – 2 I can bear the hearts to be 4 – 1. As expected, East shows out on the second spade. Now I cash K Q of hearts, everybody following. Then I play to dummy's 10 of spades and my three diamonds go away on the J 10 7 of hearts.

These maneuvers were necessary, for this was the full hand:

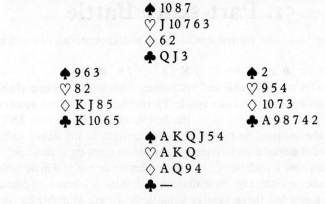

```
                    ♠ 10 8 7
                    ♡ J 10 7 6 3
                    ◇ 6 2
                    ♣ Q J 3
      ♠ 9 6 3                      ♠ 2
      ♡ 8 2                        ♡ 9 5 4
      ◇ K J 8 5                    ◇ 10 7 3
      ♣ K 10 6 5                   ♣ A 9 8 7 4 2
                    ♠ A K Q J 5 4
                    ♡ A K Q
                    ◇ A Q 9 4
                    ♣ —
```

Post-mortem

The bidding convention that we used on this hand is valuable on occasions and can be adapted to any two club system. The jump rebid, following a two club opening, sets the suit and asks partner to name his Aces immediately. Any subsequent enquiry asks for Kings. It may be possible, as on this hand, to direct attention to third round control as well.

As to the play, the combination of winner-on-loser and unblock is rare but elegant.

51. Part-score Battle

Playing in a pairs contest against keen and experienced opposition I hold:

♠ 10 9 7 6 5 2   ♡ K J 8   ◇ 7 6   ♣ Q 4

Both sides are vulnerable and my partner deals and opens **one club.** East passes and I respond **one spade.** Partner raises this to **two spades** and now East, having passed on the first round, comes in with **2NT.** That is the 'unusual no-trump' showing strength in the unbid suits, hearts and diamonds, and asking his partner to compete if possible.

If I pass now I shall be of two minds whether or not to defend with three spades against, say, three diamonds. I think it's better to take a slight risk and bid **three spades** voluntarily. It will probably be one down but they may not be able to double and the heart honors should be well placed. West considers for a moment over three spades but eventually passes, and so do North and East. The bidding has been:

South	West	North	East
—	—	1♣	pass
1♠	pass	2♠	2NT
3♠	pass	pass	pass

West leads the 5 of hearts and North puts down a poor hand:

♠ A K 8 4
♡ 7 4 3
◇ Q 9 3
♣ A 10 8

♡ 5 led

♠ 10 9 7 6 5 2
♡ K J 8
◇ 7 6
♣ Q 4

This may not be too bad if I can get out for only 100 points, for they can probably make nine or ten tricks in diamonds and possibly in hearts. East wins the first trick with the Ace of hearts and returns the 2. It's possible he has the Queen and there is no likelihood of a ruff, so I finesse the Jack. West wins with the Queen and returns a heart to my King.

That's two heart and two diamond losers for certain, probably a club and possibly even a spade. East is likely to be short in spades or even void but I haven't the nerve to take a deep finesse on the first round. I must just study for a moment whether I have any chance of avoiding two down (which would be very bad on a part-score hand) if the spades are 3 – 0 and I don't finesse. I would have a chance if I could eliminate diamonds and throw West in to lead away from the King of clubs, which he may or may not have.

There's a slight problem about that, though. Suppose I lead a spade to dummy and East shows void. Then if I play a diamond from the table West will win and play the Queen of spades. If West has two entries in diamonds he will win the second round as well, cash the Jack of spades and exit with a diamond. That will be the end of my elimination play.

It can't cost and I think it may gain to lead a diamond from my own hand. That's what I'm going to do. West goes up with the King and in response to a signal from his partner continues with the Jack. I cover with the Queen and ruff the third round. Now I lead the 10 of spades but there is no friendly cover. I put up the Ace from dummy and East shows out. I have a chance for an end-play, for these are the remaining cards:

$$\spadesuit \text{ K 8 4}$$
$$\heartsuit \text{ —}$$
$$\diamondsuit \text{ —}$$
$$\clubsuit \text{ A 10 8}$$

$$\spadesuit \text{ 9 7 6 5}$$
$$\heartsuit \text{ —}$$
$$\diamondsuit \text{ —}$$
$$\clubsuit \text{ Q 4}$$

West is thrown in on the third round of Spades. He exits with a club and I play low from dummy. When the Queen wins I am one down. That should not be too bad a result, as examination of the full hand will show:

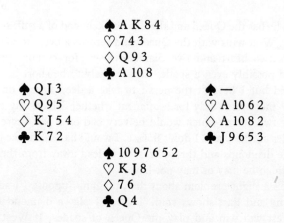

♠ A K 8 4
♥ 7 4 3
♦ Q 9 3
♣ A 10 8

♠ Q J 3   ♠ —
♥ Q 9 5   ♥ A 10 6 2
♦ K J 5 4   ♦ A 10 8 2
♣ K 7 2   ♣ J 9 6 5 3

♠ 10 9 7 6 5 2
♥ K J 8
♦ 7 6
♣ Q 4

Post-mortem

East's vulnerable intervention of 2NT was daring but typical of part-score tactics in a pairs contest. The same can be said of South's three spades. Had South passed at that point West would have bid three diamonds (better than passing 2NT) and would have been better placed thereafter to double a competitive three spades.

The main point of the play was South's lead of a diamond as soon as he got in with the King of hearts. Declarer spoils the timing of his intended elimination play if he leads a trump first, and goes two down against best defense. Say he exits from dummy with the Queen of diamonds, West wins and leads the Queen of spades. When the next diamond is led from table West wins again with the Jack, cashes the Jack of spades and exits with a diamond. Then South cannot escape the loss of a club trick.

52. Submarine Journey

Playing in a multiple team contest against opponents who are strangers to me I hold:

♠ A Q 9 5   ♡ A 4 3   ◇ K 7 6   ♣ A 9 2

We are vulnerable, they not. East, on my right, deals and opens **three diamonds.** This is a familiar situation in which one cannot be sure of doing the right thing. However, it would be timid to pass, so I **double.** My partner and I play a double at this level as primarily for penalties. West comes in with **three hearts** and this appears to give partner a problem. Eventually he bids **four diamonds,** the enemy suit, and East passes. With my defensive hand I don't like the way things are going, but all I can do is bid **four spades.** This is passed all round, so the bidding has been:

South	West	North	East
—	—	—	3◇
double	3♡	4◇	pass
4♠	pass	pass	pass

West leads the 5 of diamonds and partner's hand, like mine, turns out to be balanced:

♠ K 6 4
♡ 9 5 2
◇ A 8 3
♣ K Q 7 6

◇ 5 led

♠ A Q 9 5
♡ A 4 3
◇ K 7 6
♣ A 9 2

Yes, we would have done better to defend and pick up a safe 500 or more that way. Four spades will be all right if the suits break evenly, but probably they won't. To begin with, I can't see anything better than to take the first trick with the King of diamonds and test the trumps.

All follow to the first two rounds of spades but on the third round East discards a diamond. So West has four spades and, I imagine, six hearts. That means the clubs will probably be 4 – 2. I am one trick short, but if East has the long diamonds and long clubs perhaps I can squeeze him. To do that I must rectify the count, as they say, by losing three tricks before the squeeze begins. That can be done easily enough by giving up the trump and ducking two rounds of hearts.

To avoid complications I play the fourth trump right away, discarding a diamond from the table. West exits with a club and I win with the Queen in dummy. Now, according to plan, I lead a low heart. East puts in the Queen and I duck. West considers whether to overtake but eventually plays low. The position is now:

East exits with a diamond to dummy's Ace, West discarding a heart. (Had East played a club at this point I would have had to play the diamond myself before ducking the heart). I lead a low heart from dummy and duck again. West exits with a club to my Ace and now the Ace of hearts squeezes East in the minor suits. I have made the contract for the loss of two hearts and one spade, the full hand being:

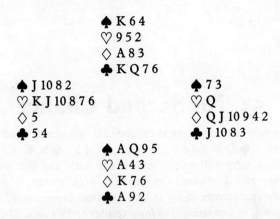

♠ K 6 4
♡ 9 5 2
♢ A 8 3
♣ K Q 7 6

♠ J 10 8 2   ♠ 7 3
♡ K J 10 8 7 6 ♡ Q
♢ 5   ♢ Q J 10 9 4 2
♣ 5 4   ♣ J 10 8 3

♠ A Q 9 5
♡ A 4 3
♢ K 7 6
♣ A 9 2

Post-mortem

The hand contains a trap that is not mentioned in the narrative. When declarer sees the possibility of developing a submarine squeeze by ducking two rounds of hearts, he may think of exiting with a heart instead of with the last trump. That will not matter if West leads the Jack of spades, as a player with the master trump will usually do. But if West is shrewd enough to continue hearts instead the timing will be different. East will have room for an extra discard and South will not be able to bring any pressure to bear.

53. No Second Chance

Playing rubber bridge against experienced opponents, I hold:

♠ Q 10 9 7 6 2   ♡ A 8 3   ♢ J 3   ♣ K 4

With both sides vulnerable, my partner deals and bids **one club**. East passes and I respond **one spade**. West comes in with **two diamonds** and partner raises to **two spades**. There should be a fair play for game, so I go straight to **four spades** and all pass. The bidding has been:

South	West	North	East
—	—	1♣	pass
1♠	2♢	2♠	pass
4♠	pass	pass	pass

West opens the King of diamonds and partner puts down:

♠ A K J
♡ J 7 5 2
♢ Q 5
♣ A 8 6 3

♢ K led

♠ Q 10 9 7 6 2
♡ A 8 3
♢ J 3
♣ K 4

Not an ideal dummy as we seem to be in danger of losing two diamonds and two hearts. West cashes a second diamond and East, having played the 9 on the first round, completes an echo with the 6. West switches to the Jack of clubs and I let this run up to the King.

Now how am I going to avoid losing two tricks in hearts ? West may have K Q alone. Failing that, there are elimination possibilities if either defender has a doubleton K x or Q x. As West has the long diamonds he is more likely to be short in hearts. Then of course he may be able to unblock—not if he has K 10 or Q 10, but with K x or Q x he can throw his honor under the Ace.

I have to consider what is the best point at which to lay down the Ace of hearts. Obviously I don't want to wait until the possibility of an elimination is obvious. At the same time West might regard it as suspicious if I were to lay down the Ace of hearts immediately. I think a rather more plausible sequence would be to cross to the King of spades and then come back to the Ace of hearts as though I were regaining the lead for a possible trump finesse.

All follow when I play a spade to the King and when a heart is returned to the Ace East plays the 4 and West the 9. Now I have to assume that West has failed to unblock from Q 9 or K 9. There are two ways of proceeding with the elimination play. If West has a singleton spade and three clubs, together with seven diamonds and two hearts, the best line is to play a club to the Ace and ruff a club and then to exit with a heart. On the other hand, if West has two trumps and two clubs he may well think of discarding his heart honor when I ruff the third club. But if he has a singleton trump and three clubs he may fail to discard the heart when I play a second trump. So I'm going to play another round of trumps at this point.

West follows to the second trump and so does East. These cards are left:

♠ J
♡ J 7 5
◇ —
♣ A 8 6

♠ Q 10 9 7
♡ 8 3
◇ —
♣ 4

I play the Ace of clubs and all follow. A third club would be a mistake now because I am taking West to be 2 – 2 – 7 – 2 with a top heart left and I mustn't give him the chance to discard that heart. After the Ace of clubs I lead a low heart. West wins with the Queen and leads a diamond. That gives me a ruff and discard, so I make the contract for the loss of two diamonds and one heart. West could not recover from his first mistake of not dropping the Queen of hearts under the Ace, for this was the full hand:

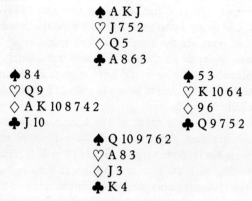

```
                    ♠ A K J
                    ♡ J 7 5 2
                    ◇ Q 5
                    ♣ A 8 6 3
  ♠ 8 4                            ♠ 5 3
  ♡ Q 9                            ♡ K 10 6 4
  ◇ A K 10 8 7 4 2                 ◇ 9 6
  ♣ J 10                           ♣ Q 9 7 5 2
                    ♠ Q 10 9 7 6 2
                    ♡ A 8 3
                    ◇ J 3
                    ♣ K 4
```

Post-mortem

The first point about this hand was the way in which the play of the Ace of hearts was timed. The elimination possibilities contained in the heart situation are well known and so is the defensive play of unblocking with an honor. Therefore declarer has to consider a sequence of play that may cause the defenders to take their eye off the ball.

The other point is that declarer's count of the hand showed that a third round of clubs before the throw-in would be a mistake. Had a third club been played West would not have failed to disembarrass himself of the Queen of hearts.

54. Slender Clue

Playing in a pairs event against opponents of moderate strength I hold as dealer:

♠ K 10 2   ♡ K 9 5 3 2   ◇ K 3   ♣ A K J

Neither side is vulnerable. As we play a weaker no-trump at that score, I open **one heart**. Partner responds **one spade**. In general I like to support my partner's major suit, but this hand is too good for two spades and unsuitable for three spades. I bid **2NT,** which in Acol shows about 17 to 18 points after a response at the level of one. It is not an ideal bid, but suppressing the support for partner's major may turn to my advantage in the play. After some consideration partner passes 2NT, so the bidding has been:

South	West	North	East
1♡	pass	1♠	pass
2NT	pass	pass	pass

West leads the 2 of clubs and the reason for partner's hesitation over 2NT is apparent when the dummy goes down:

♠ A 9 5 4
♡ J
◇ Q 7 5 2
♣ 8 6 5 3

♣ 2 led

♠ K 10 2
♡ K 9 5 3 2
◇ K 3
♣ A K J

Partner has 7 points, normally enough for a raise to 3NT in this sequence, but he has made allowance for his poor distribution and singleton in my suit. Moreover, it does not pay to strain for close games in a pairs contest. I shall be happy to make 2NT here, let alone three.

On the first trick East plays the 9 of clubs and I win with the Jack.

To make eight tricks I must make something of the hearts, puny as they are. On the lead of a low heart West plays the 6 and East covers the Jack with the Queen. East returns the 4 of clubs, West dropping what is probably a deceptive 10.

There is nothing to do but continue the hearts. On the next round West plays the 8, a spade is thrown from dummy, and East plays the 4. Abandoning his small deception in the club suit, West leads the 7, East discarding the 3 of spades.

Now comes the critical decision, whether to lead the King of hearts or a low one. If either player has A 10 left it makes no difference what I do, but from West's play of the 6 and 8 it is at any rate possible that he has either the 10 or the Ace alone. If he had had 10 8 6 he would have had no choice but to play the 6 and 8. If he had had A 8 6 might he have played the Ace? In certain circumstances—for example, if declarer's hearts were Q 9 x x x—that would be the right play! Even if he were not going to play the Ace he might have thought about it. It's not much of a clue but it may be better than nothing. So I'll try the King.

Whether there was anything in my reasoning I shall never know, but at any rate the 10 comes down and East wins with the Ace. That makes the contract safe—two spades, two hearts, one diamond and three clubs. Apparently not wanting to broach either of the other suits, East exits with a heart. I win with the 9, West discards a diamond and dummy another spade. The position is now:

♠ A 9
♡ —
◇ Q 7 5
♣ 8

♠ K 10 2
♡ 5
◇ K 3
♣ —

I don't know whether I can squeeze another trick out of this. If I play a heart at this point I shall have to abandon one of the threat cards in dummy. I think first I will knock out the Ace of diamonds and see what they return. From East's failure to play diamonds I am placing him with the Ace. In the diagram position I lead the 3 of diamonds to dummy's Queen and East's Ace. East returns a diamond, which is what I was hoping. (It would have been better play, no doubt, for East to have held up his Ace of diamonds.)

Now I lead my last heart and West shows signs of embarrassment. Eventually he throws the 10 of diamonds. Dummy's 8 of clubs is no longer wanted. Now it is apparent that East is squeezed. His last four cards are three spades and the master diamond. When he lets go a spade I make the last three tricks in that suit, ending up with an overtrick.

This was the full hand:

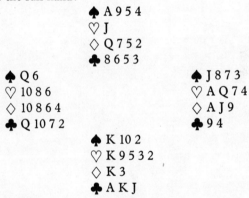

Post-mortem

This was the four-card ending that produced the extra trick:

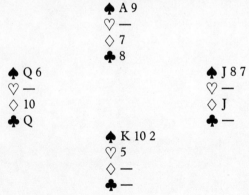

It will be seen that West had no good discard on the 5 of hearts. He should, in fact, have tried a spade, for when he threw the diamond his partner was sure to be squeezed. The position is known as a guard squeeze because West had to keep a guard to his Queen of spades to protect his partner from a finesse.

55. Choice Deferred

My partner in this game of rubber bridge is a somewhat unreliable bidder and the opposition is not particularly strong. In third position I hold:

♠ 8 6 5 3 2 ♡ 9 ◇ A Q 5 3 ♣ A J 6

It is game all and my partner opens **one heart.** With the opponents silent, I respond **one spade** and partner raises to **three spades.**

This is a situation I never care for. My two Aces suggest a slam but the trump holding is unsatisfactory. I feel that I must make one try so I bid **four clubs** to see what that produces.

It produces a prompt **4NT,** Blackwood. I suppose I must see it through. After **five hearts** partner gives me no more leeway. He goes straight to **six spades.**

The bidding has been:

South	West	North	East
—	—	1♡	pass
1♠	pass	3♠	pass
4♣	pass	4NT	pass
5♡	pass	6♠	pass
pass	pass		

West leads the 9 of diamonds and partner's hand is not exactly what I wanted to see:

♠ A K J
♡ A Q 7 4 2
◇ K 6
♣ Q 7 4

◇ 9 led

♠ 8 6 5 3 2
♡ 9
◇ A Q 5 3
♣ A J 6

If I play a straightforward game shall I have enough tricks? That is, suppose I win with King of diamonds, cash two spades and ruff the fourth diamond. I'll have to lose a trump and then I'll need the heart finesse or three club tricks. An end play may develop but it is rather nebulous. Instead, how about ruffing some hearts with my small trumps? If I do get over-ruffed it may be by the hand that has the long trumps. If by any chance I can bring down the King of hearts in three rounds I shall have enough tricks without the club finesse, assuming that the spades are 3 – 2.

I win the diamond lead in hand, cross to Ace of hearts, ruff a heart and return to the Ace of spades. On this trick East drops the 9. When a third heart is played from the table East ruffs with the Queen of spades. That alters the complexion of the hand. Let's look at the position after East's ruff:

♠ K J
♡ Q 7
◇ K
♣ Q 7 4

♠ 8 6 5
♡ —
◇ Q 5 3
♣ A J 6

I still have to discard and I am not sure what to play. East had a doubleton heart and, I imagine, a doubleton spade, for he dropped the 9 on the first round and is now ruffing with the Queen. He could be false-carding but he is not a particularly subtle player and I don't think it's likely.

If my count of the spades and hearts is correct then East must have length in both minor suits. That means there is no chance of bringing down a doubleton King of clubs. Furthermore, if West has the last two trumps I cannot ruff a diamond without establishing his 10 of spades. Whether I discard a diamond or a club I am going to be a trick short, even assuming that the club finesse is right.

It seems an odd thing to do with three trumps in my hand and two in dummy, but could there be any advantage in under-ruffing? As I am playing some sort of reverse dummy and can ruff another heart, the trick should come back. If I preserve my holding in diamonds and clubs, I may well be able to squeeze East.

Yes, that's the play. In the diagram position I under-ruff with the 5 of spades. East exits with the Jack of diamonds and I win in dummy with the King. I play a heart from table and East discards a diamond. I ruff and return to the King of spades and now East discards a club. This is the position when the last trump is played:

```
            ♠ J
            ♡ Q
            ◇ —
            ♣ Q 7 4


            ♠ —
            ♡ —
            ◇ Q 5
            ♣ A J 6
```

On the lead of the Jack of spades East is plainly in trouble. When eventually he discards a club I throw my diamond. A club finesse follows and when the King falls under the Ace on the next trick I make the remainder, having lost only to the Queen of trumps. This was the full hand:

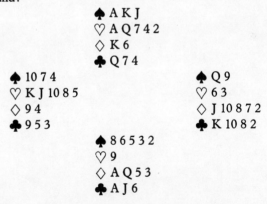

```
                    ♠ A K J
                    ♡ A Q 7 4 2
                    ◇ K 6
                    ♣ Q 7 4
  ♠ 10 7 4                        ♠ Q 9
  ♡ K J 10 8 5                    ♡ 6 3
  ◇ 9 4                           ◇ J 10 8 7 2
  ♣ 9 5 3                         ♣ K 10 8 2
                    ♠ 8 6 5 3 2
                    ♡ 9
                    ◇ A Q 5 3
                    ♣ A J 6
```

Post-mortem

The under-ruff to preserve possibilities of a squeeze is uncommon but worth noting. As the cards lie, of course, the contract can be made more simply in a number of ways. In fact, if declarer finesses the Queen of hearts and plays off A K of spades he can squeeze East for thirteen tricks.

As the play went, a clever defender in East's position would have declined the opportunity to ruff the third heart. In due course declarer would finesse the Jack of spades and then the timing for a squeeze would be wrong.

56. Bold Conclusion

On this hand from a mixed pairs event my partner and the opponents are all good players. I hold as dealer:

♠ A 10 6   ♡ A J 3   ◇ K Q 9 7 4   ♣ A J

We are vulnerable but the hand is too strong for 1NT according to my methods, so I open **one diamond.** The opponents are silent and partner, after some deliberation, responds **two diamonds.** Now I jump to **3NT.** The bidding has been brief:

North	West	South	East
—	—	1◇	pass
2◇	pass	3NT	pass
pass	pass		

West opens the 6 of hearts. Observing that with anyone else she would have responded one spade, partner puts down:

♠ Q 7 4 2
♡ Q
◇ J 8 3 2
♣ Q 10 5 4

♡ 6 led

♠ A 10 6
♡ A J 3
◇ K Q 9 7 4
♣ A J

Partner is right in her estimate that I much prefer a response of two diamonds to one spade. I can see no sense whatsoever in bidding bad suits on bad hands when there is a sound alternative.

Dummy's Queen of hearts holds the first trick, East playing the 2. Now I can count four probable tricks in diamonds, two in hearts and two black Aces. Obviously the safe way to play for a ninth trick is to take a club finesse before clearing the Ace of diamonds. If the finesse loses, West will not be able to continue hearts to advantage.

At trick 2 therefore I finesse the Jack of clubs and it holds the trick.

That doesn't tell me who has the King because West would probably hold off in any event. Now I lead the King of diamonds, West plays the 10 and East the 5. On the next round of diamonds West discards a low club and East tops dummy's Jack with the Ace. East returns the 9 of hearts.

I am safe for nine tricks now and the question is whether to go up with the Ace of hearts, keeping the Jack as an exit card, or to hold up the Ace until the third round. It seems clear from the play that West began with six hearts to the K 10 and East with three small. The prospects for an end-play are somewhat uncertain. I think it would be better to hold up so as to exhaust East of hearts and then see how they discard on the diamonds. West tops the Jack of hearts with the King and returns a heart, East following suit. After two more rounds of diamonds the position is as follows:

♠ Q 7 4
♡ —
♢ —
♣ Q 10

♠ A 10 6
♡ —
♢ 7
♣ A

On the last two tricks West has discarded a heart and the 5 of spades and East has thrown a club. On the fifth diamond West discards the 8 of spades, North the 4 and East the 3.

The problem now is whether I can afford to play for an overtrick by taking two rounds of spades and not cashing the Ace of clubs. First I'll see what happens on the Ace of spades. West follows with the Jack and East with the 9. Now if I play a spade and West has the King of spades plus two hearts I shall be one down. On the other hand, if East has the King of spades I can make an overtrick.

Apart from the fact that West might have overcalled if he had had four spades and six hearts, there are two strong indications from the play. West's first discard was a club. Surely, if he had been 4 – 6 – 1 – 2, he would have let go a spade first. Secondly, there are still three clubs out and it is most unlikely that East has them all. His natural play would be to discard down to K x of clubs, not K x x.

At total-point scoring I might not risk it, but in a pairs one has to follow one's judgment on such occasions. I play a spade and all is well. East has the King and I make the last two tricks with the Ace of clubs and 10 of spades, scoring an overtrick. This was the full hand:

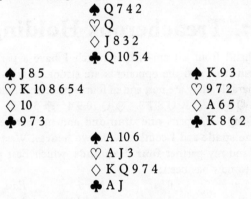

Post-mortem

Taking the club finesse at trick 2 was a matter of ordinary technique. If declarer plays first on diamonds and the hearts are cleared by a lead through the A J it becomes too dangerous to take the club finesse.

The ending is typical of many where the play for an overtrick, though superficially risky, is safe enough if the right inferences are drawn. Most players in these situations are either too lazy to work out the lie of the cards or too cowardly to put their conclusions to the test. The right approach is to take the risk that once in twenty times one has misread the position. The overtrick on the other nineteen will fully compensate in match-pointed events.

West's discarding on this hand was not in fact the best. If he throws all his clubs and keeps one more spade the lie of the cards cannot be read with any certainty.

57. Treacherous Holding

On this hand from a team-of-four match I have a partner whose bidding I can trust and the opponents are strong, aggressive players. We are vulnerable, they are not, and in fourth position I hold:

♠ Q 8 5   ♡ K Q 8 7 3   ◇ Q 10 9 4   ♣ 5

West, on my left, opens **one diamond** and my partner **doubles**. East bids **one spade** and I come in with **two hearts**. West bids **three diamonds** and my partner **four diamonds**, which East passes. The bidding up to now has been:

South	West	North	East
—	1◇	double	1♠
2♡	3◇	4◇	pass
?			

Though I don't think it's likely, I must just consider for a moment whether partner's four diamonds can possibly be a request to me to mention one of the black suits. (East's one spade, of course, could easily be psychic at the score.) No, if partner had a very strong two-suiter he wouldn't double—he would either cue-bid two diamonds or jump in one of the suits. I am going to take his four diamonds as a slam suggestion almost certainly including first round control of diamonds.

I have full value for my bid of two hearts and my K Q in that suit must be very important cards. I accept his slam invitation and jump to **five hearts**.

After a pass by West partner goes **five spades**. That can't be an attempt to play in spades. With that sort of hand he would have bid a direct four spades over West's three diamonds. I must take it as a grand slam try. No doubt he has A K of spades, good hearts headed by the Ace, probably a void in diamonds and Ace of clubs. There may be some work in the play but I am going to respect his bidding and go to **seven hearts**.

The full auction has been:

South	West	North	East
—	1◇	double	1♠
2♡	3◇	4◇	pass
5♡	pass	5♠	pass
7♡	pass	pass	pass

West leads the King of diamonds and I await partner's hand with some anxiety:

♠ A K 7 3
♡ A J 10 5 2
◇ —
♣ A J 10 3

◇ K led

♠ Q 8 5
♡ K Q 8 7 3
◇ Q 10 9 4
♣ 5

Yes, that's about what I expected. Most players would have over-called with two diamonds immediately but I agree with my partner that on a three-suited hand a double is just as good.

Not counting any ruffs there are nine tricks on top and I have to find four more. Can I negotiate four ruffs in diamonds? I think so, if the trumps break. I can ruff the first trick, then a heart to the Queen, ruff a second diamond, back to Queen of spades, ruff a third diamond, then Ace and another club, etc. Yes, that looks all right.

Dummy ruffs the first lead with the 2 of hearts and East follows with the 2 of diamonds. I lead the 5 of hearts to the Queen and West shows out, discarding a diamond.

Well, that's the end of one dream. I can't ruff three more diamonds with dummy's A J 10 because then I shan't have enough high trumps to draw East's remaining 9 x. I can ruff two more diamonds and the extra trick will have to come either from a spade break or from a squeeze or possibly from setting up a diamond winner by leading through West.

As a first move, I shall lead the Queen of diamonds. West will have to cover and there is just a chance that East may have J x. West duly covers the Queen with the Ace, dummy ruffs and East drops the 3. I play the

Ace of hearts from table and West discards another diamond. After Ace of clubs and a club ruff, no honor appearing, the position is as follows:

♠ A K 7 3
♡ J
♢ —
♣ J 10

♠ Q 8 5
♡ K 8
♢ 10 9
♣ —

At this point I lead the 10 of diamonds and West plays the 8. Now all the indications are that West began with six diamonds to the A K J and that I can safely run this 10 of diamonds. I don't think West has seven diamonds because with a suit of that length he would have pre-empted against vulnerable opponents. Also, East did not echo in diamonds. He played the 2 and then the 3.

Still, I can't be sure about the Jack of diamonds. West is likely to have it, but that isn't good enough for a grand slam. Are there any other possibilities? I don't need this finesse if the spades are 3 – 3. And if West has four spades, I'll be able to squeeze him in spades and diamonds. I need the diamond finesse only if West has a doubleton spade, six diamonds and something like five clubs headed by the King.

Now is that likely? That would leave East with four spades to the Jack or 10 and 4 – 3 – 3 – 3 distribution. And he bid one spade on the first round, didn't he? With such holdings players invariably make their psychic bid in the suit of which they hold three small. Another factor pointing in the same direction is that if West had had five clubs he would surely have discarded one on either the first or second round of hearts. Also, he might have bid three clubs instead of three diamonds on the second round.

In short, I don't think it's necessary to risk this diamond finesse now. I ruff the 10 of diamonds with the Jack of hearts and East follows with the 5. So the finesse would have won, but I don't think it will matter. I return to hand by ruffing a third club and then draw the last trump with the Queen of hearts. West, looking unhappy, discards a spade.

When all follow to the Queen and King of spades I can lay down my cards, the full hand being:

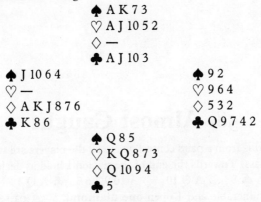

```
              ♠ A K 7 3
              ♡ A J 10 5 2
              ◇ —
              ♣ A J 10 3
♠ J 10 6 4                    ♠ 9 2
♡ —                          ♡ 9 6 4
◇ A K J 8 7 6                ◇ 5 3 2
♣ K 8 6                      ♣ Q 9 7 4 2
              ♠ Q 8 5
              ♡ K Q 8 7 3
              ◇ Q 10 9 4
              ♣ 5
```

Post-mortem

As is remarked in the narrative, South would have made the contract more simply had he run the 10 of diamonds. This deal actually occurred in a match between Britain and Denmark in the European championship of 1951. The only slight difference was that on that occasion East had the Jack of diamonds instead of the 3, which was held by his partner. The British N-S pair did brilliantly to reach seven hearts against the opening bid, but declarer's holding in diamonds proved treacherous. Assuming (as was certainly likely) that West's diamonds would be headed by the A K J, South ran the 10 of diamonds at the critical point and lost to East's Jack. As the analysis above shows, this finesse should not have been taken, for there was very strong evidence that West had at least three spades.

58. Almost Caught

This hand is from a pairs contest where all the players are supposedly of master class. Towards the end of the session I hold as dealer:

♠ 8   ♡ A Q 10   ◇ A 10 9 7 6 3   ♣ A Q 4

We are vulnerable and I open **one diamond**. West passes and my partner raises to **three diamonds**. That's a natural bid with us, not forcing. I could bid three hearts, which might lead to 3NT, but I am really too good to stop there. Playing match-points I naturally don't intend to languish in five diamonds, so I'll go straight to **six diamonds**, giving nothing away. Our bidding has been short if not accurate:

South	West	North	East
1◇	pass	3◇	pass
6◇	pass	pass	pass

West leads the 10 of spades and partner's hand is nothing to cheer about:

♠ A J 4
♡ 7 6 4 2
◇ Q 5 4 2
♣ K 10

♠ 10 led

♠ 8
♡ A Q 10
◇ A 10 9 7 6 3
♣ A Q 4

He had rather an awkward bid over one diamond. He is too good for two diamonds or 1NT and to respond one heart on 7 x x x is not part of our methods. I'm sure some of them will be playing this hand in four hearts, at that. I've seen it many times.

To make six diamonds I need a finesse or two. There is a safety play to lose only one trick in the trump suit but this is no moment for such luxuries. As there may be some sort of elimination ending I plan to take the spade Ace, ruff a spade with the 6 and then lay down the trump Ace.

Alas, East shows out on the Ace of diamonds, discarding a spade. I follow with the 7 of diamonds. West goes up with the King and plays a third spade, which I ruff with the 9.

With very little risk now I can play for an elimination ending that will save me from going down two even if both heart honors are wrong. I play three rounds of clubs, discarding a heart from the table as the opponents follow suit. Then I lead the 10 of diamonds to dummy's Queen, reaching this position:

♠ —
♡ 7 6 4
◇ 5
♣ —

♠ —
♡ A Q 10
◇ 3
♣ —

Now I lead a heart from dummy and finesse the 10, expecting to lose the trick and concede one down, but the 10 wins! Am I going to make this contract after all? I cross to the 5 of diamonds, West discarding a heart and East a club. When I play a heart from dummy at trick 12, East puts on the 8—and I nearly break my wrist pulling back the Queen which I had ready to play.

What's this 8 of hearts? I thought I was finessing East for the K J but I can see what has happened. Expecting me to finesse the heart again, West has come down to the singleton King of hearts and the thirteenth spade. It was a clever plan to put me two down and would surely have succeeded had East played his part by putting in the Jack. Feeling quite sorry for West, I go up with the Ace of hearts and drop the King, making an "impossible" contract. This was the full hand:

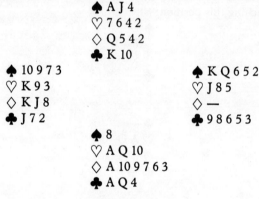

♠ A J 4
♡ 7 6 4 2
♢ Q 5 4 2
♣ K 10

♠ 10 9 7 3   ♠ K Q 6 5 2
♡ K 9 3   ♡ J 8 5
♢ K J 8   ♢ —
♣ J 7 2   ♣ 9 8 6 5 3

♠ 8
♡ A Q 10
♢ A 10 9 7 6 3
♣ A Q 4

Post-mortem

That was bad luck for West. Towards the end of a pairs when one has not been doing too well is the time to experiment with a desperate play of that sort. Had East been awake and played the Jack of hearts at trick 12, South would have finessed the Queen and West would have made the last two tricks to score 200 and a 'top' on the board.

Note, meanwhile, South's careful preservation of the trump 3 as an entry to dummy.

59. Show of Disinterest

In a team-of-four match against opponents of average strength I hold as dealer:

♠ A K Q 9 2   ♡ A 10   ◇ A K 3   ♣ J 10 4

We are vulnerable, the opponents not. According to my notions, it is appropriate to open with a suit bid when the suit needs support, but when the suit is reasonably self-supporting like the spades in the present example I like to open no-trump if the hand is in other respects suitable. Thus on the present hand I wouldn't consider any opening other than **2NT**. Partner raises to **3NT** and all pass, making a simple auction:

South	West	North	East
2NT	pass	3NT	pass
pass	pass		

West opens the 6 of hearts and I see that partner had little to spare for his raise:

```
          ♠ 7 5 4
          ♡ Q J 9
          ◇ J 9 8 7 2
          ♣ 9 5


♡ 6 led


          ♠ A K Q 9 2
          ♡ A 10
          ◇ A K 3
          ♣ J 10 4
```

I go up with the Queen of hearts from dummy and East plays the 5. As I shall be home if the spades break, I play a spade to the Ace, East dropping the 10. On the King of spades East discards the 2 of hearts. I am not quite sure about the heart position yet, but I may as well see what happens on the Queen of spades. This time East throws the 3 of clubs.

Now there are two possibilities. I can play off Ace and King of diamonds in the hope of dropping the Queen, or I can give up the fourth spade and hope that they won't find their club tricks. In view of the discarding—East's signal in hearts and his discard of a low club—it seems most unlikely that West, who did not lead a club originally, will switch to that suit now. Establishing another spade will give me only eight tricks, but meanwhile I'll be forcing East to two more discards and something favorable may arise.

West wins the fourth round of spades with the Jack and I discard a diamond from the table. Though an old trick, this show of disinterest in dummy's anemic diamond suit may persuade an opponent with Q x x to unguard the suit. For the moment, however, East throws the 6 of clubs. West, as expected, continues with the 4 of hearts, East plays the 7 and I win with the Ace. These are the remaining cards:

♠ —
♡ J
◇ J 9 8 7
♣ 9 5

♠ 2
♡ —
◇ A K 3
♣ J 10 4

On the fifth West spade discards the 7 of clubs. To throw another diamond from dummy would be overdoing it, I think. A declarer with something like A x would normally keep four to the Jack in the opposite hand. So I discard a club and East, after some thought, lets go the 8 of clubs.

Now again I have to consider whether or not to play off the top diamonds. Despite my puny attempt at deception by throwing a diamond from table, neither defender has thrown one and I find that a little sinister. East was not too happy about relinquishing this last club, and if he had had three diamonds not headed by the Queen he would have thrown one of those in preference. There are only four clubs still out and I am inclined to place East with a singleton honor, together with two winning hearts and, very likely, three diamonds to the Queen. If East has the Ace of clubs, and the rest of my assessment is correct, I can end-play him for sure. And if East has the King or Queen, it's still possible that West will fail to go up with the Ace in second position. At any rate I feel so certain that the Queen of diamonds is guarded, I plan to exit with a club.

Since I don't want to encourage West to play an honor, I lead a low club toward dummy's 9. West plays the 2 and East wins with the King. East cashes the King and 8 of hearts, and I discard the J 10 of clubs. That makes four tricks for the defense. East exits with the 5 of diamonds at trick 11. I hold my breath and let it ride to dummy's Jack—successfully, for the full hand is:

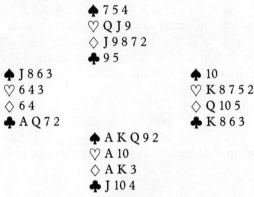

♠ 7 5 4
♡ Q J 9
♢ J 9 8 7 2
♣ 9 5

♠ J 8 6 3   ♠ 10
♡ 6 4 3   ♡ K 8 7 5 2
♢ 6 4   ♢ Q 10 5
♣ A Q 7 2   ♣ K 8 6 3

♠ A K Q 9 2
♡ A 10
♢ A K 3
♣ J 10 4

Post-mortem

The defense made some mistakes here, but to some extent they were induced by declarer's bidding and play.

1. East's discards on the second and third rounds of spades made it safe for declarer to force out the fourth spade even though the clubs were wide open.

2. As the play proceeded, it became increasingly likely that East was guarding the diamond Queen. The sequence of his discards suggested, moreover, that he had five hearts and four clubs.

3. West could have defeated the contract, of course, by going up with his Ace of clubs from A Q x on the club lead. That was a difficult play and the main fault was East's in coming down to the King of clubs single instead of a low one. Another reason why East should have kept a low club and not the King is that partner's clubs might have been headed by the A J.

60. Championship Echo

Playing in a team-of-four match against first-class opponents, I hold as dealer:

♠ K 9 2　♡ A K 6　◇ J 9 8　♣ A 5 3 2

Neither side is vulnerable and as we play a fairly weak no-trump at that score I open **1NT**. West passes and partner raises to **2NT**. Despite the poor distribution and lack of intermediates, I am close to maximum in terms of high cards, so I advance to **3NT**.

The bidding has been:

South	West	North	East
1NT	pass	2NT	pass
3NT	pass	pass	pass

West leads the 5 of spades and partner puts down a similarly featureless hand:

♠ A Q 10 4
♡ J 9 5
◇ 7 6 2
♣ K 10 7

♠ 5 led

♠ K 9 2
♡ A K 6
◇ J 9 8
♣ A 5 3 2

We have 25 points between us and we're going to need them all. I play a low spade from dummy, East plays the 6 and I win with the 9. That gives me eight tricks on top, but if I duck a club for a ninth they are likely to take at least four tricks in diamonds. I might run off the spades to see what East discards, but one disadvantage of that is that West quite probably has a five-card suit and the other is that I may want to go from hand to hand in spades. I think that the best way to produce some sort of tension in a possible end-game is to give them their tricks in diamonds and see what develops. There is also a slight chance that if I play boldly on diamonds they will turn their attack to some other suit.

To the second trick, then, I lead the Jack of diamonds. West wins with the Queen and East plays the 5. West plays another spade and dummy's 10 holds the trick, East discarding the 3 of hearts. I play another diamond, won by West's 10. West exits with a third spade and East discards the 7 of hearts. Once more I lead diamonds, East plays the King and West overtakes with the Ace. With West on lead, these are the remaining cards:

    ♠ Q
    ♡ J 9 5
    ◇ —
    ♣ K 10 7

    ♠ —
    ♡ A K 6
    ◇ —
    ♣ A 5 3 2

I know that West began with five spades and the play of the diamonds suggests that he has the thirteenth. That places East with three diamonds originally and one spade. He must have at least five hearts since he discarded two. He may have five hearts and four clubs or six hearts and three clubs.

West is giving much consideration to his next play. I imagine he is wondering whether or not to cash his thirteenth diamond. I hope he does because that will make the timing right for a squeeze against East in hearts and clubs.

Eventually, however, West exits with a spade to dummy's Queen. East throws the 8 of hearts and I discard the 6 of hearts so that I still have the possibility of dropping the Queen of hearts in two rounds or of ducking a club to East. When I lead a heart to the Ace East drops the 2 and West the 4.

This is where I have to make the critical decision. East's discard of a third heart on the fourth round of spades suggests that he began with six hearts headed by the Q 10. If so, the clubs will be 3 – 3 and my best play will be to lead a club and attempt to duck it into East's hand. Then I'll make my ninth trick with the long club.

But there is something strange about the play of the hearts. If East had had Q 10 8 7 3 2 would he have been so bashful about encouraging a heart lead? More likely, he would have signaled in hearts right away. Then is it possible that with only five hearts he would have discarded three of them instead of letting go a club? Yes it is, really, because he would see that I could promote a third club trick if he discarded one.

Now that I think about it, there's one other reason why I think the clubs must be 4 – 2 and the hearts 5 – 2. That is that if West had had three clubs to an honor he would not have been so concerned about squeezing his partner by playing off the last diamond.

So finally I play off the King of hearts. East's Queen drops and I make a ninth trick with dummy's Jack of hearts. This was the full hand:

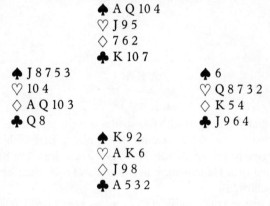

```
                    ♠ A Q 10 4
                    ♡ J 9 5
                    ◇ 7 6 2
                    ♣ K 10 7
   ♠ J 8 7 5 3                      ♠ 6
   ♡ 10 4                           ♡ Q 8 7 3 2
   ◇ A Q 10 3                       ◇ K 5 4
   ♣ Q 8                            ♣ J 9 6 4
                    ♠ K 9 2
                    ♡ A K 6
                    ◇ J 9 8
                    ♣ A 5 3 2
```

Post-mortem

This deal is based on one that occurred in the match for the world championship played between Britain and America in January 1955. It is a good example of how the play goes in expert circles on borderline no-trump hands. Among the points to note are declarer's repeated play of diamonds in order to advance the play while not losing more than four tricks; West's refusal to play the thirteenth diamond, which would prepare a squeeze on his partner; and East's unguarding of the hearts in preference to throwing a club.

In the match the play was the same as that shown above until close to the finish. At the point shown in the second diagram West led the spade to dummy's Queen, East discarded the 8 of hearts and South the 6 of hearts. Declarer then played a heart to the Ace.

This is where the play divided from that suggested in the narrative. Instead of cashing the King of hearts the British declarer led a low club. West played the 8, North the 10 and East the Jack. East exited with the club and now South had to make the decision whether to play for the clubs to divide or for the Queen of hearts to fall. He guessed rightly, going up with the Ace of clubs and then laying down the King of hearts.

Both sides made a slight mistake in the end-game. When declarer led the low club towards dummy's K 10 7 it would have been a killing stroke for West to go up with his Queen. Declarer would have to cover with the King and would then be cut off from the Jack of hearts. No doubt, when he led the low club South thought he was postponing the critical decision. In fact, the play was a technical error.

61. Timely Concession

My opponents on this hand from a pairs event are good players but not quite in the top class. West deals and I hold:

♠ J 8 4 ♡ 3 ◇ A K J 8 5 ♣ Q J 9 3

Neither side is vulnerable and after a pass by West my partner opens **one heart**. East passes and I respond **two diamonds**. Partner bids **three diamonds.** With my losers in the black suits I'm not keen on five diamonds. It could well be right to pass three diamonds but I must play with the room and bid **3NT**. All pass, so the bidding has been:

South	West	North	East
—	pass	1♡	pass
2◇	pass	3◇	pass
3NT	pass	pass	pass

After some thought West leads the 8 of clubs and dummy goes down:

♠ A 5
♡ A Q 10 6 4
◇ 10 7 6 2
♣ A 10

♣ 8 led

♠ J 8 4
♡ 3
◇ A K J 8 5
♣ Q J 9 3

Partner is quite strong for his bidding. We're lucky to have escaped a spade lead but even so the contract is no lay-down. If I finesse this club and East wins he'll probably return a spade. Then I'll have to make all the diamonds. It might be a better idea to conceal my strength in clubs by going up with the Ace and concealing my 3. But if East has the 2 and plays it, that may encourage West to continue clubs when he is in.

On the Ace of clubs East plays the 5 and I drop my 9 according to plan. Now if I bang out Ace, King and another diamond and they don't break, the enemy will have the chance of two discards and will probably discover that their future lies in spades, not clubs. How about finessing the Jack of diamonds right away? If it wins, so much the better, and if it loses there's a good chance that West will continue clubs. It is true that I am giving up the chance to drop a singleton Queen in West's hand, but that's not very important.

At the second trick, therefore, I finesse the Jack of diamonds. West does win and, as hoped, leads the 2 of clubs. East plays the King and switches to the 6 of spades. I don't think it's likely that he has led away from the K Q. My Jack may come in useful later so for the moment I will put in the 8 spot. West plays the 9 and I duck in dummy. West exits with the 2 of spades to dummy's Ace, East dropping the 3. Now I play off diamonds and clubs up to this position:

♠ —
♡ A Q 10
♢ —
♣ —

♠ J
♡ 3
♢ —
♣ J

West has turned up with three diamonds, so my early finesse cost nothing. The play and discards have also marked West with 8 7 x x of clubs. East has discarded two spades and two hearts, so at this point I am disposed to read each defender for a spade honor and two hearts. I still haven't made up my mind about the King of hearts.

On the Jack of clubs West throws the Queen of spades and East the Jack of hearts. Now if I take the Ace of hearts that will be nine tricks and at least an average result on the board. There is also the chance, in theory, that East has been squeezed after the discard of the Queen of spades and that his King of hearts is now going to fall.

But I don't really believe that. If West, at the finish, had had two small hearts and the Queen of spades he would surely have thrown a heart so as not to expose his partner to the squeeze. To do otherwise would be extremely careless or extremely clever and West is neither. It seems a safe inference that he holds the heart King, so I'm going to finesse the Queen of hearts for an overtrick. The finesse wins, the full hand being:

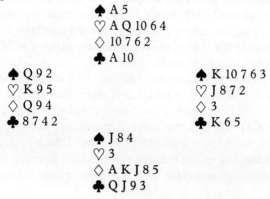

♠ A 5
♡ A Q 10 6 4
◇ 10 7 6 2
♣ A 10

♠ Q 9 2   ♠ K 10 7 6 3
♡ K 9 5   ♡ J 8 7 2
◇ Q 9 4   ◇ 3
♣ 8 7 4 2   ♣ K 6 5

♠ J 8 4
♡ 3
◇ A K J 8 5
♣ Q J 9 3

Post-mortem

One way of preventing a switch to a dangerous suit is to encourage the enemy to continue leading a suit which actually has no future for them.

The play of the Ace of clubs at trick 1 and the 9 from hand was the best way to give West the idea that he had made a promising lead.

The early finesse in diamonds could have lost a trick had West held Queen of diamonds single or Q x, but as South had had the benefit of a favorable lead and could expect a club continuation it was good tactics to finesse the diamond immediately.

The analysis at the finish established almost beyond doubt that West had thrown the Queen of spades in order to keep K x of hearts. As often happens when the play for an overtrick seems risky, there is a perfectly safe inference—once you think of it.

62. Rash Venture

In a keenly fought game of rubber bridge my side is not vulnerable and has nothing below the line. The opponents are vulnerable and have a part score of 40. I hold as dealer:

♠ A Q 2   ♡ 8 5 2   ♢ K 4   ♣ A 10 8 7 3

In these part score situations I like to open 1NT when possible, but my partner has insisted on a strong no-trump throughout, so perhaps that would be unwise. Instead, I shall venture a psychic **one heart.** If ever there is a time to make such a bid, this is it—not vulnerable against vulnerable opponents who have a part score!

West overcalls with **one spade** and my partner bids **two spades.** I don't altogether like the sound of that. No doubt he is going to raise the hearts in a moment! After a pass by East I bid **2NT.** West competes again with **three clubs** and now my partner bids **three diamonds.** East appears to quiver for a moment before passing.

I'm slightly tempted to pass three diamonds before he puts me in six hearts or something of that sort. However, it's possible that if he hears me bid no-trump again he will realize that my hearts are more or less non-existent. So I bid **3NT** and West passes. Partner considers for a while, then bids **four hearts.** As expected, East **doubles.** All pass and this is the sad story of the auction:

South	West	North	East
1♡	1♠	2♠	pass
2NT	3♣	3♢	pass
3NT	pass	4♡	double
pass	pass	pass	

West leads the 7 of hearts and partner puts down:

♠ 8
♥ A Q 9 4
♦ A J 9 8 6 3
♣ Q 4

♥ 7 led

♠ A Q 2
♥ 8 5 2
♦ K 4
♣ A 10 8 7 3

One thing about this bidding is that it isn't difficult to place the cards. West must have at least six spades and probably five clubs. He may have two red singletons or, slightly more probable on the lead, a doubleton heart and a void in diamonds.

I play a low heart from dummy and East wins with the Jack, no doubt a false card. East returns the 5 of spades. I'm not going to be able to draw trumps and establish diamonds, so I may as well make as many tricks as I can by ruffing. I go up with the Ace of spades and ruff the 2 of spades with dummy's 9 of hearts.

If West's distribution is 6 – 1 – 1 – 5 my best line now will be to take two diamond ruffs in my hand. But I think it's more likely that he is 6 – 2 – 0 – 5. With two singletons he might well have led the diamond and also, if East had had five trumps, it would have been better defense on his part to return a trump at trick 2. To confirm that view, I cash the Ace of hearts. East plays the 3 and West follows with the 6. Now I play a club to the Ace and ruff the Queen of spades with dummy's last heart, West playing the King of spades and East the Jack. That leaves the cards as follows:

♠ —
♡ —
♢ A J 9 8 6 3
♣ Q

♠ —
♡ 8
♢ K 4
♣ 10 8 7 3

This hand is not going to be a calamity, after all. I can play it almost as double dummy from now on. East must have K 10 of hearts and all five diamonds.

In the diagram position I lead the 8 of diamonds from dummy. If East plays low I'm going to let that run, then come to hand with the King of diamonds and exit with a trump. East seems to be aware of that, for he puts in the 10, which I take with the King. There are several ways of making three more tricks now. Choosing one of the more artistic, I lead the 4 of diamonds to the Ace and return the Jack. East covers with the Queen and instead of ruffing I discard a club. East makes his two good hearts and then has to lead from the 7 5 of diamonds into dummy's 9 6.

That leaves me one down—not such a bad result when one looks at the full diagram:

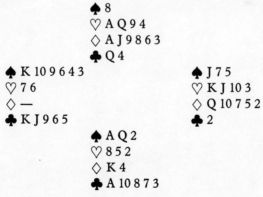

♠ 8
♡ A Q 9 4
♢ A J 9 8 6 3
♣ Q 4

♠ K 10 9 6 4 3
♡ 7 6
♢ —
♣ K J 9 6 5

♠ J 7 5
♡ K J 10 3
♢ Q 10 7 5 2
♣ 2

♠ A Q 2
♡ 8 5 2
♢ K 4
♣ A 10 8 7 3

Once declarer had taken note of the likely distribution, the hand played surprisingly well. East thought he might have saved a trick by unblocking with the 10 of hearts under the Ace and keeping the 3 as an exit card. (South had played the 2 on the first trick.) That would not have affected the result so long as South took care not to be left in his own hand with nothing but clubs to lead. By forgoing the ruff of East's diamond Queen South forced East to retain the lead. East was end-played and eventually had to give South back two diamond tricks for one!

63. Desperate Defense

On this hand from rubber bridge my opponents are first-class players, my partner not so strong. This is my hand:

♠ A J 7 6 4   ♡ 8 5 2   ◇ 10   ♣ Q 9 6 2

With both sides vulnerable I deal and pass. West opens **one diamond**, my partner **doubles** and East bids **one heart**. Some players like you to give them two spades on this sort of hand but in my opinion a free bid of **one spade** is quite enough. We have no game if partner cannot speak again. West bids **two diamonds** and partner **two spades**. Now I am worth four spades, but as my partner is probably overbidding I shall keep something in reserve and say **three spades** only. North raises this to **four spades** and all pass. The bidding has been:

South	West	North	East
pass	1◇	double	1♡
1♠	2◇	2♠	pass
3♠	pass	4♠	pass
pass	pass		

West leads the King of diamonds and partner displays:

♠ K Q 10
♡ A 10 6 4
◇ Q 6 3
♣ A 7 3

◇ K led

♠ A J 7 6 4
♡ 8 5 2
◇ 10
♣ Q 9 6 2

As I suspected, he was barely worth the first raise to two spades, let alone the final four spades. There would have been more sense to

3NT. Now it looks as though I must lose a diamond, two hearts and at least one club.

East plays the 9 of diamonds under the King and West switches to the 7 of hearts. That looks like a singleton and as my general idea at this stage is to keep East out of the lead I go up with the Ace and draw three rounds of trumps. On the third round East completes an echo in hearts.

Since East played a high diamond on the first trick I am inclined to place West with seven diamonds, three trumps, a singleton heart and two clubs. Now I begin to see a small glimmer of light. If West has a doubleton King of clubs, which seems likely, I can throw him in on the second round and he will have to give dummy a trick with the Queen of diamonds. I might do even better, for if West's clubs are K 10 or K J then my Q 9 will become a tenace over East. Miraculous as it may seem, ten tricks are beginning to appear on the horizon!

Now, when I finally lead a low club toward the dummy, it is West who goes into a trance. Yes, I *was* a bit slow in thinking all this out. West is right with me and I realize he is going to unblock by throwing the King of clubs. After a while he does so. I win with the Ace and now this is the position:

♠ —
♡ 10 6 4
◇ Q 6
♣ 7 3

♠ A 7
♡ 8 5
◇ —
♣ Q 9 6

If West has the Jack of clubs left this unblock won't make any difference. I play the 7 from table and now East goes into committee with himself. Eventually, muttering something about having read somebody's book, he plays the Jack of clubs.

Well! I'm sorry I wrote that book. I must cover with the Queen and West follows with the 10. My 9 6 of clubs are a major tenace over East's 8 x but now I can't get back to dummy to lead the 3!

Two more rounds of trumps may achieve something, however. On the Ace of spades East discards the Jack of hearts and on the 7 of spades the 2 of diamonds. Now I throw him in with a heart and after making two heart tricks he has to lead a club into my 9 6. I finesse the 6 and so make the contract, the full hand being:

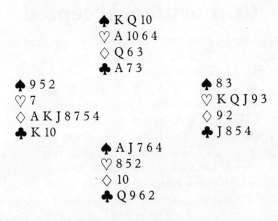

♠ K Q 10
♥ A 10 6 4
♦ Q 6 3
♣ A 7 3

♠ 9 5 2
♥ 7
♦ A K J 8 7 5 4
♣ K 10

♠ 8 3
♥ K Q J 9 3
♦ 9 2
♣ J 8 5 4

♠ A J 7 6 4
♥ 8 5 2
♦ 10
♣ Q 9 6 2

Post-mortem

The result would have been the same if at the finish East had kept a heart and a diamond with his two clubs instead of two hearts. After winning with the King of hearts he would have had to lead a diamond to his partner's Ace and West would then have had to concede a trick to dummy's Queen of diamonds.

North's comment at the end of the play showed how little he appreciated the desperate throws by the defense.

"You were lucky to find the club honors all falling together, weren't you!" was all he said.

64. Fortune Accepted

My partner in this pairs tournament is an earnest performer and the opponents, so far as I know, not especially formidable. With neither side vulnerable, I pick up as dealer:

♠ A Q 9 4 3   ♡ A K 3   ◇ K 10 6   ♣ A 4

Since we are doing fairly well at this stage of the contest, I reject any notion of 2NT and open an orthodox **one spade**. West overcalls with **two diamonds** and this is passed by North and East. I could double now or bid 2NT. The **double** is slightly better since partner could have a weak hand with long hearts. Over my double West competes again with **three diamonds**. Partner thinks awhile, consults the ceiling, and eventually gives me **three spades**. I have an idea that my hand isn't quite as good as it looks, but I must go on to **four spades**.

The bidding has been:

South	West	North	East
1♠	2◇	pass	pass
double	3◇	3♠	pass
4♠	pass	pass	pass

West opens the 5 of hearts and a little nervously partner puts down:

♠ K 10 6 5
♡ J 7 4
◇ 5 4
♣ 10 8 7 5

♡ 5 led

♠ A Q 9 4 3
♡ A K 3
◇ K 10 6
♣ A 4

The lead could be anything, but as East is not likely to have a doubleton Queen of hearts I may as well put up dummy's Jack. A little to my surprise, it holds the trick. I play a spade to the Ace and all follow.

The contract is in no danger now, for I can draw trumps and lose, at most, two diamonds and a club. There is a chance for an overtrick if I can end-play West in clubs and force him to lead diamonds. He is undoubtedly short in clubs and if he has K Q alone, for example, or the singleton King, I may be able to manage it.

Against very strong opponents I would have to be careful about the sequence of play lest West have an opportunity to discard a high club. I don't think that the present West is likely to perform any prodigies of unblocking, so I will take the simple course and draw a second trump with the Queen.

The trumps turn out to be 2 – 2. I play off two top hearts and again all follow, West playing the Queen on the third round. The following cards are left:

        ♠ K 10
        ♡ —
        ♢ 5 4
        ♣ 10 8 7 5

        ♠ 9 4 3
        ♡ —
        ♢ K 10 8
        ♣ A 4

Could West be 2 – 3 – 6 – 2? Just possible, if his clubs were K Q. But then he might have led a club in preference to a heart from Q x x. It is altogether more likely that he has seven diamonds and a singleton club. After all, he did bid three diamonds very much under the gun.

If he has a singleton King of clubs I can just play a small club from hand. But he may have a singleton Queen, and in that case it is better to lead the club from dummy before East realizes what is happening. It is true that by crossing to dummy I give West a chance to disembarrass himself of the high club, but I don't expect him to do that.

In the diagram position I lead a spade to the King, West discarding a diamond. On the lead of the 7 of clubs East plays the 9 and I duck, as planned. West wins with the Queen and has to play diamonds, so I end up with an overtrick, the full hand being:

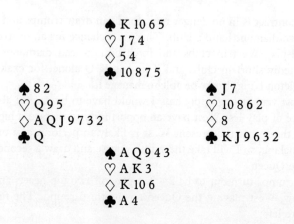

```
                    ♠ K 10 6 5
                    ♡ J 7 4
                    ♢ 5 4
                    ♣ 10 8 7 5
        ♠ 8 2                        ♠ J 7
        ♡ Q 9 5                      ♡ 10 8 6 2
        ♢ A Q J 9 7 3 2              ♢ 8
        ♣ Q                          ♣ K J 9 6 3 2
                    ♠ A Q 9 4 3
                    ♡ A K 3
                    ♢ K 10 6
                    ♣ A 4
```

Post-mortem

Three factors contributed to the overtrick—a lucky lead, a count of West's distribution, and the strategic move of leading the club from dummy rather than from hand.

Both defenders could have done better—West by throwing the Queen of clubs on the third trump, and East by going up with the King when the club was led. Neither play was at all easy.

65. Second String

Both partner and opponents on this hand from rubber bridge are capable and aggressive players. As South I hold:

♠ — ♡ A ◇ J 9 8 6 ♣ A K Q 9 8 7 6 3

At game all West deals and opens **three hearts.** After some thought my partner overcalls with **four hearts.** We usually play that to show a two-suiter of some sort. While I am wondering how many clubs to bid, East jumps to **six hearts.** I don't suppose for a moment that they can make that, but I am going to stretch them to the limit by bidding **seven clubs.** It is just possible we can make it and more than likely that they will go to seven hearts. But no, East **doubles.** Both West and North think for a long while before they pass the double. The bidding has been brief but exciting:

South	West	North	East
—	3♡	4♡	6♡
7♣	pass	pass	double
pass	pass	pass	

West opens the King of hearts. Saying, "You'll be furious with me," partner puts down:

> ♠ K 10 8 6 4
> ♡ —
> ◇ A K 7 5 3 2
> ♣ J 4

♡ K led

> ♠ —
> ♡ A
> ◇ J 9 8 6
> ♣ A K Q 9 8 7 6 3

Actually, he has rather a suitable hand. No trouble at all if the diamonds break. If they don't, can I make up the tricks in spades? There are some possibilities. At any rate, it costs nothing to ruff the heart and lead a spade from table. They may make a mistake.

When I play a low spade from dummy at trick 2 East gives it a long look and eventually plays low. I ruff and the 9 falls from West. That's not unhopeful. If West has Q 9 or J 9 alone I can establish a spade trick by force and there may be a squeeze for a thirteenth. The next trick is a low club to dummy's Jack and East shows out, discarding a heart.

That makes it rather more likely that East will have Q 10 x of diamonds. Let's see what happens to the King of spades. East covers with the Ace, I ruff high and West drops the Queen. I thought that might happen. Of course, if West has Q J 9 another ruff will set up two tricks. On the whole I think it is more likely that the Q 9 is a doubleton and that West is 2 – 8 – 0 – 3. In that case there may be a trump squeeze against East. For the moment I can lead out trumps and watch the discards.

After four more rounds of clubs the following cards are left:

♠ 10 8 6
♡ —
◇ A K
♣ —

♠ —
♡ —
◇ J 9 8 6
♣ 6

West has thrown nothing but hearts. East has discarded two spades and two hearts, the 9 and Jack. Now I play a diamond to the King and West, as I feared, shows out. I lead the 10 of spades from dummy and East plays the 7. This is the moment of decision. Has East had to come down to J x of spades to guard his diamonds, or is the Jack of spades still in West's hand?

Let's look at the bidding first. West has one of these two hands:
(1) ♠ Q J 9   ♡ K Q 10 x x x x   ◇ —   ♣ 10 x x
(2) ♠ Q 9   ♡ K Q 10 x x x x x   ◇ —   ♣ 10 x x

He opened three hearts at game all. The second hand is more likely but the other, in this game, is possible.

East began with one of these two hands:
(1) ♠ A x x x x   ♡ J 9 x x x   ◇ Q 10 x   ♣ —
(2) ♠ A J x x x x   ♡ J 9 x x   ◇ Q 10 x   ♣ —
There again the second hand is slightly more probable.

What of the play? The only card that may have significance is East's low spade at trick 2. That would be natural if he had A J x x x x because he would expect his partner to have led a singleton 9 if he held it. But from A x x x x East would have rather more reason to go up with the Ace.

That makes three small indications all pointing in the same direction —that East holds the spade Jack. So I run the 10 and it holds the trick. I ruff out the Jack of spades, return to the Ace of diamonds and discard my last diamond on dummy's fifth spade. East, as seemed probable all the time, had been caught in a trump squeeze, the full hand being:

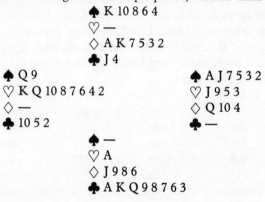

♠ K 10 8 6 4
♡ —
◇ A K 7 5 3 2
♣ J 4

♠ Q 9
♡ K Q 10 8 7 6 4 2
◇ —
♣ 10 5 2

♠ A J 7 5 3 2
♡ J 9 5 3
◇ Q 10 4
♣ —

♠ —
♡ A
◇ J 9 8 6
♣ A K Q 9 8 7 6 3

Post-mortem

There were two steps towards the making of this contract: first, declarer had to appreciate the possibility of establishing tricks in spades, and second, he had to have some understanding of the technique of the trump squeeze.

The standard procedure in a trump squeeze is to play off all the trumps but one and to retain two entry cards to the opposite hand. Thus in the present deal the A K of diamonds had to be retained in dummy up to and beyond the moment of the squeeze. If South had played a diamond earlier to test the position he would not have been able to bring pressure to bear on East at the finish.

66. Dangerous Height

My partner in this pairs contest is a studious player of the modern school. We are vulnerable and I hold:

♠ K J 10   ♡ 10   ◇ A Q 8 4 2   ♣ K Q J 6

My partner deals and opens **one club.** East passes and I force with **two diamonds,** for in our system we show a big hand at once rather than try to catch up later. West passes and partner's rebid is **two hearts.**

The obvious move now is to show club support, but in view of my spade holding and the fact that we are playing a match-pointed pairs I propose to bid **2NT.** One advantage of that bid is that when I support clubs later partner will realize that I have a guard in spades. We may possibly finish in a high no-trump contract.

Partner raises to **3NT** and now I bid **four clubs.** If partner bids four diamonds or four spades I shall bid simply five clubs and leave it to him to choose the final contract. But he bids **4NT.** I take that to be natural, not conventional, and I have no more to say.

The bidding has been:

South	West	North	East
—	—	1♣	pass
2◇	pass	2♡	pass
2NT	pass	3NT	pass
4♣	pass	4NT	pass
pass	pass		

West leads the 4 of clubs and partner displays a most indifferent hand:

♠ A 8 5
♡ K Q 4 2
◇ 10 6 3
♣ A 3 2

♣ 4 led

♠ K J 10
♡ 10
◇ A Q 8 4 2
♣ K Q J 6

In my opinion it is much better to pass that sort of hand, especially when vulnerable and dealer. For so many players these days, life is bounded by the number of points they hold. To make game you need some playing tricks, not just a barren assortment of high cards!

Four no-trump is no lay-down despite this neutral lead. I am wondering whether to make the safety play in diamonds for three sure tricks—that is, Ace first and then low toward the 10 x. No, I don't think I can afford that. If the Ace of hearts is wrong they can set up enough tricks to beat me. I must take the best chance of making four tricks in diamonds.

On the first club dummy plays low, East plays the 9 and I win with the Queen. I cash Ace of diamonds, lead a low club to the Ace and return the 6 of diamonds. Now the worst happens: East shows out, discarding a low heart. I play low and West wins with the 9. West exits with a low club, East following suit. On the thirteenth club West discards a spade, dummy a heart, and East another heart. The position is now:

♠ A 8 5
♡ K Q 4
◇ 10
♣ —

♠ K J 10
♡ 10
◇ Q 8 4
♣ —

I'm sure that West has the Ace of hearts as otherwise he would have led a heart when he was in. If I were in 3NT the play would be simple. I would lead a heart to dummy's Queen and then return a diamond, leaving West to play. As it is, I can't afford to play a diamond into West's K J. To make five more tricks I have to find the Queen of spades and somehow end-play West in hearts and diamonds.

First I must decide which way to finesse the spades. West has turned up with the majority of high cards so far, and to that extent East is more likely to have the spade Queen. On the other hand, East is obviously long in hearts and he hasn't thrown a spade. It is quite likely that West's holding in the major suits is four spades and two hearts.

His opening lead is perhaps another slight indication. Holding three or four spades to the Queen, together with honors in hearts and diamonds, he would certainly choose the club lead. With no high card in spades he might possibly have led a spade.

If I'm going to play West for the Queen of spades it is convenient to take that finesse right away. I run the 10 of spades and it wins the trick. Now I switch to the 10 of hearts. West plays low and dummy's Queen wins. Whether West began with three spades and three hearts, or four spades and two hearts, I have him now. I return a low spade to the King and a third round to the Ace. West follows throughout. That means that his last three cards must be the Ace of hearts and K J of diamonds. I exit with a low heart and make my tenth trick with the Queen of diamonds.

This was the full hand:

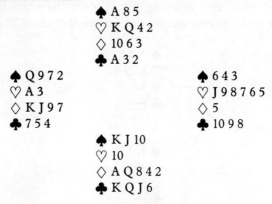

Post-mortem

Having opened his very poor hand, North should have rebid 2NT over the force of two diamonds. After three clubs by South, three hearts by North, South might then have closed the bidding at 3NT.

Ten tricks seemed remote when East showed out on the second diamond but then a number of favorable inferences came to light. West's failure to play hearts surely marked him with the Ace and his opening club lead suggested that he had the Queen of spades. All that South had to do thereafter was keep a count of West's hand.

222

67. Retaining the Loser

My partner on this occasion is a stranger of whose methods I know nothing. It is the first hand of the rubber and I hold:

♠ K Q 9 8 7 3   ♡ K 7 2   ◇ Q 9 8 5   ♣ —

Partner opens **one club** and after a pass by East I respond **one spade**. West passes and partner introduces **two hearts**. Whether that is meant to show a big hand or not I don't know, but I can't bid less than **three spades**. West suddenly interposes a **double**. Partner considers a while and finally passes. I have nothing more to say, so the bidding has been:

South	West	North	East
—	—	1♣	pass
1♠	pass	2♡	pass
3♠	double	pass	pass
pass			

West leads the Ace of clubs and without any sign of remorse partner puts down:

> ♠ —
> ♡ A J 6 4
> ◇ K J 10
> ♣ Q J 8 7 5 2

♣ A led

> ♠ K Q 9 8 7 3
> ♡ K 7 2
> ◇ Q 9 8 5
> ♣ —

If that's how he bids I'm glad he's not at the wheel in four hearts doubled. Not that three spades is likely to be a success. I must make what tricks I can in the side suits, together with a few trumps. After ruffing the first club I play a diamond to the King. This holds and I ruff another club. (Although West normally leads the King from A K, I imagine he is false-carding on this occasion. I don't think he would lead the unsupported Ace of dummy's suit).

Faintly hoping that West will let it pass, I lead a small diamond to the J 10 but West has seen his partner's 2 on the preceding round and goes up with the Ace. He switches to the 8 of hearts. It's unlikely to win but I put in dummy's Jack. East covers with the Queen and I win with the King. Both opponents follow when I play a diamond to the Jack. When I ruff a third round of clubs West drops the King.

It's going as well as can be expected so far. Now I play to the Ace of hearts in dummy and the position is as follows:

♠ —
♡ 6 4
♢ —
♣ Q J 8

♠ K Q 9
♡ 7
♢ Q
♣ —

West is known to have begun with three diamonds and three clubs. He could have four spades and a heart left, but more likely he has nothing but trumps. The way the bidding was going, he wouldn't have doubled three spades without a commanding hand.

The more trumps he has, the better my chance. I have lost only one trick so far and now I must decide what to throw on the Queen of clubs. The losing heart is the obvious card. Or is it? West will ruff the club and probably exit with a middle trump—or possibly with a low trump to his partner's 10. But if I retain the heart I can force West to ruff it at the next trick with no fear that East will be able to over-ruff and then play through me.

On the Queen of clubs, therefore, I discard the master diamond. West ruffs low and exits with the Jack of spades. I win with the King and play the heart. West has to ruff and concede a ninth trick to the Queen of spades, the full hand being:

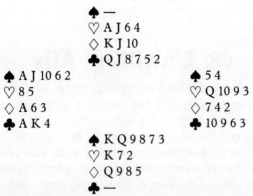

♠ —
♡ A J 6 4
◇ K J 10
♣ Q J 8 7 5 2

♠ A J 10 6 2   ♠ 5 4
♡ 8 5   ♡ Q 10 9 3
◇ A 6 3   ◇ 7 4 2
♣ A K 4   ♣ 10 9 6 3

♠ K Q 9 8 7 3
♡ K 7 2
◇ Q 9 8 5
♣ —

I was able to congratulate my partner on his discretion in passing three spades doubled.

"Oh, I wasn't going to bid 3NT with a void of your suit," he answered virtuously.

Had South played inaccurately at the finish, an interesting defensive point would have arisen. This was the position round the table five cards from the end:

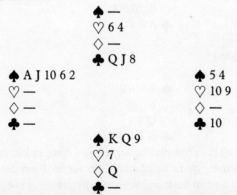

♠ —
♡ 6 4
◇ —
♣ Q J 8

♠ A J 10 6 2   ♠ 5 4
♡ —   ♡ 10 9
◇ —   ◇ —
♣ —   ♣ 10

♠ K Q 9
♡ 7
◇ Q
♣ —

If declarer discards a heart on the Queen of clubs, West must ruff with the 6, not the 2. He exits with the Jack of spades to South's King. When South leads the diamond West is able to ruff low and East over-ruffs with the 5 to gain the lead at the critical moment.

68. Unwilling Ally

My opponents on this hand from rubber bridge are capable players, my partner also a good player but belonging to the scientific school. With both sides vulnerable I pick up:

♠ A 7 6 2 ♡ K ◇ Q 9 7 ♣ K 8 6 5 3

My partner opens **one heart** and after a pass by East I respond **two clubs**. With the opponents remaining silent, partner raises to **three clubs**. I don't see much point in introducing three spades now so I bid **3NT** and all pass. The bidding has gone:

South	West	North	East
—	—	1♡	pass
2♣	pass	3♣	pass
3NT	pass	pass	pass

West opens the Queen of hearts and partner displays this moderate holding:

♠ J 4
♡ A 9 7 3
◇ K 10 8 4
♣ A 7 4

♡ Q led

♠ A 7 6 2
♡ K
◇ Q 9 7
♣ K 8 6 5 3

"I like to open 1NT, but playing with you I have to bid one heart," observes my partner, quite unashamed. So far as I am concerned, I don't like these 12-point no-trumps, either vulnerable or not. As dealer, vulnerable, it wouldn't occur to me to open this hand at all!

On the Queen of hearts East plays the 6 and I win with the King. If I give up a club and the clubs are 3 – 2 I'll have seven tricks on top but I may or may not have time to establish a trick in diamonds. In any event I shall probably need to find the Jack of diamonds to make nine tricks.

Suppose I play on diamonds first. If I find the Jack that will give me eight tricks on top, with some chance of making a ninth trick from hearts or from a squeeze.

At trick 2 I run the 9 of diamonds and lose to East's Jack. East switches to the 5 of spades. I play low and West wins with the Queen. West returns the 8 of spades and East plays the King on dummy's Jack. To have any chance now, I must assume that East has five spades and that West has the Ace of diamonds. I can't afford to give them another spade trick, so I win with the Ace.

Both opponents play low on the Queen of diamonds. When I lead a third diamond now, West goes up with the Ace and East discards the 3 of spades. West exits with a fourth diamond to dummy's King, East discards the 2 of clubs and I throw a spade. The position is now:

♠ —
♡ A 9 7
◇ —
♣ A 7 4

♠ 7
♡ —
◇ —
♣ K 8 6 5 3

I have lost three tricks so far and if I can duck a club into West's hand I can probably make the remainder. Somehow I don't think that's going to be possible. That club discard by East is very sinister. I know that East began with five spades and two diamonds and I should think that he also had four clubs and two hearts.

East played the 6 of hearts on the first trick and his second heart may well be the 8. That would explain why West did not continue hearts. He would know that after the play of the Jack, won by the Ace, dummy's 9 7 would be equals against the 10. Well then, what about leading the 9 of hearts from dummy? Yes, but not immediately. First I must lay down the Ace of clubs to remove West's exit card.

On the Ace of clubs East plays the 9 and West the 10. I continue with the 9 of hearts from dummy and East, as I was hoping, drops the 8. West wins with the Jack and returns a small heart. We are now down to four cards:

♠ —
♡ A 7
♢ —
♣ 7 4

♠ 7
♡ —
♢ —
♣ K 8 6

The finesse of the 7 of hearts wins and the Ace of hearts then squeezes East in spades and clubs, giving me my ninth trick. This was the full hand:

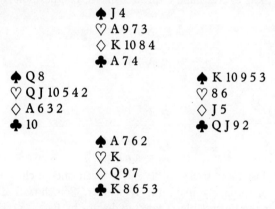

♠ J 4
♡ A 9 7 3
♢ K 10 8 4
♣ A 7 4

♠ Q 8
♡ Q J 10 5 4 2
♢ A 6 3 2
♣ 10

♠ K 10 9 5 3
♡ 8 6
♢ J 5
♣ Q J 9 2

♠ A 7 6 2
♡ K
♢ Q 9 7
♣ K 8 6 5 3

Post-mortem

Declarer had to base his play on the hope that the player with the Ace of diamonds would have a doubleton spade. On that assumption, which proved correct, it would have been a mistake to hold up twice in spades. Had the defense been allowed to win a second spade they could have defeated the contract in a number of ways.

Declarer's accurate card-reading in this hand deserves a little study. Note how the fall of the 6 of hearts from East at trick 1 suggested the possibility that his second heart would be the 8. Even without the indication, declarer would have had to play for that chance. Note, too, how declarer rightly read the club distribution. East's discard of a low club on the fourth round of diamonds gave evidence that he had begun with at least four since, with $5 - 3 - 2 - 3$ distribution, East would surely have discarded a heart.

The general count of the hand showed that declarer had to cash the Ace of clubs before exiting with the 9 of hearts in order to force the heart return from West.

69. Unwanted Possession

My partner on this hand of rubber bridge is a player of notoriously poor judgment. It is therefore with some apprehension that I contemplate this indeterminate two-suiter:

♠ 6 4   ♡ K Q J 9 3   ◇ —   ♣ Q 10 8 6 5 4

We are vulnerable and my alarm is not lessened when West, on my left, deals and opens **three clubs**. My partner overcalls with **3NT** and East passes. In view of my club holding it is evident that the bid of 3NT is for a take-out. I bid a cautious **four hearts** and partner now introduces **five diamonds**.

I wonder whether I ought to pass before someone doubles. It would be a difficult decision with a good partner—quite impossible with a bad one. It may be foolish but I'm going to bid **five hearts.**

It *was* foolish. Partner's next move is **six diamonds** and now East **doubles.** I can but pass and prepare my apologies but it's not all over. After many nervous glances over his spectacles, partner transfers to **six hearts.** East **doubles** almost in the same moment and all pass. The bidding has been:

South	West	North	East
—	3♣	3NT	pass
4♡	pass	5◇	pass
5♡	pass	6◇	double
pass	pass	6♡	double
pass	pass	pass	

West leads the King of clubs and partner's hand is in a way better than I was expecting:

♠ A Q 7 3
♡ A 10
◇ A K 10 7 5 4 3
♣ —

♣ K led

♠ 6 4
♡ K Q J 9 3
◇ —
♣ Q 10 8 6 5 4

Digressing for a moment, I don't mind 3NT for a take-out over a major suit but over a minor it loses too much bidding space. To my mind, a better system than any of the optional doubles or popular conventional methods is to play a double of three clubs or three diamonds as primarily for a take-out and a double of three spades or three hearts as primarily for penalties.

On North's present hand it is better to overcall three clubs with a cue bid of four clubs. That suggests a more unbalanced type of hand. When on the next round North bids five diamonds over South's four hearts, it is easier for South to pass.

Exactly how I am going to play six hearts I don't know yet. At any rate, I must ruff the first club with the Ace of hearts. East follows suit, so I can take it that the clubs are 6 – 1.

Perhaps it's one of those hands on which one has to ruff one diamond and concede another. On the surface, if both red suits are not worse than 4 – 2 I can come to 12 tricks by way of five hearts, five diamonds, Ace of spades and a club ruff. But entries are a problem. I would like to give up the very first round of diamonds but I can't be sure of ducking the trick into East's hand. A spade lead from West would be very in- convenient. I am going to begin with Ace, King and another diamond and see what transpires.

Both opponents follow to the top diamonds and I discard two clubs. On a third diamond East plays the Queen. Is there any advantage in letting him hold this trick? Not really, because if the diamonds are 4 – 2 West will ruff his partner's trick and lead a spade. So I ruff the diamond with the 9 of hearts and, a little to my surprise, West follows with the Jack of diamonds.

That's good in one way but perhaps bad in another. If East has only four cards in the minors he may well have five hearts and four spades to the King. Furthermore, West is more likely to be 3 – 1 – 3 – 6 than 2 – 2 – 3 – 6. Can I do anything about it if East has five trumps ? I think perhaps I can. One fortunate thing about this hand is that East, having a singleton club, is entirely cut off from his partner.

The position at the moment is as follows:

♠ A Q 7 3
♡ 10
♢ 10 7 5 4
♣ —

♠ 6 4
♡ K Q J 3
♢ —
♣ Q 10 8

If I draw trumps, and they are not 5 – 1, I make an overtrick with no difficulty at all. But life isn't like that. Besides, East is looking quite pleased with himself still. I can make the contract even if the hearts are 5 – 1, and that's what I'm going to assume.

I lead the 3 of hearts to dummy's 10. West follows, I am glad to see, for the hearts could have been 6 – 0 as well! Now comes the decisive moment. I play a winning diamond from dummy and East discards a spade, West a club. Better! East ruffs the next diamond and looks aggrieved when I leave him in possession of the trick. It is plain now that whether he leads a heart or a spade I can make the rest of the tricks. I show him my cards and he concedes the contract, the full hand being:

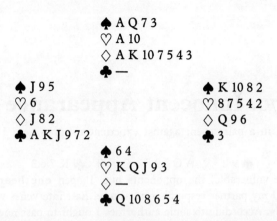

```
                    ♠ A Q 7 3
                    ♡ A 10
                    ◇ A K 10 7 5 4 3
                    ♣ —
   ♠ J 9 5                          ♠ K 10 8 2
   ♡ 6                              ♡ 8 7 5 4 2
   ◇ J 8 2                          ◇ Q 9 6
   ♣ A K J 9 7 2                    ♣ 3
                    ♠ 6 4
                    ♡ K Q J 9 3
                    ◇ —
                    ♣ Q 10 8 6 5 4
```

Post-mortem

Declarer's analysis of the distribution confirms a point that has been mentioned before. When opponents double one high contract after this sort of bidding sequence they generally have still better defense (or think they have) against the other. Six diamonds, as it happens, would have been a lay-down.

Had the diamonds proved to be 4 – 2 South would have had to cut his losses, taking care not to let West into the lead. The best continuation, after ruffing the third diamond, would have been to lead the top trumps and try to throw the lead to East on the fourth round.

70. Innocent Appearance

Playing in a pairs event against experienced opposition, I hold as dealer:

♠ 9 2   ♡ A Q J 9 5   ◇ K 8   ♣ K 7 6 3

We are vulnerable, the opponents not. I open **one heart,** West passes and my partner responds **one spade.** East intervenes with **two diamonds.** According to some authorities I ought to pass now, as my hand is not much better than a minimum opening. To my mind, when there is competitive bidding it is all the more important to say one's piece at a low level. I bid **two hearts,** therefore, and partner raises to **four hearts.** It is evident that on this occasion my free rebid has not affected the result. The bidding has been:

South	West	North	East
1♡	pass	1♠	2◇
2♡	pass	4♡	pass
pass	pass		

West leads the 7 of diamonds and partner goes down with a useful hand:

```
              ♠ A K 6 5
              ♡ 10 8 4 2
              ◇ 6 4 3
              ♣ A 8


◇ 7 led


              ♠ 9 2
              ♡ A Q J 9 5
              ◇ K 8
              ♣ K 7 6 3
```

East wins the first trick with the Ace of diamonds and returns the Queen. I cross to the King of spades and run the 8 of hearts. When this holds, I finesse the Queen and this time West discards a club.

Eleven tricks are certain, but at the moment I don't see any good play for a twelfth. If East had been short of hearts I would have ruffed two clubs, but now it seems certain that East will over-ruff. He over-called in diamonds and has turned up with three hearts, so he is most unlikely to have four clubs. In fact, West's discard of a club probably means that he has at least five. If I am not going to ruff clubs, I may as well play off the Ace of hearts. On this trick West discards a diamond and East's King falls. These are the remaining cards:

♠ A 6 5
♥ 10
♦ 6
♣ A 8

♠ 9
♥ J 9
♦ —
♣ K 7 6 3

Up to now I have not been thinking about West. If he has fourth round control of both black suits I should be able to bring some pressure to bear on him. Suppose I play a spade to the Ace and ruff a spade, then cross to the Ace of clubs and ruff a diamond? That's no good because I can't get back to dummy to play the 10 of hearts.

Another possibility is to play Ace and King of clubs, ruff a club in dummy, back to my hand with a diamond ruff and then play the last trump. But then West will discard a spade, relying on partner to guard that suit.

To exert real pressure on West, I must keep a trump in both hands. Suppose I cross to dummy with a club and immediately ruff a diamond? Yes, that's the answer.

When I cross to the Ace of clubs and return to hand by ruffing a diamond West is in obvious difficulties. He finally throws a club. Now I play King of clubs and ruff a club in dummy. After the Ace of spades a spade ruff puts me in hand to make the last club for a second over-trick. West was caught in a ruffing squeeze at the finish, the full hand being:

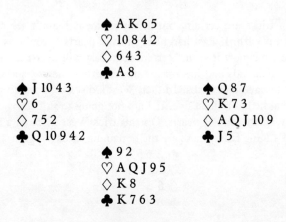

```
              ♠ A K 6 5
              ♡ 10 8 4 2
              ◇ 6 4 3
              ♣ A 8
♠ J 10 4 3                    ♠ Q 8 7
♡ 6                           ♡ K 7 3
◇ 7 5 2                       ◇ A Q J 10 9
♣ Q 10 9 4 2                  ♣ J 5
              ♠ 9 2
              ♡ A Q J 9 5
              ◇ K 8
              ♣ K 7 6 3
```

Post-mortem

This was the position after South had drawn the Ace of hearts:

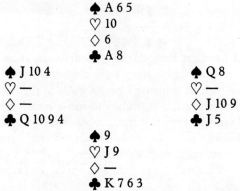

```
              ♠ A 6 5
              ♡ 10
              ◇ 6
              ♣ A 8
♠ J 10 4                      ♠ Q 8
♡ —                           ♡ —
◇ —                           ◇ J 10 9
♣ Q 10 9 4                    ♣ J 5
              ♠ 9
              ♡ J 9
              ◇ —
              ♣ K 7 6 3
```

The innocent-seeming diamond ruff was the only way to turn the screw on West. When both hands contain potential winners that may be established by ruffing, it is usually right to play for a position in which both dummy and declarer have one trump left.

71. Debatable Hold-up

Playing rubber bridge against opponents of fair strength, I hold in second position:

♠ A K Q   ♡ A Q 10 5   ◇ K J 7   ♣ J 9 5

We are vulnerable, they are not. East passes and I open a rather poor **2NT**. This is raised to **3NT** and that concludes the bidding:

South	West	North	East
—	—	—	pass
2NT	pass	3NT	pass
pass	pass		

After drawing out one card, then another, West finally produces the 9 of hearts and partner displays moderate support:

♠ J 10 7
♡ 6 4
◇ A 8 5
♣ 10 8 6 4 2

♡ 9 led

♠ A K Q
♡ A Q 10 5
◇ K J 7
♣ J 9 5

Assuming that the lead is top of nothing, I can count eight tricks. Then there is the diamond finesse and it should be possible to establish some tricks in clubs. That will take some time and I suppose it's possible that the enemy will be able to get their hearts going meanwhile. For example, if the lead is from a doubleton and East has two entries in clubs they may set up two heart tricks before I can enjoy the long clubs.

I wonder if this is a hand on which I should hold up with three controls in the enemy suit? Possibly, as I can afford to lose a heart and three clubs. If the 9 of hearts wins they are sure to continue the suit. I'll try that.

East plays the 3 on the first trick and when the 9 holds West continues with the 7. I take this with the 10 and lead the 9 of clubs. West studies this card for a moment, then plays the 3. East wins with the Queen and switches to the 6 of diamonds.

Yes, I should have foreseen that. The hold-up on the first trick may turn out to have been a calamitous error. Now I've got to decide who has the Queen of diamonds. The only indication I have is that East appears to have four or five hearts to the K J and at least one honor in clubs. It's even more likely that he has two honors, for if West had had A K x he wouldn't have thought twice about playing low. On the whole I think West is more likely to have the diamond Queen so I am going to refuse the finesse and put up the King.

West takes the next round of clubs with the King. That leaves the cards as follows:

```
              ♠ J 10 7
              ♡ —
              ◇ A 8
              ♣ 10 8 6



              ♠ A K Q
              ♡ A Q
              ◇ J 7
              ♣ 5
```

Now West makes a good play by leading the Queen of diamonds which I have to win in dummy. That takes away my entry to dummy's long clubs, but if East has the club Ace I can throw him in. After taking the Ace of diamonds I cash three spades and the diamond Jack. East discards a heart on the third round of spades. At trick 11 I play a club and scramble my ninth trick when East has to lead into the A Q of hearts.

Well, the hold-up worked, the way the cards were lying:

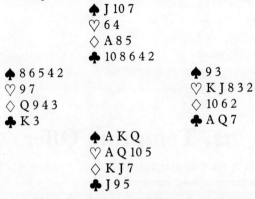

♠ J 10 7
♥ 6 4
♦ A 8 5
♣ 10 8 6 4 2

♠ 8 6 5 4 2
♥ 9 7
♦ Q 9 4 3
♣ K 3

♠ 9 3
♥ K J 8 3 2
♦ 10 6 2
♣ A Q 7

♠ A K Q
♥ A Q 10 5
♦ K J 7
♣ J 9 5

Post-mortem

Though it led to some interesting play and turned out well, it is doubtful whether the hold-up at the first trick was correct. For it to gain, the hearts have to be 5 – 2 and West has to have a doubleton honor in clubs. Meanwhile, the diamond hazard is increased. If South has not already lost a trick he can try the Jack of diamonds when East leads the suit and the contract will not necessarily be defeated if the finesse goes wrong, for he can let the Queen win.

72. Tempting Offer

Playing in a team-of-four match against opponents who are not particularly strong, I hold second in hand:

♠ K J 9 4   ♡ J 6   ◇ K 5 2   ♣ A Q 10 2

Both sides are vulnerable and after a pass by East I open **one club**. Partner responds **one diamond** and I rebid **one spade**. Partner raises to **three spades**. There will probably be some finesses in this, but I must go to **four spades**. The bidding has been:

South	West	North	East
—	—	—	pass
1♣	pass	1◇	pass
1♠	pass	3♠	pass
4♠	pass	pass	pass

West opens the 4 of diamonds and a fair dummy goes down:

♠ Q 10 7 5
♡ A 4
◇ A 10 7 6 3
♣ J 4

◇ 4 led

♠ K J 9 4
♡ J 6
◇ K 5 2
♣ A Q 10 2

This lead looks like a singleton, but I can be grateful that they haven't led a heart. There are several ways of playing this. I can go up with Ace of diamonds and finesse a club. If it loses I can still dispose of the heart loser in dummy, but if East has the Ace of spades my King of diamonds may be ruffed. On the other hand, if I take the diamond in hand I have no convenient way of entering dummy for the club finesse. I can play a spade, but then they will knock out the Ace of hearts before I have touched clubs. Another possibility is to win in hand with the King of diamonds and lead a low club, abandoning the finesse. But then again I may run into diamond ruffs unnecessarily.

It is hard to assess all these chances so I will follow the natural line of going up with the Ace of diamonds and finessing in clubs. East plays the 8 of diamonds under the Ace and covers the Jack of clubs with the King. Now I don't have to rush for the heart discard, so after winning with the Ace of clubs I lead the 9 of spades. This holds the trick and I follow with the 4 of spades to dummy's 10. Now a slight shock as East shows out, discarding the 7 of hearts! The contract has suddenly become difficult again. These are the remaining cards:

♠ Q 7
♡ A 4
♢ 10 7 6 3
♣ 4

♠ K J
♡ J 6
♢ K 5
♣ Q 10 2

I can discard a heart from dummy on the 10 of clubs and can take a ruff on the table in either hearts or clubs. But then I shall be in dummy and badly placed. If at that point I lead a diamond the King will be ruffed, West will draw the Ace of spades, and I shall still have a diamond and one other trick to lose. Alternatively, in the diagram position, I can play a trump, but then West will return a trump and again I shall be a trick short.

I wonder if I can do anything with the long diamond in dummy. Suppose I play a diamond right away. West will ruff, draw the Ace of spades and lead a heart. Then I shall be an entry short to make anything of the fifth diamond.

Still, that does give me an idea. It looks odd, but suppose I were to duck a diamond. If East has the King of hearts and not the K Q he may fall for the temptation of giving his partner a diamond ruff. Then, if my calculations are correct, I shall be a tempo ahead.

I'm going to try this because I don't think there's any other way of doing it. I play a diamond from dummy, East plays the 9 and I duck. West discards the 5 of hearts. East studies this for some while but then makes what seems to him the obvious play of a diamond to give West a ruff. West draws the Ace of spades and exits with a heart to dummy's Ace. Now the situation has improved:

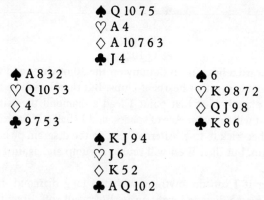

```
              ♠ Q
              ♡ 4
              ◇ 10 7
              ♣ 4


              ♠ K
              ♡ J
              ◇ —
              ♣ Q 10 2
```

I ruff a diamond with the King of spades, play the Queen and 10 of clubs, and make the last two tricks with dummy's Queen of spades and 10 of diamonds. This was the full hand:

```
                      ♠ Q 10 7 5
                      ♡ A 4
                      ◇ A 10 7 6 3
                      ♣ J 4
        ♠ A 8 3 2                      ♠ 6
        ♡ Q 10 5 3                     ♡ K 9 8 7 2
        ◇ 4                            ◇ Q J 9 8
        ♣ 9 7 5 3                      ♣ K 8 6
                      ♠ K J 9 4
                      ♡ J 6
                      ◇ K 5 2
                      ♣ A Q 10 2
```

Post-mortem

East did not defend well, but the situation was quite complex and many players would have done the same.

Declarer's stratagem of ducking a diamond when he was sure that the King would be ruffed is worth noting. A similar position sometimes arises in a side suit which is distributed as follows:

10 x x x x

x   A Q J 9

K x x

West leads his singleton. East wins with the Ace and returns the Queen. By playing low South gains a tempo which may help him to establish the long card in dummy.

73. Invitation Declined

Playing in a rubber game where the standard of play is high throughout, I am last to speak and hold:

♠ K 9 2 ♥ K 8 3 ♦ A Q 7 ♣ A Q 6 4

Both sides are vulnerable and after three passes I open **1NT.** Partner raises to **3NT,** making a brief auction:

South	West	North	East
—	pass	pass	pass
1NT	pass	3NT	pass
pass	pass		

West opens the 4 of hearts and partner puts down a fair hand:

♠ Q 10 7 4
♥ A 7
♦ 10 8 6 2
♣ K J 5

♥ 4 led

♠ K 9 2
♥ K 8 3
♦ A Q 7
♣ A Q 6 4

There are seven tricks on top and at least one more can be developed in spades. It looks as though the Jack of spades is going to be the critical card. As there is no other suit to fear, I must hold up in hearts. East's Queen wins the first trick and he returns the 10 to dummy's Ace, West playing the 2.

If I can force out the Ace of spades from either side the contract will be safe, assuming that West has the long hearts. At trick 3 I lead a low spade from dummy to the King and it holds the trick. The obvious play now is to return a spade and finesse the 10. If East has no more than three hearts it won't matter if he has both Ace and Jack of spades. However, I am chary of drawing the inference that West does not have the Ace of spades. He is quite good enough a player to hold up, expecting me to finesse the 10. Then the hearts will be cleared and he will come in with the Ace to make two more heart tricks.

So far as I can see, it will cost nothing to take the diamond finesse before playing a second spade. If the finesse wins that will be nine tricks, and if it loses I can still play East for the Ace of spades. The advantage of playing on diamonds first is that if I lose a spade finesse to the Jack and the hearts are cleared I won't know what to do next—finesse the Queen of diamonds or play another spade.

Having worked this out, I cross to the club King and finesse the Queen of diamonds. The finesse wins and now the contract is safe. The following cards are left:

♠ Q 10 7
♡ —
♢ 10 8 6
♣ J 5

♠ 9 2
♡ K
♢ A 7
♣ A Q 6

I lead a low spade and West plays low. This is the guess that I did not want to take earlier. One point that did not occur to me then is that if East had had the Ace of spades he might have thought of playing it when I led the low spade from dummy at trick 3. From his point of view his partner might have the King of hearts, and the King of spades might be my ninth trick. That's one reason for going up with the Queen now. Another is that if West played low from A x x I can teach him a little lesson. Next time he will think twice before employing this stratagem.

The Queen of spades wins the trick and I return a spade. When both opponents follow I have eleven tricks on top, the full hand being:

```
              ♠ Q 10 7 4
              ♡ A 7
              ◇ 10 8 6 2
              ♣ K J 5
♠ A 6 5                      ♠ J 8 3
♡ J 9 6 4 2                  ♡ Q 10 5
◇ J 3                        ◇ K 9 5 4
♣ 10 7 2                     ♣ 9 8 3
              ♠ K 9 2
              ♡ K 8 3
              ◇ A Q 7
              ♣ A Q 6 4
```

Post-mortem

Despite the result, West's duck on the first round of spades was, of course, the right play. Most players are up to that little trick nowadays and when the King wins in such a situation declarer should not too readily finesse the 10 on the way back. Taking a long view, when defenders know that declarer may go up with the Queen on the way back, as South did on this hand, they will be wary of attempting this particular coup.

74. Desperate Assumption

Playing in a multiple team event against opponents of average strength, I hold in third position:

♠ 8 5   ♡ Q 10 2   ◇ A K J 5   ♣ A 9 5 2

With opponents vulnerable, my partner deals and opens **one spade**. East passes and I respond **two diamonds**. Partner rebids **two spades** and I go to **3NT,** which is passed all round. The bidding has been:

South	West	North	East
—	—	1♠	pass
2◇	pass	2♠	pass
3NT	pass	pass	pass

West leads the 4 of hearts and North is seen to have a minimum bid:

♠ K Q J 6 4 2
♡ A 5
◇ 9 3
♣ J 6 4

♡ 4 led

♠ 8 5
♡ Q 10 2
◇ A K J 5
♣ A 9 5 2

Well, I hope the King of hearts is right, that's all. Disillusionment comes quickly. East wins the first heart with the King and returns the 3, removing dummy's only entry.

Now I have no prospect of making nine tricks without bringing in the spades and very little chance of doing that. I come to hand with a diamond and lead a spade, on which West plays the 3. Now I don't see that it can do me any good to go up with a spade honor. If East has the Ace guarded he will obviously hold off. There is one chance, and one chance only, of making tricks in spades and that is to find East with the singleton Ace.

Following this desperate assumption, I play a low spade from the table. Luck is with me—or, as they say, there would be no story. East wins with the Ace of spades and returns a heart, knocking out my Queen. Now I have all the remaining tricks but one in top cards. Before running off the spades I may as well cash the Ace of clubs. Then I shall be able to take a diamond finesse at the finish without risking the contract.

After the Ace of clubs and four more rounds of spades these cards are left:

On the last spade East discards the Queen of clubs and I the 9 of clubs. West, who had discarded a heart on the fifth spade, now throws a diamond. The King of clubs is still out and I think it is possible that East's discard of the Queen was a mistake. At any rate, I am going to be satisfied with a minimum of ten tricks and go up with the King of diamonds. It turns out, as I suspected, that East's discard of the Queen of clubs squeezed his partner, for the Queen of diamonds now falls under the King and I finish up with two overtricks. This was the full hand:

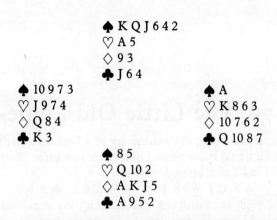

♠ K Q J 6 4 2
♡ A 5
◇ 9 3
♣ J 6 4

♠ 10 9 7 3   ♠ A
♡ J 9 7 4   ♡ K 8 6 3
◇ Q 8 4   ◇ 10 7 6 2
♣ K 3   ♣ Q 10 8 7

♠ 8 5
♡ Q 10 2
◇ A K J 5
♣ A 9 5 2

Post-mortem

The play in spades demonstrates a little-known tactical point. These are some other combinations where the only chance, assuming that there is no side entry to the dummy, is to play the right-hand opponent for a singleton Ace:

(1)   K Q 10 x x x

J 9 x x   A

                 x x

(2)   K Q x x x x

J 10 x   A

                 x x

(3)   K J x x x x

Q 10 x   A

                 x x

75. The Little Old Ladies

The occasion, a big pairs tournament at a French resort; the opponents, two little old ladies whom I have never seen before. Both sides are vulnerable and I pick up as dealer:

♠ K Q J   ♡ K J 10   ◇ K 10 6 2   ♣ A K 7

This 20-point hand with only one Ace is by no means ideal for **2NT,** but against the present opposition I will take the chance.

West passes and partner responds **three diamonds.** That is mildly constructive, but having opened sub-minimum I mustn't force it. Even little old ladies can cash two Aces when they have them. I bid **3NT.**

Partner raises to **6NT.** That's enough for me. The full bidding:

South	West	North	East
2NT	pass	3◇	pass
3NT	pass	6NT	pass
pass	pass		

West opens the Jack of clubs and partner puts down:

♠ A 6 4
♡ A 7 5
◇ Q J 9 5 3
♣ 4 3

♣ J led

♠ K Q J
♡ K J 10
◇ K 10 6 2
♣ A K 7

East plays the 5 of clubs. I win with the King and force out the Ace of diamonds. A club comes back. Both follow to a second round of diamonds.

So I have to find the Queen of hearts, with no count and no indication of any kind. I could play off three more rounds of diamonds, but it is unlikely that that would help.

One possibility is to lead the Jack of hearts in the hope of tempting a cover should West hold the Queen. But even little old ladies are unlikely to fall for that.

On the other hand, she may *hesitate* and then produce a small heart....

But what would that mean? Unfortunately, I don't know her habits. Some of these little old ladies are very tricky: they hesitate when they haven't got Queens. On the other hand, she may hesitate and be quite honest, actually holding the Queen.

So I shall have to guess, unless ....

Yes, I have it! I'll lead the Jack of spades and see what this little old lady does when she does not hold the Queen.

On the Jack of spades, a tiny hesitation. I put on the Ace, return to hand with a diamond and lead the Jack of hearts.

No hesitation now, none whatever.

Finesse!

Successfully, for this is the full hand:

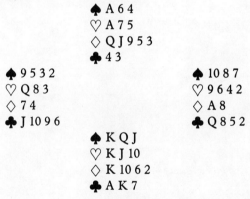

```
              ♠ A 6 4
              ♡ A 7 5
              ◇ Q J 9 5 3
              ♣ 4 3
♠ 9 5 3 2                      ♠ 10 8 7
♡ Q 8 3                        ♡ 9 6 4 2
◇ 7 4                          ◇ A 8
♣ J 10 9 6                     ♣ Q 8 5 2
              ♠ K Q J
              ♡ K J 10
              ◇ K 10 6 2
              ♣ A K 7
```

Post-mortem

In so far as this little fable has a moral, it is that it is foolish as well as (if done with conscious intent) unethical to form these revealing habits of play. I am thinking of West's hesitation when the Jack of spades was led.

There are many situations where, without any thought of deceiving, players give free indications. For example, when a defender to 3NT hovers from one lead to another before finally settling on an indeterminate 5, he tells the world that as likely as not he is leading from a short suit. In a trump contract, when a defender leads after long thought you can just about dismiss the possibility of his having selected an obvious lead like a singleton.

The most difficult opponents are those who maintain an even tempo in both bidding and play. Of course, after a long sequence of bidding, the player on lead sometimes has to consider strategic possibilities, and that takes time. But when the bidding has been 1NT – 3NT, a player who hesitates over his lead is not deliberating, he is just dithering.

From the other side of the table, one should train oneself to observe these variations in behavior and to draw the appropriate inferences.

A CATALOGUE OF SELECTED DOVER BOOKS
IN ALL FIELDS OF INTEREST

A CATALOGUE OF SELECTED DOVER BOOKS
IN ALL FIELDS OF INTEREST

AMERICA'S OLD MASTERS, James T. Flexner. Four men emerged unexpectedly from provincial 18th century America to leadership in European art: Benjamin West, J. S. Copley, C. R. Peale, Gilbert Stuart. Brilliant coverage of lives and contributions. Revised, 1967 edition. 69 plates. 365pp. of text.

21806-6 Paperbound $3.00

FIRST FLOWERS OF OUR WILDERNESS: AMERICAN PAINTING, THE COLONIAL PERIOD, James T. Flexner. Painters, and regional painting traditions from earliest Colonial times up to the emergence of Copley, West and Peale Sr., Foster, Gustavus Hesselius, Feke, John Smibert and many anonymous painters in the primitive manner. Engaging presentation, with 162 illustrations. xxii + 368pp.

22180-6 Paperbound $3.50

THE LIGHT OF DISTANT SKIES: AMERICAN PAINTING, 1760-1835, James T. Flexner. The great generation of early American painters goes to Europe to learn and to teach: West, Copley, Gilbert Stuart and others. Allston, Trumbull, Morse; also contemporary American painters—primitives, derivatives, academics—who remained in America. 102 illustrations. xiii + 306pp. 22179-2 Paperbound $3.50

A HISTORY OF THE RISE AND PROGRESS OF THE ARTS OF DESIGN IN THE UNITED STATES, William Dunlap. Much the richest mine of information on early American painters, sculptors, architects, engravers, miniaturists, etc. The only source of information for scores of artists, the major primary source for many others. Unabridged reprint of rare original 1834 edition, with new introduction by James T. Flexner, and 394 new illustrations. Edited by Rita Weiss. 6⅝ x 9⅝.

21695-0, 21696-9, 21697-7 Three volumes, Paperbound $13.50

EPOCHS OF CHINESE AND JAPANESE ART, Ernest F. Fenollosa. From primitive Chinese art to the 20th century, thorough history, explanation of every important art period and form, including Japanese woodcuts; main stress on China and Japan, but Tibet, Korea also included. Still unexcelled for its detailed, rich coverage of cultural background, aesthetic elements, diffusion studies, particularly of the historical period. 2nd, 1913 edition. 242 illustrations. lii + 439pp. of text.

20364-6, 20365-4 Two volumes, Paperbound $6.00

THE GENTLE ART OF MAKING ENEMIES, James A. M. Whistler. Greatest wit of his day deflates Oscar Wilde, Ruskin, Swinburne; strikes back at inane critics, exhibitions, art journalism; aesthetics of impressionist revolution in most striking form. Highly readable classic by great painter. Reproduction of edition designed by Whistler. Introduction by Alfred Werner. xxxvi + 334pp.

21875-9 Paperbound $3.00

VISUAL ILLUSIONS: THEIR CAUSES, CHARACTERISTICS, AND APPLICATIONS, Matthew Luckiesh. Thorough description and discussion of optical illusion, geometric and perspective, particularly; size and shape distortions, illusions of color, of motion; natural illusions; use of illusion in art and magic, industry, etc. Most useful today with op art, also for classical art. Scores of effects illustrated. Introduction by William H. Ittleson. 100 illustrations. xxi + 252pp.
21530-X Paperbound $2.00

A HANDBOOK OF ANATOMY FOR ART STUDENTS, Arthur Thomson. Thorough, virtually exhaustive coverage of skeletal structure, musculature, etc. Full text, supplemented by anatomical diagrams and drawings and by photographs of undraped figures. Unique in its comparison of male and female forms, pointing out differences of contour, texture, form. 211 figures, 40 drawings, 86 photographs. xx + 459pp. 5⅜ x 8⅜.
21163-0 Paperbound $3.50

150 MASTERPIECES OF DRAWING, Selected by Anthony Toney. Full page reproductions of drawings from the early 16th to the end of the 18th century, all beautifully reproduced: Rembrandt, Michelangelo, Dürer, Fragonard, Urs, Graf, Wouwerman, many others. First-rate browsing book, model book for artists. xviii + 150pp. 8⅜ x 11¼.
21032-4 Paperbound $2.50

THE LATER WORK OF AUBREY BEARDSLEY, Aubrey Beardsley. Exotic, erotic, ironic masterpieces in full maturity: Comedy Ballet, Venus and Tannhauser, Pierrot, Lysistrata, Rape of the Lock, Savoy material, Ali Baba, Volpone, etc. This material revolutionized the art world, and is still powerful, fresh, brilliant. With *The Early Work*, all Beardsley's finest work. 174 plates, 2 in color. xiv + 176pp. 8⅛ x 11.
21817-1 Paperbound $3.00

DRAWINGS OF REMBRANDT, Rembrandt van Rijn. Complete reproduction of fabulously rare edition by Lippmann and Hofstede de Groot, completely reedited, updated, improved by Prof. Seymour Slive, Fogg Museum. Portraits, Biblical sketches, landscapes, Oriental types, nudes, episodes from classical mythology—All Rembrandt's fertile genius. Also selection of drawings by his pupils and followers. "Stunning volumes," *Saturday Review*. 550 illustrations. lxxviii + 552pp. 9⅛ x 12¼.
21485-0, 21486-9 Two volumes, Paperbound $10.00

THE DISASTERS OF WAR, Francisco Goya. One of the masterpieces of Western civilization—83 etchings that record Goya's shattering, bitter reaction to the Napoleonic war that swept through Spain after the insurrection of 1808 and to war in general. Reprint of the first edition, with three additional plates from Boston's Museum of Fine Arts. All plates facsimile size. Introduction by Philip Hofer, Fogg Museum. v + 97pp. 9⅜ x 8¼.
21872-4 Paperbound $2.00

GRAPHIC WORKS OF ODILON REDON. Largest collection of Redon's graphic works ever assembled: 172 lithographs, 28 etchings and engravings, 9 drawings. These include some of his most famous works. All the plates from *Odilon Redon: oeuvre graphique complet,* plus additional plates. New introduction and caption translations by Alfred Werner. 209 illustrations. xxvii + 209pp. 9⅛ x 12¼.
21966-8 Paperbound $4.50

DESIGN BY ACCIDENT; A BOOK OF "ACCIDENTAL EFFECTS" FOR ARTISTS AND DESIGNERS, James F. O'Brien. Create your own unique, striking, imaginative effects by "controlled accident" interaction of materials: paints and lacquers, oil and water based paints, splatter, crackling materials, shatter, similar items. Everything you do will be different; first book on this limitless art, so useful to both fine artist and commercial artist. Full instructions. 192 plates showing "accidents," 8 in color. viii + 215pp. 8⅜ x 11¼.   21942-9 Paperbound $3.50

THE BOOK OF SIGNS, Rudolf Koch. Famed German type designer draws 493 beautiful symbols: religious, mystical, alchemical, imperial, property marks, runes, etc. Remarkable fusion of traditional and modern. Good for suggestions of timelessness, smartness, modernity. Text. vi + 104pp. 6⅛ x 9¼.   20162-7 Paperbound $1.25

HISTORY OF INDIAN AND INDONESIAN ART, Ananda K. Coomaraswamy. An unabridged republication of one of the finest books by a great scholar in Eastern art. Rich in descriptive material, history, social backgrounds; Sunga reliefs, Rajput paintings, Gupta temples, Burmese frescoes, textiles, jewelry, sculpture, etc. 400 photos. viii + 423pp. 6⅜ x 9¾.   21436-2 Paperbound $5.00

PRIMITIVE ART, Franz Boas. America's foremost anthropologist surveys textiles, ceramics, woodcarving, basketry, metalwork, etc.; patterns, technology, creation of symbols, style origins. All areas of world, but very full on Northwest Coast Indians. More than 350 illustrations of baskets, boxes, totem poles, weapons, etc. 378 pp.   20025-6 Paperbound $3.00

THE GENTLEMAN AND CABINET MAKER'S DIRECTOR, Thomas Chippendale. Full reprint (third edition, 1762) of most influential furniture book of all time, by master cabinetmaker. 200 plates, illustrating chairs, sofas, mirrors, tables, cabinets, plus 24 photographs of surviving pieces. Biographical introduction by N. Bienenstock. vi + 249pp. 9⅞ x 12¾.   21601-2 Paperbound $4.00

AMERICAN ANTIQUE FURNITURE, Edgar G. Miller, Jr. The basic coverage of all American furniture before 1840. Individual chapters cover type of furniture—clocks, tables, sideboards, etc.—chronologically, with inexhaustible wealth of data. More than 2100 photographs, all identified, commented on. Essential to all early American collectors. Introduction by H. E. Keyes. vi + 1106pp. 7⅞ x 10¾.   21599-7, 21600-4 Two volumes, Paperbound $11.00

PENNSYLVANIA DUTCH AMERICAN FOLK ART, Henry J. Kauffman. 279 photos, 28 drawings of tulipware, Fraktur script, painted tinware, toys, flowered furniture, quilts, samplers, hex signs, house interiors, etc. Full descriptive text. Excellent for tourist, rewarding for designer, collector. Map. 146pp. 7⅞ x 10¾.   21205-X Paperbound $2.50

EARLY NEW ENGLAND GRAVESTONE RUBBINGS, Edmund V. Gillon, Jr. 43 photographs, 226 carefully reproduced rubbings show heavily symbolic, sometimes macabre early gravestones, up to early 19th century. Remarkable early American primitive art, occasionally strikingly beautiful; always powerful. Text. xxvi + 207pp. 8⅜ x 11¼.   21380-3 Paperbound $3.50

ALPHABETS AND ORNAMENTS, Ernst Lehner. Well-known pictorial source for decorative alphabets, script examples, cartouches, frames, decorative title pages, calligraphic initials, borders, similar material. 14th to 19th century, mostly European. Useful in almost any graphic arts designing, varied styles. 750 illustrations. 256pp. 7 x 10.   21905-4 Paperbound $4.00

PAINTING: A CREATIVE APPROACH, Norman Colquhoun. For the beginner simple guide provides an instructive approach to painting: major stumbling blocks for beginner; overcoming them, technical points; paints and pigments; oil painting; watercolor and other media and color. New section on "plastic" paints. Glossary. Formerly *Paint Your Own Pictures.* 221pp.   22000-1 Paperbound $1.75

THE ENJOYMENT AND USE OF COLOR, Walter Sargent. Explanation of the relations between colors themselves and between colors in nature and art, including hundreds of little-known facts about color values, intensities, effects of high and low illumination, complementary colors. Many practical hints for painters, references to great masters. 7 color plates, 29 illustrations. x + 274pp.
                                                      20944-X Paperbound $2.75

THE NOTEBOOKS OF LEONARDO DA VINCI, compiled and edited by Jean Paul Richter. 1566 extracts from original manuscripts reveal the full range of Leonardo's versatile genius: all his writings on painting, sculpture, architecture, anatomy, astronomy, geography, topography, physiology, mining, music, etc., in both Italian and English, with 186 plates of manuscript pages and more than 500 additional drawings. Includes studies for the Last Supper, the lost Sforza monument, and other works. Total of xlvii + 866pp. 7⅞ x 10¾.
                        22572-0, 22573-9 Two volumes, Paperbound $10.00

MONTGOMERY WARD CATALOGUE OF 1895. Tea gowns, yards of flannel and pillow-case lace, stereoscopes, books of gospel hymns, the New Improved Singer Sewing Machine, side saddles, milk skimmers, straight-edged razors, high-button shoes, spittoons, and on and on . . . listing some 25,000 items, practically all illustrated. Essential to the shoppers of the 1890's, it is our truest record of the spirit of the period. Unaltered reprint of Issue No. 57, Spring and Summer 1895. Introduction by Boris Emmet. Innumerable illustrations. xiii + 624pp. 8½ x 11⅝.
                                                      22377-9 Paperbound $6.95

THE CRYSTAL PALACE EXHIBITION ILLUSTRATED CATALOGUE (LONDON, 1851). One of the wonders of the modern world—the Crystal Palace Exhibition in which all the nations of the civilized world exhibited their achievements in the arts and sciences—presented in an equally important illustrated catalogue. More than 1700 items pictured with accompanying text—ceramics, textiles, cast-iron work, carpets, pianos, sleds, razors, wall-papers, billiard tables, beehives, silverware and hundreds of other artifacts—represent the focal point of Victorian culture in the Western World. Probably the largest collection of Victorian decorative art ever assembled—indispensable for antiquarians and designers. Unabridged republication of the Art-Journal Catalogue of the Great Exhibition of 1851, with all terminal essays. New introduction by John Gloag, F.S.A. xxxiv + 426pp. 9 x 12.
                                                      22503-8 Paperbound $5.00

A HISTORY OF COSTUME, Carl Köhler. Definitive history, based on surviving pieces of clothing primarily, and paintings, statues, etc. secondarily. Highly readable text, supplemented by 594 illustrations of costumes of the ancient Mediterranean peoples, Greece and Rome, the Teutonic prehistoric period; costumes of the Middle Ages, Renaissance, Baroque, 18th and 19th centuries. Clear, measured patterns are provided for many clothing articles. Approach is practical throughout. Enlarged by Emma von Sichart. 464pp.   21030-8 Paperbound $3.50.

ORIENTAL RUGS, ANTIQUE AND MODERN, Walter A. Hawley. A complete and authoritative treatise on the Oriental rug—where they are made, by whom and how, designs and symbols, characteristics in detail of the six major groups, how to distinguish them and how to buy them. Detailed technical data is provided on periods, weaves, warps, wefts, textures, sides, ends and knots, although no technical background is required for an understanding. 11 color plates, 80 halftones, 4 maps. vi + 320pp. 6⅛ x 9⅛.   22366-3 Paperbound $5.00

TEN BOOKS ON ARCHITECTURE, Vitruvius. By any standards the most important book on architecture ever written. Early Roman discussion of aesthetics of building, construction methods, orders, sites, and every other aspect of architecture has inspired, instructed architecture for about 2,000 years. Stands behind Palladio, Michelangelo, Bramante, Wren, countless others. Definitive Morris H. Morgan translation. 68 illustrations. xii + 331pp.   20645-9 Paperbound $3.00

THE FOUR BOOKS OF ARCHITECTURE, Andrea Palladio. Translated into every major Western European language in the two centuries following its publication in 1570, this has been one of the most influential books in the history of architecture. Complete reprint of the 1738 Isaac Ware edition. New introduction by Adolf Placzek, Columbia Univ. 216 plates. xxii + 110pp. of text. 9½ x 12¾.
                          21308-0 Clothbound $12.50

STICKS AND STONES: A STUDY OF AMERICAN ARCHITECTURE AND CIVILIZATION, Lewis Mumford.One of the great classics of American cultural history. American architecture from the medieval-inspired earliest forms to the early 20th century; evolution of structure and style, and reciprocal influences on environment. 21 photographic illustrations. 238pp.   20202-X Paperbound $2.00

THE AMERICAN BUILDER'S COMPANION, Asher Benjamin. The most widely used early 19th century architectural style and source book, for colonial up into Greek Revival periods. Extensive development of geometry of carpentering, construction of sashes, frames, doors, stairs; plans and elevations of domestic and other buildings. Hundreds of thousands of houses were built according to this book, now invaluable to historians, architects, restorers, etc. 1827 edition. 59 plates. 114pp. 7⅞ x 10¾.
                          22236-5 Paperbound $3.50

DUTCH HOUSES IN THE HUDSON VALLEY BEFORE 1776, Helen Wilkinson Reynolds. The standard survey of the Dutch colonial house and outbuildings, with constructional features, decoration, and local history associated with individual homesteads. Introduction by Franklin D. Roosevelt. Map. 150 illustrations. 469pp. 6⅝ x 9¼.   21469-9 Paperbound $5.00

THE ARCHITECTURE OF COUNTRY HOUSES, Andrew J. Downing. Together with Vaux's *Villas and Cottages* this is the basic book for Hudson River Gothic architecture of the middle Victorian period. Full, sound discussions of general aspects of housing, architecture, style, decoration, furnishing, together with scores of detailed house plans, illustrations of specific buildings, accompanied by full text. Perhaps the most influential single American architectural book. 1850 edition. Introduction by J. Stewart Johnson. 321 figures, 34 architectural designs. xvi + 560pp.
22003-6 Paperbound $4.00

LOST EXAMPLES OF COLONIAL ARCHITECTURE, John Mead Howells. Full-page photographs of buildings that have disappeared or been so altered as to be denatured, including many designed by major early American architects. 245 plates. xvii + 248pp. 7⅞ x 10¾.
21143-6 Paperbound $3.50

DOMESTIC ARCHITECTURE OF THE AMERICAN COLONIES AND OF THE EARLY REPUBLIC, Fiske Kimball. Foremost architect and restorer of Williamsburg and Monticello covers nearly 200 homes between 1620-1825. Architectural details, construction, style features, special fixtures, floor plans, etc. Generally considered finest work in its area. 219 illustrations of houses, doorways, windows, capital mantels. xx + 314pp. 7⅞ x 10¾.
21743-4 Paperbound $4.00

EARLY AMERICAN ROOMS: 1650-1858, edited by Russell Hawes Kettell. Tour of 12 rooms, each representative of a different era in American history and each furnished, decorated, designed and occupied in the style of the era. 72 plans and elevations, 8-page color section, etc., show fabrics, wall papers, arrangements, etc. Full descriptive text. xvii + 200pp. of text. 8⅜ x 11¼.
21633-0 Paperbound $5.00

THE FITZWILLIAM VIRGINAL BOOK, edited by J. Fuller Maitland and W. B. Squire. Full modern printing of famous early 17th-century ms. volume of 300 works by Morley, Byrd, Bull, Gibbons, etc. For piano or other modern keyboard instrument; easy to read format. xxxvi + 938pp. 8⅜ x 11.
21068-5, 21069-3 Two volumes, Paperbound $10.00

KEYBOARD MUSIC, Johann Sebastian Bach. Bach Gesellschaft edition. A rich selection of Bach's masterpieces for the harpsichord: the six English Suites, six French Suites, the six Partitas (Clavierübung part I), the Goldberg Variations (Clavierübung part IV), the fifteen Two-Part Inventions and the fifteen Three-Part Sinfonias. Clearly reproduced on large sheets with ample margins; eminently playable. vi + 312pp. 8⅛ x 11.
22360-4 Paperbound $5.00

THE MUSIC OF BACH: AN INTRODUCTION, Charles Sanford Terry. A fine, nontechnical introduction to Bach's music, both instrumental and vocal. Covers organ music, chamber music, passion music, other types. Analyzes themes, developments, innovations. x + 114pp.
21075-8 Paperbound $1.50

BEETHOVEN AND HIS NINE SYMPHONIES, Sir George Grove. Noted British musicologist provides best history, analysis, commentary on symphonies. Very thorough, rigorously accurate; necessary to both advanced student and amateur music lover. 436 musical passages. vii + 407 pp.
20334-4 Paperbound $2.75

JOHANN SEBASTIAN BACH, Philipp Spitta. One of the great classics of musicology, this definitive analysis of Bach's music (and life) has never been surpassed. Lucid, nontechnical analyses of hundreds of pieces (30 pages devoted to St. Matthew Passion, 26 to B Minor Mass). Also includes major analysis of 18th-century music. 450 musical examples. 40-page musical supplement. Total of xx + 1799pp.
(EUK) 22278-0, 22279-9 Two volumes, Clothbound $17.50

MOZART AND HIS PIANO CONCERTOS, Cuthbert Girdlestone. The only full-length study of an important area of Mozart's creativity. Provides detailed analyses of all 23 concertos, traces inspirational sources. 417 musical examples. Second edition. 509pp.
21271-8 Paperbound $3.50

THE PERFECT WAGNERITE: A COMMENTARY ON THE NIBLUNG'S RING, George Bernard Shaw. Brilliant and still relevant criticism in remarkable essays on Wagner's Ring cycle, Shaw's ideas on political and social ideology behind the plots, role of Leitmotifs, vocal requisites, etc. Prefaces. xxi + 136pp.
(USO) 21707-8 Paperbound $1.50

DON GIOVANNI, W. A. Mozart. Complete libretto, modern English translation; biographies of composer and librettist; accounts of early performances and critical reaction. Lavishly illustrated. All the material you need to understand and appreciate this great work. Dover Opera Guide and Libretto Series; translated and introduced by Ellen Bleiler. 92 illustrations. 209pp.
21134-7 Paperbound $2.00

BASIC ELECTRICITY, U. S. Bureau of Naval Personel. Originally a training course, best non-technical coverage of basic theory of electricity and its applications. Fundamental concepts, batteries, circuits, conductors and wiring techniques, AC and DC, inductance and capacitance, generators, motors, transformers, magnetic amplifiers, synchros, servomechanisms, etc. Also covers blue-prints, electrical diagrams, etc. Many questions, with answers. 349 illustrations. x + 448pp. 6½ x 9¼.
20973-3 Paperbound $3.50

REPRODUCTION OF SOUND, Edgar Villchur. Thorough coverage for laymen of high fidelity systems, reproducing systems in general, needles, amplifiers, preamps, loudspeakers, feedback, explaining physical background. "A rare talent for making technicalities vividly comprehensible," R. Darrell, *High Fidelity*. 69 figures. iv + 92pp.
21515-6 Paperbound $1.25

HEAR ME TALKIN' TO YA: THE STORY OF JAZZ AS TOLD BY THE MEN WHO MADE IT, Nat Shapiro and Nat Hentoff. Louis Armstrong, Fats Waller, Jo Jones, Clarence Williams, Billy Holiday, Duke Ellington, Jelly Roll Morton and dozens of other jazz greats tell how it was in Chicago's South Side, New Orleans, depression Harlem and the modern West Coast as jazz was born and grew. xvi + 429pp.
21726-4 Paperbound $3.00

FABLES OF AESOP, translated by Sir Roger L'Estrange. A reproduction of the very rare 1931 Paris edition; a selection of the most interesting fables, together with 50 imaginative drawings by Alexander Calder. v + 128pp. 6½x9¼.
21780-9 Paperbound $1.50

AGAINST THE GRAIN (A REBOURS), Joris K. Huysmans. Filled with weird images, evidences of a bizarre imagination, exotic experiments with hallucinatory drugs, rich tastes and smells and the diversions of its sybarite hero Duc Jean des Esseintes, this classic novel pushed 19th-century literary decadence to its limits. Full unabridged edition. Do not confuse this with abridged editions generally sold. Introduction by Havelock Ellis. xlix + 206pp.　　　　22190-3 Paperbound $2.00

VARIORUM SHAKESPEARE: HAMLET. Edited by Horace H. Furness; a landmark of American scholarship. Exhaustive footnotes and appendices treat all doubtful words and phrases, as well as suggested critical emendations throughout the play's history. First volume contains editor's own text, collated with all Quartos and Folios. Second volume contains full first Quarto, translations of Shakespeare's sources (Belleforest, and Saxo Grammaticus), Der Bestrafte Brudermord, and many essays on critical and historical points of interest by major authorities of past and present. Includes details of staging and costuming over the years. By far the best edition available for serious students of Shakespeare. Total of xx + 905pp.
21004-9, 21005-7, 2 volumes, Paperbound $7.00

A LIFE OF WILLIAM SHAKESPEARE, Sir Sidney Lee. This is the standard life of Shakespeare, summarizing everything known about Shakespeare and his plays. Incredibly rich in material, broad in coverage, clear and judicious, it has served thousands as the best introduction to Shakespeare. 1931 edition. 9 plates. xxix + 792pp.　　　　(USO) 21967-4 Paperbound $3.75

MASTERS OF THE DRAMA, John Gassner. Most comprehensive history of the drama in print, covering every tradition from Greeks to modern Europe and America, including India, Far East, etc. Covers more than 800 dramatists, 2000 plays, with biographical material, plot summaries, theatre history, criticism, etc. "Best of its kind in English," *New Republic*. 77 illustrations. xxii + 890pp.
20100-7 Clothbound $8.50

THE EVOLUTION OF THE ENGLISH LANGUAGE, George McKnight. The growth of English, from the 14th century to the present. Unusual, non-technical account presents basic information in very interesting form: sound shifts, change in grammar and syntax, vocabulary growth, similar topics. Abundantly illustrated with quotations. Formerly *Modern English in the Making*. xii + 590pp.
21932-1 Paperbound $3.50

AN ETYMOLOGICAL DICTIONARY OF MODERN ENGLISH, Ernest Weekley. Fullest, richest work of its sort, by foremost British lexicographer. Detailed word histories, including many colloquial and archaic words; extensive quotations. Do not confuse this with the Concise Etymological Dictionary, which is much abridged. Total of xxvii + 830pp. 6½ x 9¼.
21873-2, 21874-0 Two volumes, Paperbound $7.90

FLATLAND: A ROMANCE OF MANY DIMENSIONS, E. A. Abbott. Classic of science-fiction explores ramifications of life in a two-dimensional world, and what happens when a three-dimensional being intrudes. Amusing reading, but also useful as introduction to thought about hyperspace. Introduction by Banesh Hoffmann. 16 illustrations. xx + 103pp.　　　　20001-9 Paperbound $1.00

POEMS OF ANNE BRADSTREET, edited with an introduction by Robert Hutchinson. A new selection of poems by America's first poet and perhaps the first significant woman poet in the English language. 48 poems display her development in works of considerable variety—love poems, domestic poems, religious meditations, formal elegies, "quaternions," etc. Notes, bibliography. viii + 222pp.

22160-1 Paperbound $2.50

THREE GOTHIC NOVELS: THE CASTLE OF OTRANTO BY HORACE WALPOLE; VATHEK BY WILLIAM BECKFORD; THE VAMPYRE BY JOHN POLIDORI, WITH FRAGMENT OF A NOVEL BY LORD BYRON, edited by E. F. Bleiler. The first Gothic novel, by Walpole; the finest Oriental tale in English, by Beckford; powerful Romantic supernatural story in versions by Polidori and Byron. All extremely important in history of literature; all still exciting, packed with supernatural thrills, ghosts, haunted castles, magic, etc. xl + 291pp.

21232-7 Paperbound $2.50

THE BEST TALES OF HOFFMANN, E. T. A. Hoffmann. 10 of Hoffmann's most important stories, in modern re-editings of standard translations: Nutcracker and the King of Mice, Signor Formica, Automata, The Sandman, Rath Krespel, The Golden Flowerpot, Master Martin the Cooper, The Mines of Falun, The King's Betrothed, A New Year's Eve Adventure. 7 illustrations by Hoffmann. Edited by E. F. Bleiler. xxxix + 419pp.

21793-0 Paperbound $3.00

GHOST AND HORROR STORIES OF AMBROSE BIERCE, Ambrose Bierce. 23 strikingly modern stories of the horrors latent in the human mind: The Eyes of the Panther, The Damned Thing, An Occurrence at Owl Creek Bridge, An Inhabitant of Carcosa, etc., plus the dream-essay, Visions of the Night. Edited by E. F. Bleiler. xxii + 199pp.

20767-6 Paperbound $1.50

BEST GHOST STORIES OF J. S. LeFANU, J. Sheridan LeFanu. Finest stories by Victorian master often considered greatest supernatural writer of all. Carmilla, Green Tea, The Haunted Baronet, The Familiar, and 12 others. Most never before available in the U. S. A. Edited by E. F. Bleiler. 8 illustrations from Victorian publications. xvii + 467pp.

20415-4 Paperbound $3.00

MATHEMATICAL FOUNDATIONS OF INFORMATION THEORY, A. I. Khinchin. Comprehensive introduction to work of Shannon, McMillan, Feinstein and Khinchin, placing these investigations on a rigorous mathematical basis. Covers entropy concept in probability theory, uniqueness theorem, Shannon's inequality, ergodic sources, the E property, martingale concept, noise, Feinstein's fundamental lemma, Shanon's first and second theorems. Translated by R. A. Silverman and M. D. Friedman. iii + 120pp.

60434-9 Paperbound $2.00

SEVEN SCIENCE FICTION NOVELS, H. G. Wells. The standard collection of the great novels. Complete, unabridged. *First Men in the Moon, Island of Dr. Moreau, War of the Worlds, Food of the Gods, Invisible Man, Time Machine, In the Days of the Comet.* Not only science fiction fans, but every educated person owes it to himself to read these novels. 1015pp. (USO) 20264-X Clothbound $6.00

LAST AND FIRST MEN AND STAR MAKER, TWO SCIENCE FICTION NOVELS, Olaf Stapledon. Greatest future histories in science fiction. In the first, human intelligence is the "hero," through strange paths of evolution, interplanetary invasions, incredible technologies, near extinctions and reemergences. Star Maker describes the quest of a band of star rovers for intelligence itself, through time and space: weird inhuman civilizations, crustacean minds, symbiotic worlds, etc. Complete, unabridged. v + 438pp. (USO) 21962-3 Paperbound $2.50

THREE PROPHETIC NOVELS, H. G. WELLS. Stages of a consistently planned future for mankind. *When the Sleeper Wakes,* and *A Story of the Days to Come,* anticipate *Brave New World* and *1984,* in the 21st Century; *The Time Machine,* only complete version in print, shows farther future and the end of mankind. All show Wells's greatest gifts as storyteller and novelist. Edited by E. F. Bleiler. x + 335pp. (USO) 20605-X Paperbound $2.50

THE DEVIL'S DICTIONARY, Ambrose Bierce. America's own Oscar Wilde—Ambrose Bierce—offers his barbed iconoclastic wisdom in over 1,000 definitions hailed by H. L. Mencken as "some of the most gorgeous witticisms in the English language." 145pp. 20487-1 Paperbound $1.25

MAX AND MORITZ, Wilhelm Busch. Great children's classic, father of comic strip, of two bad boys, Max and Moritz. Also Ker and Plunk (Plisch und Plumm), Cat and Mouse, Deceitful Henry, Ice-Peter, The Boy and the Pipe, and five other pieces. Original German, with English translation. Edited by H. Arthur Klein; translations by various hands and H. Arthur Klein. vi + 216pp. 20181-3 Paperbound $2.00

PIGS IS PIGS AND OTHER FAVORITES, Ellis Parker Butler. The title story is one of the best humor short stories, as Mike Flannery obfuscates biology and English. Also included, That Pup of Murchison's, The Great American Pie Company, and Perkins of Portland. 14 illustrations. v + 109pp. 21532-6 Paperbound $1.25

THE PETERKIN PAPERS, Lucretia P. Hale. It takes genius to be as stupidly mad as the Peterkins, as they decide to become wise, celebrate the "Fourth," keep a cow, and otherwise strain the resources of the Lady from Philadelphia. Basic book of American humor. 153 illustrations. 219pp. 20794-3 Paperbound $1.50

PERRAULT'S FAIRY TALES, translated by A. E. Johnson and S. R. Littlewood, with 34 full-page illustrations by Gustave Doré. All the original Perrault stories—Cinderella, Sleeping Beauty, Bluebeard, Little Red Riding Hood, Puss in Boots, Tom Thumb, etc.—with their witty verse morals and the magnificent illustrations of Doré. One of the five or six great books of European fairy tales. viii + 117pp. 8⅛ x 11. 22311-6 Paperbound $2.00

OLD HUNGARIAN FAIRY TALES, Baroness Orczy. Favorites translated and adapted by author of the *Scarlet Pimpernel.* Eight fairy tales include "The Suitors of Princess Fire-Fly," "The Twin Hunchbacks," "Mr. Cuttlefish's Love Story," and "The Enchanted Cat." This little volume of magic and adventure will captivate children as it has for generations. 90 drawings by Montagu Barstow. 96pp. 22293-4 Paperbound $1.95

THE RED FAIRY BOOK, Andrew Lang. Lang's color fairy books have long been children's favorites. This volume includes Rapunzel, Jack and the Bean-stalk and 35 other stories, familiar and unfamiliar. 4 plates, 93 illustrations x + 367pp.
21673-X Paperbound $2.50

THE BLUE FAIRY BOOK, Andrew Lang. Lang's tales come from all countries and all times. Here are 37 tales from Grimm, the Arabian Nights, Greek Mythology, and other fascinating sources. 8 plates, 130 illustrations. xi + 390pp.
21437-0 Paperbound $2.50

HOUSEHOLD STORIES BY THE BROTHERS GRIMM. Classic English-language edition of the well-known tales — Rumpelstiltskin, Snow White, Hansel and Gretel, The Twelve Brothers, Faithful John, Rapunzel, Tom Thumb (52 stories in all). Translated into simple, straightforward English by Lucy Crane. Ornamented with headpieces, vignettes, elaborate decorative initials and a dozen full-page illustrations by Walter Crane. x + 269pp.
21080-4 Paperbound **$2.00**

THE MERRY ADVENTURES OF ROBIN HOOD, Howard Pyle. The finest modern versions of the traditional ballads and tales about the great English outlaw. Howard Pyle's complete prose version, with every word, every illustration of the first edition. Do not confuse this facsimile of the original (1883) with modern editions that change text or illustrations. 23 plates plus many page decorations. xxii + 296pp.
22043-5 Paperbound $2.50

THE STORY OF KING ARTHUR AND HIS KNIGHTS, Howard Pyle. The finest children's version of the life of King Arthur; brilliantly retold by Pyle, with 48 of his most imaginative illustrations. xviii + 313pp. 6⅛ x 9¼.
21445-1 Paperbound $2.50

THE WONDERFUL WIZARD OF OZ, L. Frank Baum. America's finest children's book in facsimile of first edition with all Denslow illustrations in full color. The edition a child should have. Introduction by Martin Gardner. 23 color plates, scores of drawings. iv + 267pp.
20691-2 Paperbound $2.50

THE MARVELOUS LAND OF OZ, L. Frank Baum. The second Oz book, every bit as imaginative as the Wizard. The hero is a boy named Tip, but the Scarecrow and the Tin Woodman are back, as is the Oz magic. 16 color plates, 120 drawings by John R. Neill. 287pp.
20692-0 Paperbound $2.50

THE MAGICAL MONARCH OF MO, L. Frank Baum. Remarkable adventures in a land even stranger than Oz. The best of Baum's books not in the Oz series. 15 color plates and dozens of drawings by Frank Verbeck. xviii + 237pp.
21892-9 Paperbound $2.25

THE BAD CHILD'S BOOK OF BEASTS, MORE BEASTS FOR WORSE CHILDREN, A MORAL ALPHABET, Hilaire Belloc. Three complete humor classics in one volume. Be kind to the frog, and do not call him names . . . and 28 other whimsical animals. Familiar favorites and some not so well known. Illustrated by Basil Blackwell. 156pp.
(USO) 20749-8 Paperbound $1.50

EAST O' THE SUN AND WEST O' THE MOON, George W. Dasent. Considered the best of all translations of these Norwegian folk tales, this collection has been enjoyed by generations of children (and folklorists too). Includes True and Untrue, Why the Sea is Salt, East O' the Sun and West O' the Moon, Why the Bear is Stumpy-Tailed, Boots and the Troll, The Cock and the Hen, Rich Peter the Pedlar, and 52 more. The only edition with all 59 tales. 77 illustrations by Erik Werenskiold and Theodor Kittelsen. xv + 418pp.   22521-6 Paperbound $3.50

GOOPS AND HOW TO BE THEM, Gelett Burgess. Classic of tongue-in-cheek humor, masquerading as etiquette book. 87 verses, twice as many cartoons, show mischievous Goops as they demonstrate to children virtues of table manners, neatness, courtesy, etc. Favorite for generations. viii + 88pp. 6½ x 9¼.
                        22233-0 Paperbound $1.25

ALICE'S ADVENTURES UNDER GROUND, Lewis Carroll. The first version, quite different from the final *Alice in Wonderland*, printed out by Carroll himself with his own illustrations. Complete facsimile of the "million dollar" manuscript Carroll gave to Alice Liddell in 1864. Introduction by Martin Gardner. viii + 96pp. Title and dedication pages in color.   21482-6 Paperbound $1.25

THE BROWNIES, THEIR BOOK, Palmer Cox. Small as mice, cunning as foxes, exuberant and full of mischief, the Brownies go to the zoo, toy shop, seashore, circus, etc., in 24 verse adventures and 266 illustrations. Long a favorite, since their first appearance in St. Nicholas Magazine. xi + 144pp. 6⅝ x 9¼.
                        21265-3 Paperbound $1.75

SONGS OF CHILDHOOD, Walter De La Mare. Published (under the pseudonym Walter Ramal) when De La Mare was only 29, this charming collection has long been a favorite children's book. A facsimile of the first edition in paper, the 47 poems capture the simplicity of the nursery rhyme and the ballad, including such lyrics as I Met Eve, Tartary, The Silver Penny. vii + 106pp. (USO) 21972-0 Paperbound
                        $1.25

THE COMPLETE NONSENSE OF EDWARD LEAR, Edward Lear. The finest 19th-century humorist-cartoonist in full: all nonsense limericks, zany alphabets, Owl and Pussycat, songs, nonsense botany, and more than 500 illustrations by Lear himself. Edited by Holbrook Jackson. xxix + 287pp.   (USO) 20167-8 Paperbound $2.00

BILLY WHISKERS: THE AUTOBIOGRAPHY OF A GOAT, Frances Trego Montgomery. A favorite of children since the early 20th century, here are the escapades of that rambunctious, irresistible and mischievous goat—Billy Whiskers. Much in the spirit of *Peck's Bad Boy*, this is a book that children never tire of reading or hearing. All the original familiar illustrations by W. H. Fry are included: 6 color plates, 18 black and white drawings. 159pp.   22345-0 Paperbound $2.00

MOTHER GOOSE MELODIES. Faithful republication of the fabulously rare Munroe and Francis "copyright 1833" Boston edition—the most important Mother Goose collection, usually referred to as the "original." Familiar rhymes plus many rare ones, with wonderful old woodcut illustrations. Edited by E. F. Bleiler. 128pp. 4½ x 6⅜.   22577-1 Paperbound $1.00

TWO LITTLE SAVAGES; BEING THE ADVENTURES OF TWO BOYS WHO LIVED AS INDIANS AND WHAT THEY LEARNED, Ernest Thompson Seton. Great classic of nature and boyhood provides a vast range of woodlore in most palatable form, a genuinely entertaining story. Two farm boys build a teepee in woods and live in it for a month, working out Indian solutions to living problems, star lore, birds and animals, plants, etc. 293 illustrations. vii + 286pp.

20985-7 Paperbound $2.50

PETER PIPER'S PRACTICAL PRINCIPLES OF PLAIN & PERFECT PRONUNCIATION. Alliterative jingles and tongue-twisters of surprising charm, that made their first appearance in America about 1830. Republished in full with the spirited woodcut illustrations from this earliest American edition. 32pp. $4\frac{1}{2}$ x $6\frac{3}{8}$.

22560-7 Paperbound $1.00

SCIENCE EXPERIMENTS AND AMUSEMENTS FOR CHILDREN, Charles Vivian. 73 easy experiments, requiring only materials found at home or easily available, such as candles, coins, steel wool, etc.; illustrate basic phenomena like vacuum, simple chemical reaction, etc. All safe. Modern, well-planned. Formerly *Science Games for Children*. 102 photos, numerous drawings. 96pp. $6\frac{1}{8}$ x $9\frac{1}{4}$.

21856-2 Paperbound $1.25

AN INTRODUCTION TO CHESS MOVES AND TACTICS SIMPLY EXPLAINED, Leonard Barden. Informal intermediate introduction, quite strong in explaining reasons for moves. Covers basic material, tactics, important openings, traps, positional play in middle game, end game. Attempts to isolate patterns and recurrent configurations. Formerly *Chess*. 58 figures. 102pp.   (USO) 21210-6 Paperbound $1.25

LASKER'S MANUAL OF CHESS, Dr. Emanuel Lasker. Lasker was not only one of the five great World Champions, he was also one of the ablest expositors, theorists, and analysts. In many ways, his Manual, permeated with his philosophy of battle, filled with keen insights, is one of the greatest works ever written on chess. Filled with analyzed games by the great players. A single-volume library that will profit almost any chess player, beginner or master. 308 diagrams. xli x 349pp.

20640-8 Paperbound $2.75

THE MASTER BOOK OF MATHEMATICAL RECREATIONS, Fred Schuh. In opinion of many the finest work ever prepared on mathematical puzzles, stunts, recreations; exhaustively thorough explanations of mathematics involved, analysis of effects, citation of puzzles and games. Mathematics involved is elementary. Translated bv F. Göbel. 194 figures. xxiv + 430pp.   22134-2 Paperbound $3.50

MATHEMATICS, MAGIC AND MYSTERY, Martin Gardner. Puzzle editor for Scientific American explains mathematics behind various mystifying tricks: card tricks, stage "mind reading," coin and match tricks, counting out games, geometric dissections, etc. Probability sets, theory of numbers clearly explained. Also provides more than 400 tricks, guaranteed to work, that you can do. 135 illustrations. xii + 176pp.

20335-2 Paperbound $1.75

MATHEMATICAL PUZZLES FOR BEGINNERS AND ENTHUSIASTS, Geoffrey Mott-Smith. 189 puzzles from easy to difficult—involving arithmetic, logic, algebra, properties of digits, probability, etc.—for enjoyment and mental stimulus. Explanation of mathematical principles behind the puzzles. 135 illustrations. viii + 248pp.
20198-8 Paperbound $1.75

PAPER FOLDING FOR BEGINNERS, William D. Murray and Francis J. Rigney. Easiest book on the market, clearest instructions on making interesting, beautiful origami. Sail boats, cups, roosters, frogs that move legs, bonbon boxes, standing birds, etc. 40 projects; more than 275 diagrams and photographs. 94pp.
20713-7 Paperbound $1.00

TRICKS AND GAMES ON THE POOL TABLE, Fred Herrmann. 79 tricks and games— some solitaires, some for two or more players, some competitive games—to entertain you between formal games. Mystifying shots and throws, unusual caroms, tricks involving such props as cork, coins, a hat, etc. Formerly *Fun on the Pool Table*. 77 figures. 95pp.
21814-7 Paperbound $1.00

HAND SHADOWS TO BE THROWN UPON THE WALL: A SERIES OF NOVEL AND AMUSING FIGURES FORMED BY THE HAND, Henry Bursill. Delightful picturebook from great-grandfather's day shows how to make 18 different hand shadows: a bird that flies, duck that quacks, dog that wags his tail, camel, goose, deer, boy, turtle, etc. Only book of its sort. vi + 33pp. 6½ x 9¼. 21779-5 Paperbound $1.00

WHITTLING AND WOODCARVING, E. J. Tangerman. 18th printing of best book on market. "If you can cut a potato you can carve" toys and puzzles, chains, chessmen, caricatures, masks, frames, woodcut blocks, surface patterns, much more. Information on tools, woods, techniques. Also goes into serious wood sculpture from Middle Ages to present, East and West. 464 photos, figures. x + 293pp.
20965-2 Paperbound $2.00

HISTORY OF PHILOSOPHY, Julián Marias. Possibly the clearest, most easily followed, best planned, most useful one-volume history of philosophy on the market; neither skimpy nor overfull. Full details on system of every major philosopher and dozens of less important thinkers from pre-Socratics up to Existentialism and later. Strong on many European figures usually omitted. Has gone through dozens of editions in Europe. 1966 edition, translated by Stanley Appelbaum and Clarence Strowbridge. xviii + 505pp.
21739-6 Paperbound $3.50

YOGA: A SCIENTIFIC EVALUATION, Kovoor T. Behanan. Scientific but non-technical study of physiological results of yoga exercises; done under auspices of Yale U. Relations to Indian thought, to psychoanalysis, etc. 16 photos. xxiii + 270pp.
20505-3 Paperbound $2.50

Prices subject to change without notice.
Available at your book dealer or write for free catalogue to Dept. GI, Dover Publications, Inc., 180 Varick St., N. Y., N. Y. 10014. Dover publishes more than 150 books each year on science, elementary and advanced mathematics, biology, music, art, literary history, social sciences and other areas.